Energy Law in South Africa

Energy Law in South Africa

Second Edition

Willemien du Plessis

This book was originally published as a monograph in the International Encyclopaedia of Laws/Energy Law.

Founding Editor: Roger Blanpain
General Editor: Frank Hendrickx
Volume Editors: Kurt Deketelaere & Bram Delvaux

Wolters Kluwer

Published by:
Kluwer Law International B.V.
PO Box 316
2400 AH Alphen aan den Rijn
The Netherlands
E-mail: international-sales@wolterskluwer.com
Website: lrus.wolterskluwer.com

Sold and distributed in North, Central and South America by:
Wolters Kluwer Legal & Regulatory U.S.
7201 McKinney Circle
Frederick, MD 21704
United States of America
Email: customer.service@wolterskluwer.com

Sold and distributed in all other countries by:
Air Business Subscriptions
Rockwood House
Haywards Heath
West Sussex
RH16 3DH
United Kingdom
Email: international-customerservice@wolterskluwer.com

Printed on acid-free paper

ISBN 978-94-035-2103-9

e-Book: ISBN 978-94-035-2151-0
web-PDF: ISBN 978-94-035-2173-2

Printed in the United Kingdom.

The Author

Willemien du Plessis is Doctor of Law and Professor at the North-West University (Potchefstroom Campus), South Africa. She teaches Environmental Law and Legal History. She has published more than 200 articles and contributions in books on environmental law, land law, legal pluralism and legal history and participated in various international and national inter-university research projects on these topics. She also co-edited several books on environmental law. She participated in various governmental working groups on land reform. She is the Secretary of the South African Environmental Law Association and an evaluator for the National Research Foundation on the above-mentioned topics. She was the co-chair of the IUCN Academy of Environmental Law's Research Committee from 2009 until 2013. She is on the editorial boards of the *Resource Management Theory & Practice* (*RM Theory & Practice*), the *Botswana Law Journal* and the *South African Journal of Environmental Law and Policy*. From 2017 she serves as an International Advisory Board (IAB) member of Sustainability College Bruges (SCB), Belgium.

The Author

Table of Contents

Table of Contents

List of Abbreviations

C	Cape
CDM	Clean Development Mechanism
CSIR	South African Council for Scientific and Industrial Research
DEA	Department of Environmental Affairs
DEAT	Department of Environmental Affairs and Tourism
DEAFF	Department of Environmental Affairs, Forestry and Fisheries
DME	Department of Minerals and Energy
DMR	Department of Mineral Resources
DWAF	Department of Water Affairs and Forestry
ECA	Environment Conservation Act
EIA	Environmental impact assessment
EMPR	Environmental Management Programme Report
GDP	Gross Domestic Product
GEAR	Growth, Employment and Redistribution
GHG	Greenhouse Gas
IPP	Independent Power Producer
MEC	Member of Executive Committee of a Province
MPRDA	Mineral and Petroleum Resources Development Act
N	Natal
NEMA	National Environmental Management Act
NEMAQA	National Environmental Management: Air Quality Act
NEMBA	National Environmental Management: Biodiversity Act
NEMICMA	National Environmental Management: Integrated Coastal Management
NEMWA	National Environmental Management: Waste Act
NERSA	National Energy Regulator of South Africa
NWA	National Water Act
PELJ	*Potchefstroom Electronic Law Journal*
S Afr J Sci	*South African Journal of Science*

List of Abbreviations

s.	Section
SABS	South African Bureau of Standards
SADC	Southern African Development Community
SAHRA	South African Heritage Resources Agency
SAJELP	*South African Journal of Environmental Law and Policy*
SANEDI	South African Energy Development Institute
SANS	South African National Standards
SCA	Supreme Court of Appeal
Ss	Sections
Stats SA	Statistics South Africa
T	Transvaal
THRHR	*Tydskrif vir Hedendaags Romeins-Hollandse Reg/Journal of Contemporary Roman Dutch Law*

General Introduction

Chapter 1. General Background

§1. Geography and Population

1. South Africa is situated at the southern tip of Africa.[1] Its surface area is 1,219,602 sq km.[2] The country's neighbours are Namibia, Mozambique, Botswana, Zimbabwe, Lesotho and Swaziland. Lesotho is an integrated part of South Africa. South Africa also annexed the Prince Edward and Marion Islands approximately 1,920 km south-east of Cape Town in the Atlantic in 1947. Research is conducted in the Antarctic. South Africa is a member of the Southern African Development Community (SADC), which is negotiating *inter alia* free movement of trade, workers, academics and students, as well as import and export measures.

South Africa has a very long coastline of 3,000 km and is bordered in the south, west and east by the Atlantic and Indian oceans. Two major ocean currents have an influence on the natural environment both in the sea and on land. On the east and south coasts, the warm Mozambique-Agulhas current flows southwards, and along the west coast is the cold Benguela current. The river mouths are unsuitable for use as harbours as they are mostly barred by sand. Only the Limpopo and Orange Rivers have permanent channels, but can still not be used as harbours. The country has no navigable rivers and is mostly dependent on dams for storage of water.[3] South Africa has two major physiographic features, namely the interior plateau and the land between the plateau and the coast. The boundary is formed by the Great Escarpment, which stretches from the Cape to the Northern Province. Its height varies from 1,500 m above sea level in the Roggeveld to 3,482 m above sea level in the KwaZulu-Natal Drakensberg. The plateau has an average height of 1,200 m above sea level. The area between the escarpment and the coast varies from 80 to 240 km in width in the east and 60 to 80 km in the west.

South Africa has a temperate climate, with sunshine nearly all year round. Most of the country falls in a summer rainfall region, except the Cape, which has winter

1. Latitude: 22° to 35° S; longitude: 17 to 33 E. The following description is based on Department of Government Communication and Information System, *South Africa Yearbook 2012/2013*, 2–5 http://www.gcis.gov.za/content/resourcecentre/sa-info/yearbook2012-13 (accessed 20 Sep. 2013) (hereinafter '*SA Yearbook 2012/2013*').
2. South African Yearbook 2017/2018 'Land and its people' 2 https://www.gcis.gov.za/sites/default/files/docs/resourcecentre/yearbook/9-Environment2018.pdf (accessed 20 Apr. 2019) (hereinafter 'SA Yearbook 2017/2018').
3. *See also SA Yearbook 2012/2013* at 2–3.

rainfall. The temperature in summer can rise above 32°C, while in the lower Free State and Mpumalanga regions the temperatures frequently exceed 38°C. There is an approximate difference of 6°C in temperatures between the east and west coast. Snow is rarely seen in South Africa, except on the mountain peaks and high-lying ground. Frost occurs on the interior plateau during cold winter nights. Frost occurs for the longest period on the eastern and southern plateau bordering the escarpment (from April to October). To the north, the incidence of frost decreases and the coast is virtually frost-free. Temperatures in winter can drop to below freezing point at night but usually rise during the day to temperatures from 16°C to 22°C.

South Africa's average annual rainfall is 464 mm, which does not compare well with the world's average of 860 mm. 'About 21% of the country has a total annual rainfall of less than 200 mm, 48% between 200 and 600 mm, while only about 30% records more than 600 mm. In total, 65% of the country has an annual rainfall of less than 500 mm – usually regarded as the absolute minimum for dry-land farming.'[4] South Africa experiences long periods of drought, which may be followed by floods.[5] The rainfall is unpredictable and cannot be relied upon.[6] Water resources are therefore scarce.[7] Soils are thin and moderately fertile.[8] Only about 13% of South Africa's surface area can be used for crop production, and high-potential arable land comprises only 22% of the total arable land. Irrigation is used on 1.3 million ha.[9]

South Africa is a country with a rich biodiversity, which ranges from drought-resistant plants and animals to aquatic life.[10] South Africa's biological diversity includes[11] grasslands, natural coastal forests, scrub and alpine forest and woodland, savanna, mountain areas, wetlands and semi-arid areas alternate. Three internationally recognized biodiversity 'hotspots' are found in South Africa, namely the Cape Floristic Fynbos Kingdom (unique in nature), Maputuland-Pondoland-Albany and

4. *SA Yearbook 2012/2013* at 3–4.
5. *See* in this regard, Donna Hornby et al., *A Harvest of Dysfunction: Rethinking the Approach to Drought, Its Causes and Impacts in South Africa,* Oxfam South Africa (October 2016).
6. Also *see* WWF, *Scenarios for the Future of Water in South Africa* (March 2017) http://www.wwf.org.za/media_room/publications/?20461/Scenarios-for-the-future-of-water-in-South-Africa# (accessed 22 Mar. 2017); G. Viljoen, *South Africa's Water Crisis: The Idea of Water as Property as Both a Cause and a Solution*, 21 Law, Democracy and Development 176–200 (2017).
7. *See* in this regard, V. Wepener, W. Malherbe and N.J. Smit, *Water Resources in South Africa,* 351–400. In *Fuggle and Rabie's Environmental Management in South Africa* (King, N.D, Strydom, H.A. & F.P. Retief, eds, 3rd edn, Juta 2018).
8. DEA, *South African Outlook Report* (hereinafter '*State of the Environment*'), http://soer.deat.gov.za/State_of_the_Environment.html (accessed 20 Sep. 2013).
9. *SA Yearbook 2012/2013* at 6, 60–62. Agriculture is based on a well-developed commercial sector and a subsistence-orientated sector in the rural areas.
10. According to the SA Yearbook 2017/2018 'Environment' at 19: 'South Africa is home to some 24 000 species, around 7% of the world's vertebrate species, and 5,5% of the world's known insect species (only about half of the latter have been described). In terms of the number of endemic species of mammals, birds, reptiles and amphibians found in South Africa, the country ranks as the fifth richest in Africa and the 24th richest in the world. Marine biodiversity is also high, with more than 11 000 species found in South African waters, which is about 15% of global species. More than 25% of these species (or 3 496 species) are endemic to South Africa, many of which are threatened, especially in river ecosystems (82%) and estuaries (77%).'.
11. *SA Yearbook 2017/2018* at 15.

the Succulent Karoo (the only arid-land biodiversity hotspot in the world).[12] There is also a wide diversity of mammals, birds, insects, reptiles and amphibia, in terrestrial, coastal and marine habitats.[13]

Afforestation has had a major impact on South Africa's scarce water resources. However, it provides jobs and economic opportunities for people in the rural areas. Government sees forest production as a means to introduce Black Economic Empowerment.[14] There is a move from exploitation to sustainable forest management and the protection of natural forests and water resources.[15] There is a number of alien species that also have an impact on South Africa's water resources. Government implemented landcare and watercare projects as job creation projects to eradicate 8725 ha of alien invasive plants. At the same time, projects were introduced to restore grazing land. Government allocates an annual budget to achieve this.[16]

A large number of minerals are found in South Africa, of which gold and platinum are the most important mineral exports. South African gold accounted for 30% of the world's production, but due to the economic slump and the difficulty to gain access to the gold, it is no longer the case. Other minerals that are mined are coal, anthracite, platinum, iron ore, diamonds, chromium, manganese, vanadium, vermiculite, antimony, limestone, asbestos, fluorspar, uranium, aluminosilicates, phosphate, copper, lead and zinc. Natural gas, sillimanite, silver, andalusite, titanium and zirconium are also to be found.[17] Gold production has decreased in the last years with concomitant job losses. Platinum is the largest employer.[18]

2. According to Stats SA (Statistics South Africa), *Mid-Year Population Estimates*, 2013 South Africa had a population of 52.98 million people.[19] In 2018 Stats SA estimated the population to be 57.73 million.[20] South Africa is a multicultural and multilingual society and 51.3% of the population consists of women.[21] The cultural groups consist of the Nguni people (more or less two-thirds of the population – Zulu and Xhosa peoples), the Sotho-Tswana people (Southern, Northern and Western Sotho (Tswana)), the Tsonga people, the Venda people, Afrikaner, English, Brown people, Khoi-San and Indians, as well as other immigrants who kept their

12. Of the six Southern African 'hotspots', five are in South Africa, namely the Wolkberg, Pondoland, Maputaland, Eastern Mountain and Albany – *State of the Environment* at 4.
13. *Ibid.*
14. *SA Yearbook 2012/2013* at 76–77. Approximately 50%–60% of the forest areas are subject to land claims – *SA Yearbook 2011/12* at 62–65.
15. *SA Yearbook 2012/2013* at 66–67. A total of 80% of all forests received certification from the Forest Stewardship Council or has ISO14001 accreditation.
16. *Ibid.* at 47, 62–63.
17. Anon., *The Europa World Yearbook 2004*, Volume II 3851–3852 (45th edn, Gresham 2004); *SA Yearbook 2012/2013* at 449–457.
18. *SA Yearbook 2012/2013* at 444.
19. www.statssa.gov.za (accessed 30 Sep. 2013) (hereinafter 'Stats SA'). According to the census of 2011, South Africa had 51.8 million people.
20. SA Yearbook 2017/18 'Land and its people' at 2.
21. *Ibid.*

own cultural identity (e.g., Portuguese, Greeks, Jews, Germans, Nigerians, Ethiopians, etc.).[22] Most of the people live in the Gauteng Province (25.4%), followed by KwaZulu-Natal (19.7%). The least populated province is the Northern Cape with only 2.1% of the population.[23]

3. The Constitution of the Republic of South Africa, 1996 (hereinafter 'Constitution') 'recognizes 11 official languages, of which at least two must be used in all official documents. The languages are Afrikaans, English, IsiNdebele, IsiXhosa, IsiZulu, Sepedi, Sesotho, Setswana, SiSwati, Tshivenda and Xitsonga'.[24] IsiZulu is spoken by 24.6% of the population, IsiXhosa by 17%, Afrikaans by 12.1%, Sepedi by 9.5% and English by 8.3%. There is a tendency to use English as the common denominator at official meetings.

The South African population is a religious society and people adhere to a wide diversity of religions. The Constitution guarantees freedom of religion, belief and opinion in section 15. Only 64% of people in South Africa in 2012 professed to belong to a belief system.[25] According to a census survey, however, approximately 80% of the population is of the Christian faith,[26] while the other major religious groups include the Islam, Hindu and Jewish religions.[27] A minority of the population does not adhere to any religion at all.

Due to the apartheid system, communities still live according to racial groups, a tendency which is slowly changing. The grouping together of people in racial or cultural terms strengthened cultural and religious identity, which makes it difficult for the government to create a single South African identity without marginalizing culture.

---

22. *SA Yearbook 2011/12* at 4; Anon., *The Europa Yearbook 2004*, Volume II 3851–3852 (45th edn, Gresham 2004).
23. Stats SA, *Mid-Year Population Estimates*, 2018 <http://www.statssa.gov.za/?p=11341> (accessed 20 Apr. 2019).
24. Section 6. The national and provincial government may use any two official languages for the purposes of government, taking into account usage, practicality, expense, regional circumstances and the balance and needs and preferences of the population as a whole or in the province. Municipalities must take into account the language usage and preference of their residents. A Pan South African Language Board was established to promote the development of all official languages, as well as the Khoi, San and Nama languages and other languages commonly used by communities such as German, Greek, Gujarati, Hindi, Portuguese, Tamil, Telugu, Urdu, Arabic, Hebrew, Sanskrit and other languages used for religious purposes. The Khoi and San National Language Body was established in 1999 to promote these languages. *See SA Yearbook 2017/2018* Land and its people at 3.
25. *SA Yearbook 2012/2013* at 5. According to a Win-Gallup survey.
26. These churches can broadly be divided into African Independent (Zionist and Apostolic), Roman Catholic, Afrikaans Protestant, Lutheran, Presbyterian, Methodist, Anglican, Congregational, Pentecostal and Charismatic Churches.
27. Two-thirds of the Indian population adheres to the Hindu religion, while the remainder includes Muslims (20%) and Christians (12%). The Muslim community is the strongest under the Cape Malays, descendants of the Malayan slaves. The Jewish population is approximately 100,000. The majority are Orthodox Jews. Buddhism is adhered to by a minority of people. *See SA Yearbook 2011/12* at 3–5.

§2. Legal and Political Structure

I. Historical Background

4. Before 1994, South Africa's political dispensation was characterized by minority rule and the enforcement of the segregation policy, later known as apartheid. Since 1994, South Africa has been a sovereign, democratic state founded on the values of human dignity, the achievement of equality and the advancement of human rights and freedoms, non-racialism and non-sexism, supremacy of the Constitution and the rule of law, as well as universal adult suffrage, a national common voter's roll, regular elections and a multiparty system of democratic government to ensure accountability, responsiveness and openness.[28]

II. Political Structure

5. South Africa is a constitutional state. Three spheres of government are distinguished, namely the national, provincial and local spheres of government. These spheres of government are distinctive, interdependent and interrelated.[29] The national government consists of the President, who is the official head of the state, assisted by a Deputy-President and a National Executive.[30] The powers and functions of the President include the responsibility to assent to and sign bills; referring a bill back to the National Assembly or the Constitutional Court for reconsideration of the Bill's constitutionality; summoning the National Assembly, the National Council of Provinces or Parliament to an extraordinary sitting to conduct special business; appointing commissions of enquiry; calling national referenda; and pardoning or reprieving offenders and remit any fines, penalties or forfeitures.[31] The executive authority of the Republic is vested in the President, who exercises this authority together with the members of cabinet.[32]

The cabinet consists of the President, Deputy-President and Ministers, who are appointed by the President.[33] The Deputy-President and Ministers must be selected from members of the National Assembly. The President may appoint two ministers from outside the assembly. The Deputy-President and Ministers are responsible for the powers and functions allocated to them by the President. Members of the cabinet are collectively and individually accountable to Parliament for exercising their

28. Sections 1 and 7 of the Constitution.
29. Section 40 of the Constitution.
30. Sections 83–102.
31. Section 84.
32. Section 85 – the executive authority includes the implementation of national legislation, except where the Constitution or an Act of Parliament instructs otherwise, development and implementation of national policy, coordination of the functions of state departments and administrations, preparation and initiation of legislation and performance of any other executive function provided for in the Constitution or national legislation.
33. Section 91.

powers and performing their functions.[34] A cabinet minister may assign any power or function to be exercised or performed in terms of national legislation to a member of the Provincial Executive Council or a municipal council.[35]

Parliament consists of the National Assembly and National Council of Provinces.[36] The National Assembly and National Council of Provinces participate in the legislative process in the manner set out in the Constitution. The National Assembly is elected to represent the people and to ensure government by the people. The National Assembly elects the President and provides a public forum for public consideration of issues. The National Assembly consists of 350 to 400 women and men elected as members in terms of the prescribed electoral system.[37]

The National Council of Provinces represents the provinces to ensure that the interests of provinces are taken into account in the national sphere of government. It participates in the national legislative process and provides a national forum on issues dealing with the provinces.[38] The council consists of a single delegation from each province comprising ten delegates.[39] Ten members of local governments may also participate in the council but are not allowed to vote.[40] If a bill before National Parliament may affect the provinces, the Bill must be referred to the National Council of Provinces, which may pass, amend or reject the Bill.[41]

The legislative authority of the Republic rests in the national sphere in Parliament (section 44 of the Constitution), in the provincial sphere with the provincial legislatures (section 104) and in the local sphere of government in the municipal councils (section 156).

6. There are nine provinces in South Africa, namely the Eastern Cape, Free State, Gauteng, KwaZulu-Natal, Mpumalanga, Northern Cape, Limpopo Province, North West and Western Cape.[42] The executive power of a province is vested in the Premier of that province. The Premier, together with the other Members of the Executive Council (MECs), exercises executive authority by implementing provincial legislation in the province, implementing all national legislation that fall within the functional areas listed in Schedules 4 and 5 of the Constitution, administering

34. Section 92. Deputy Ministers may be appointed from the members of the National Assembly – s. 93. The President may in terms of s. 97 of the Constitution transfer the administration and powers and functions entrusted by legislation to certain cabinet members which he does from time to time – *see*, e.g., Proclamation 16 in *Government Gazette* 36527 of 31 May 2013 where he shared the responsibilities of the Marine Living Resources Act 18 of 1998 between the then Minister of Environmental Affairs and the Minister of Agriculture, Forestry and Fisheries.
35. Section 99.
36. Sections 42–82.
37. Section 46.
38. Section 42.
39. Section 60.
40. Section 67.
41. Sections 75–76.
42. Section 103 of the Constitution.

the province, developing and implementing provincial policy, coordinating the function of the provincial administration and its departments, preparing and initiating provincial legislation and performing any other function provided for in the Constitution or national legislation.[43]

The Premier is elected by the provincial legislature.[44] The functions of the Premier include assenting to and signing provincial bills, referring a bill back to the provincial legislature for reconsideration, referring a bill to the Constitutional Court for a decision on the Bill's constitutionality, appointing commissions of enquiry and calling a referendum in the province in accordance with national legislation.[45] The executive council consists of the Premier and between five and ten members appointed by the Premier from the members of the Provincial Legislature.[46] The MECs are responsible for the functions assigned to them by the Premier. The MECs are collectively and individually accountable to the Provincial Legislature for exercising their powers and performance.[47]

Provinces may introduce their own constitutions. Only two provinces have submitted their constitutions to the constitutional court, namely KwaZulu-Natal and the Western Cape.[48]

7. There was confusion in the Constitution of the Republic of South Africa Act 200 of 1993 (hereinafter '1993 Constitution') regarding the relationship between national and provincial government. In the 1996 Constitution, these interpretation problems have more or less been solved, as provision is made for concurrent and exclusive provincial functional areas. Section 104(1)(b) of the 1996 Constitution provides that a province may pass legislation for its province with regard to any matter within Schedule 4 (concurrent national and provincial legislative competence) and Schedule 5 (exclusive provincial legislative competence) functional areas, any matter outside the functional areas assigned to the province in terms of national legislation and any matter for which the Constitution envisages provincial legislation. In accordance with section 104(4), provincial legislation is regarded as a matter listed in the Schedule if it deals with a matter that is reasonable, necessary for, or incidental to the effective exercising of a power concerning any matter listed in Schedule 4. The same applies to parliamentary legislation in this regard.[49] A provincial legislature may also recommend to the National Assembly any legislation outside its functional areas or where an Act of Parliament prevails over a provincial law.[50] Sections 146–150 deal with the interpretation of conflicts between national and provincial legislation.

---

43. Section 125.
44. Section 128. Also *see* A. Du Plessis and O. Fuo, *Governing Authorities in the Same Boat and a Tale of Two Schedules: Marius Nel v Hessequa Local Municipality*, 20 Commonwealth Journal of Local Governance 6076 (2015).
45. Section 127.
46. Section 132.
47. Section 133.
48. Sections 142–145.
49. Section 44(3).
50. Section 104(5).

National legislation that applies uniformly in the country as a whole prevails over provincial legislation if any of the following conditions are met: (a) the matter cannot be regulated effectively by legislation enacted by the provinces individually;[51] (b) the national legislation (in order to ensure effectiveness and uniformity across the nation) establishes norms and standards, frameworks or national policies;[52] (c) the national legislation is necessary for the maintenance of national security and economic unity, the protection of the common market, the promotion of economic activities across provincial boundaries and equal opportunity or equal access to government services and the protection of the environment;[53] (d) the national legislation is aimed at preventing unreasonable action by a province that is prejudicial to the economic, health or security interests of another province or the country as a whole, or impedes the implementation of national economic policy.[54]

The functional areas of concurrent national and provincial legislative competence include disaster management, environment, health services, nature conservation (excluding national parks, national botanical gardens and marine resources), pollution control, population development, public transport and road traffic legislation, regional planning and development, soil conservation, trade, urban and rural development.[55]

The following issues matter to the extent of their compliance with section 155(3), namely to monitor local government matters, and where national and provincial governments have the legislative and executive authority to see to the effective performance by municipalities of their functions.[56] These functions include air pollution, building regulations, electricity and gas reticulation, firefighting services, municipal planning, municipal health services, pontoons, ferries, jetties, piers and harbours, storm water management systems in built-up areas, water and sanitation services limited to potable water supply systems and domestic waste water and sewage disposal systems.[57] According to Schedule 5, the following exclusive functional areas of legislative competence deal with environmental matters: provincial planning and provincial roads and traffic. The following local government issues matter to the extent of their compliance with section 155(3): cleansing, control of public nuisances, fencing, municipal roads, noise pollution and refuse removal, refuse dumps and solid waste disposal. The South Africa Local Government Association

51. Section 146(2)(a).
52. Section 146(2)(b).
53. Section 146(2)(c).
54. Section 146(3).
55. Also *see* V. Bronstein, *Mapping Legislative and Executive Powers over 'Municipal Planning': Exploring the Boundaries of Local, Provincial and National Control*, South African Law Journal 639–663 (2015).
56. *See* on the role of local government in environmental matters, A. Du Plessis, ed., *Environmental Law and Local Government*, Juta, 2015; A. Du Plessis, *A Role for Local Government in Global Environmental Governance and Transnational Environmental Law from a Subsidiarity Perspective*, 48(2) Comparative and International Law Journal of Southern Africa: 281–316 (2015); A.A. Du Plessis, *The 'Brown' Environmental Agenda and the Constitutional Duties of Local Government in South Africa: A Conceptual Introduction, Potchefstroom Electronic Law Journal* 1845–1880 (2015).
57. Also *see* L. Feris, *The Human Right to Sanitation: A Critique on the Absence of Environmental Considerations*, Review of European, Comparative & International Environmental Law (RECIEL) 24(1) (2015).

(SALGA) published, for example, a strategy on renewable energy for local governments, determining local government's contribution to energy savings and reduction of CO_2 emissions.[58] In 2015 the Department of Energy published a document on the *State of Renewable Energy in South Africa*[59] stating that South Africa's policy and legal framework provides an enabling environment to achieve the renewable energy target set for 2030.[60]

8. National government may undertake the responsibilities of provincial governments if it is necessary to maintain essential national standards or meet established minimum standards for rendering a service, maintain economic unity, maintain social security or to prevent the province from taking unreasonable action that is prejudicial to the interests of another province or the country as a whole.[61] Similarly, a province may take over an executive obligation from a municipality if it cannot or does not fulfil its functions.[62]

9. The whole of South Africa is divided into municipalities.[63] During the previous dispensation, municipalities were only to be found in urban areas or towns. The rural areas were not included in the local government structures. Matters in the rural areas were handled by regional services councils and in traditional community areas by traditional leaders.

The objects of local government are to provide democratic and accountable government to local communities, to ensure the provision of services to communities in a sustainable manner, to promote social and economic development, to promote a safe and healthy environment and to encourage the involvement of communities and community organizations in the matters of local government.[64] Local governments must be put into a position to comment on legislation that may affect their status, institutions, powers or functions.[65]

Three categories of municipalities are established. Category A municipalities include municipalities with an exclusive municipal executive and legislative authority. Category B municipalities share a municipal executive and legislative authority with a Category C municipality. A Category C municipality has municipal and

58. SALGA, *Local Government Energy Efficiency and Renewable Energy Strategy*, 2014, https://www.sustainable.org.za/uploads/files/file100.pdf (accessed 26 Apr. 2019).
59. Department of Energy, *State of Renewable Energy in South Africa*, 2015 https://www.gov.za/sites/default/files/gcis_document/201510/state-renewable-energy-south-africas.pdf (accessed 7 May 2019).
60. Also *see* T. Murombo, *Legal and Policy Barriers to Renewable and Sustainable Energy Sources in South Africa*, The Journal of World Energy Law & Business doi: 10.1093/jwelb/jww001 (2016).
61. Section 100 of the Constitution.
62. Section 136.
63. Section 151 of the Constitution.
64. Section 152. *See* in this regard, A.A. Du Plessis, *Local Government and the Pursuit of Urban Sustainability in South Africa*, 263–281. In Fuggle and Rabie's Environmental Management in South Africa (King, N.D, Strydom, H.A. & F.P. Retief, eds, 3rd edn, Juta 2018).
65. Section 154.

executive authority in an area that includes more than one municipality.[66] A municipal council is elected according to the legislation providing for elections.[67] The government may by way of an Act of Parliament provide for the recognition of national and provincial organizations representing municipalities and determine the procedure for consultation with national and provincial government, as well as designate representatives to participate in the National Council of Provinces.

A municipality has executive authority over local government matters listed in Part B of Schedule 4 and Part B of Schedule 5, as well as any other matter assigned to it by national or provincial legislation. A municipality may make and administer by-laws for the effective administration of matters falling in its area of jurisdiction. A by-law that conflicts with national or provincial legislation is invalid. A Schedule 4 and 5 Part A matter may be assigned to a municipality if that municipality has the capacity to administer it and if the matter would be administered most effectively at a local level.[68]

10. The institution, status and role of traditional leadership according to customary law are recognized, subject to the Constitution. Traditional leaders have a National House for Traditional Leaders[69] and Provincial Houses of Traditional Leaders.[70] Traditional leaders have an ex officio role in local government. There is an ongoing dispute between traditional leaders and the government with regard to the division of functions between local government and traditional authority areas. Previously traditional leaders were regarded as custodians of the land and the first address for services. In 2004 a Traditional Leadership and Governance Framework Act 41 of 2003 was promulgated to provide among other things for the recognition of traditional communities, traditional councils and traditional leaders as well as to spell out the functions and roles of traditional leaders. Section 19 states that a traditional leader 'performs the functions provided for in terms of customary law and customs of the traditional community concerned, and in applicable legislation'. In terms of customary law, a traditional leader has to see to the welfare and development of his or her people. Section 19 does not really address the conflict between customary law and legislation. National and provincial government may also provide a role for traditional leaders or councils in respect of *inter alia* land administration, agriculture, health, economic development, environment, disaster management and the management of natural resources.[71]

---

66. Section 155. *See also* the Local Government Municipal: Structures Act 117 of 1998 and the Local Government: Municipal Systems Act 32 of 2000.
67. Section 158.
68. Section 156.
69. Established in terms of s. 212(2) of the Constitution, Traditional Leadership and Governance Act 41 of 2003 and the National House of Traditional Leaders Act 22 of 2009. Traditional leaders are paid by the government – there are approximately 820 recognized traditional leaders and it is estimated that they have control over approximately 23% of the population. The Traditional and Khoi-San Leadership Act 3 of 2019 provides for the recognition of the Khoi-San leaders who were not included in the 2003 legislation.
70. *See* in this regard T.E. Scheepers & W. Du Plessis, *House of Traditional Leaders: Role, problems and future*, 3 PELJ (2000), www.nwu.ac.za/content/volume-3-2000-no1-1 (accessed 25 Jan. 2015).
71. Section 20.

III. Legal Structure

11. South Africa has an uncodified legal system that is derived from both the Roman-Dutch law and the English law, as well as indigenous legal systems. The Constitution also recognizes the personal legal systems of religion-based legal systems.[72] South Africa can therefore be regarded as a mixed legal jurisdiction. The South African law has several sources, namely the Constitution, legislation, precedent (court decisions), common law, custom, indigenous law, the religion-based legal systems and works of modern authors.[73] Not all sources have the same authority – some have binding authority and others have persuasive authority.

12. The court interprets all the different sources; therefore, court decisions (precedents or case law) form an integral part of the sources of the law. In settling disputes, the court has to ascertain the law, apply it to the case and then give judgment. The court has to take previous decisions in similar cases into account (this is also called the principle of stare decisis): 'Previous decisions create (binding) precedents which must be followed. When deciding which court decision has binding authority, the hierarchy of courts in South Africa has to be taken into account.'[74]

The highest court on constitutional matters is the Constitutional Court (established in terms of section 167 of the Constitution). The Supreme Court of Appeal (SCA) is the highest Court of Appeal, except in the case of constitutional matters.[75] It is bound by its own decisions. High Courts[76] have the second-highest authority and are bound by the decisions of the Appellate Division as well as their own decisions. A single judge is bound by the decision of a full bench (two or more judges). Provincial and local divisions of a certain province are usually not bound by judgments of other provinces. These court decisions only have persuasive authority. The lower courts are Magistrates' Courts, Traditional Courts, Labour Courts, etc. Magistrates' Courts are bound by the Appellate Court and High Court decisions in their province. The decisions of lower courts do not serve as precedents and are not reported.[77]

---

72. *See* in this regard D.H. van Zyl, *Geskiedenis van die Romeins-Hollandse Reg*, 1–9 (Butterworths 1983); L.M. Du Plessis, *An Introduction to Law* 49–50 (2nd edn, Juta 1996); D. Kleyn & F. Viljoen, *Beginner's Guide for Law Students*, 16–18 (2nd edn, Juta 1995); T. Humby, et al., *Introduction to Law and Legal Skills in South Africa*, 45–120 (Oxford University Press 2012).
73. Kleyn & Viljoen, *ibid.* at 48–97. Humby, et al., *ibid.* at 121–148.
74. Kleyn & Viljoen, *ibid.* at 64; Humby, et al., *ibid.* at 134–135.
75. Section 167 of the Constitution.
76. Previously 'Supreme Courts'. These courts were established in each province; sometimes a local division of the High Court is also present, for example formerly Witwatersrand and Durban and Coast now, e.g. Gauteng Local Division – s. 169 of the 1996 Constitution read with the Supreme Court Act 59 of 1959 and now the Superior Courts Act 10 of 2013.
77. Court decisions are found in the *South African Law Reports*, *Butterworths Constitutional Law Reports* and various others (use can be made of consolidated indices Butterworth's *Consolidated Index and Noterup to the South African Law Reports* and Juta's *Index* and *Annotations to the South African Law Reports*). The *South African Law Reports* are also available online (*Jutastat*) and the Constitutional Court decisions can also be found on the Internet www.constitutionalcourt.org.za. Until now the Constitutional Court has only decided on one energy law related case dealing with access to electricity, namely *Joseph and Others v. City of Johannesburg and Others* 2010 4 SA 55 (CC). *See also Cape Gate (Pty) Ltd and others v Eskom Holdings Soc Ltd and others* [2019] 1 All

Judges are appointed by a Judicial Service Commission consisting of the Chief Justice, the President of the Constitutional Court, one Judge President designated by the Judges President, a cabinet member responsible for the administration of justice, two practising advocates and two practising attorneys, a teacher of law designated by the teachers of law at South African universities, six persons designated by the National Assembly (three must be from opposition parties), four permanent delegates to the National Council of Provinces and four persons designated by the President after consulting all the parties in Parliament.[78] There is a single prosecuting authority that consists of a National Director of Public Prosecutions and directors of public prosecutions and prosecutors as determined by an Act of Parliament.[79]

§3. Economic Characteristics

13. South Africa is regarded as an upper-middle-income country[80] and joined the BRICS (Brasilia, Russia, India, China, South Africa) strategic partnership in 2010.[81] Despite this, 49% of South Africa's adult population has been regarded as poor according to 2015 statistics.[82] In 2018 the national level of domestic electrification was 85% and 77% of the people had access to sanitation services.[83] Low-income households have access to a basic supply of free electricity[84] and free basic water services.[85] Government introduced several social grants to assist lower-income families, such as child grants[86] and housing subsidies.

14. South Africa's GDP (gross domestic product) was estimated by the World Bank in 2015 at USD 348.27 billion, while the GNI (gross national income per capita) was 5.430 in 2017, among the highest in the world.[87] South Africa's economy is dependent on agriculture (including forestry and fishing) and industry

SA 141 (GJ) where Eskom wanted to cut off a municipality's electricity due to non-payment. However, this would have had detrimental economic effects on those rate payers whose electricity accounts with the municipality was up-to-date. New legislation and policy documents are also to be found at www.gov.za and court decisions on http://www.saflii.org/.

78. Section 178.
79. Section 179.
80. http://data.worldbank.org/country/south-africa (accessed 10 Sep. 2013).
81. www.southafrica.info/global/brics/brics-080411.htm (accessed 10 Sep. 2013).
82. *Ibid.* South Africa *Millennium Development Goals Report*, 23–40 (2010), StatsSA Five facts about poverty http://www.statssa.gov.za/?p=12075 (accessed 20 Apr. 2019).
83. http://www.statssa.gov.za/?page_id=739&id=2=1 (accessed 20 Apr. 2019).
84. *Electricity Pricing Policy*, Government Notice 1398 in *Government Gazette* 31714 of 19 Dec. 2008, para. 9.8. Various other policies are reviewed to address indigent policies, *see also* Department of Water Affairs, *Draft National Water Policy Review: Updated Policy Positions to overcome the water challenges of our developmental state to provide for improved access to water, equity and sustainability*, General Notice 888 in *Government Gazette* 36798 of 30 Aug. 2013.
85. *See* South Africa *Millennium Development Goals Report* (2010) 34–35; *Mazibuko and Others; City of Johannesburg and Others* 2010 4 SA 1 (CC).
86. *See also* www.sassa.gov.za/#ajx/index.php/social-grants/ (accessed 12 Sep. 2013); http://www.info.gov.za/aboutsa/housing.htm (accessed 12 Oct. 2013).
87. http://data.worldbank.org/country/south-africa (accessed 20 Apr. 2019).

(mining, manufacturing, construction and power). Agriculture, forestry and fisheries contributed an estimated 2.59% of the GDP in 2019, while the manufacturing industry contributed 13.53%, electricity, gas and water 2.31% and construction 3.77%.[88] The government of South Africa is committed towards a green economy, and the National Treasury committed more than ZAR 800 million towards a Green Fund over the period from 2012 to 2014. The Department of Environmental Affairs, Forestry and Fisheries (DEAFF) budget ZAR 11 billion towards the green economy in 2019.[89] This fund must be used to create 'high-quality, high-impact, job-creating green economy projects throughout the country'.[90] These projects are to be implemented in 'the environmental goods and services sector, particularly in biodiversity, waste and natural resource management services'. In 2015 the DEA commissioned a report to determine the contribution of business in biodiversity protection.[91] The study revealed that 40% of the 33 JSE listed companies have a good understanding of mainstreaming biodiversity into their business, while the other 40% had less understanding. A total of 20% of these companies had undertaken detailed risk assessments of their activities' impact on the environment. The extractives industries in this research displayed a better understanding of their dependency on biodiversity than the other listed companies.[92]

15. Energy is derived mainly from coal-based electricity, supplemented by nuclear power and hydroelectric power. Natural gas is converted to liquid fuel, and the exploitation of petroleum reserves commenced in 1997 south-west of the Southern Cape. The import of mineral fuels contributes 9.6% of the total imports in 1996 and in 2019, 18.2%.[93] South Africa is currently exploring the possibility of hydraulic fracturing and gas exploration as a future contributor to energy.[94]

16. Mining contributed an estimated 8.5% of the GDP in 2018 and 8.8% in 2011, but its overall contribution may be higher.[95] The mineral industry is export-orientated.

In 2019/2020, the central 'budget deficit' remains substantial at 4.5% of the GDP. The largest risk to the budget deficit is the financial risk posed by Eskom, the country's only electricity utility.[96]

88. https://www.southafricanmi.com/south-africas-gdp.html (accessed 20 Apr. 2019).
89. National Treasury *Environment Budget 2019 Estimates of National Expenditure Vote 27* at 4 http://www.treasury.gov.za/documents/national%20budget/2019/enebooklets/Vote%2027%20Environmental%20Affairs.pdf (accessed 20 Apr. 2019).
90. *SA Yearbook 2012/2013* at 141.
91. NBBN, *Overview of current approaches and practices of South African businesses to the mainstreaming of biodiversity: a preliminary baseline assessment*, Report of the National Biodiversity and Business Network (February 2015).
92. *Ibid.* Executive Summary.
93. http://www.worldstopexports.com/south-africas-top-10-imports/ (accessed 20 Apr. 2019).
94. Lameez Omarjee, *Government to move ahead with shale gas exploration and exploitation – Mantashe, fin24,* 16 May 2018 https://www.fin24.com/Economy/government-to-move-ahead-with-shale-gas-exploration-and-exploitation-mantashe-20180516 (accessed 20 Apr. 2019).
95. http://www.worldstopexports.com/south-africas-top-10-imports/ (accessed 20 Apr. 2019).
96. *SA Yearbook 2012/2013* at 254.

17. Despite the apparent mineral and economic soundness, the relative income per household is still very low. A total of 55.5% of the people living in South Africa have an income lower than ZAR 992 per month.[97] Various reasons can be given, namely the apartheid system that benefited only a few, the sanctions imposed on South Africa in the 1980s and the general economic condition in the world. Unemployment was at a rate of 24.7% of South Africa's economically active population in the third quarter of 2013.[98] Parliament introduced an Employment Tax Incentive Act[99] to provide for a youth wage subsidy, enticing employers to appoint inexperienced youth in their industries, firms or companies to obtain some experience and to make them more employable in future. Government has also introduced various youth development projects and internships to assist young people and women in South Africa to develop new skills and to enter the job market.[100]

In 1994, the government initiated a Reconstruction and Development Plan (RDP), which was later amended by the long-term strategy named Growth, Employment and Redistribution (GEAR). The emphasis is on fiscal discipline, reductions in the budgetary deficit and removal of exchange controls. GEAR was, however, not developed from a sustainable development perspective – the strategy will have to be implemented in such a manner that the environment is not further degraded – GEAR should contribute to rather than prevent sustainable development.[101]

By 1999, positive changes in the economy could be seen. The inflation rate was the lowest in thirty years and the real GDP increased. In 2012–2013, the consumer inflation rate fluctuated between 5.5% and 6.5%.[102] In 2005, the value of the rand against major currencies seemed to have increased and stabilized;[103] however, in 2013 it experienced again a downward spiral.[104] In 2019 the inflation rate was 4.5%.[105]

---

97. StatsSA, *Poverty trends in South Africa: An examination of absolute poverty between 2006 and 2015* (StatsSA 2017) at 14 http://www.statssa.gov.za/publications/Report-03-10-06/Report-03-10-06 2015.pdf (accessed 20 Apr. 2019). The government introduced a skills levy to finance the National Skills Fund established in terms of the Skills Development Act 97 of 1998 and the Skills Development Levies Act 9 of 1999. This money may be used to enhance people's skills to ensure continued employment or to help people to become entrepreneurs.
98. http://beta2.statssa.gov.za/ (accessed 10 Nov. 2013).
99. 26 of 2013.
100. *See*, e.g., www.dti.gov.za/financial_assistance/financial_assistance.jsp (accessed 12 Nov. 2013).
101. Department of Environmental Affairs and Tourism (DEAT), *State of the Environment South Africa 1999 – An Overview* 9–10 (Government Printer 1999).
102. Anon, *Proposals to narrow budget deficit from 4.5% to 4% by 2022*, *SANews*, 20 Feb. 2019, https://www.sanews.gov.za/south-africa/proposals-narrow-budget-deficit-45-4-2022 (accessed 20 Apr. 2019); *SA Yearbook 2012–2013* at 138.
103. Anon, *The Europa World Yearbook 2004*, Volume II 3851–3852 (45th edn, Gresham 2004). In 2002 the 'Rand reached an all-time low against the US dollar'.
104. D. Stratton, *Fluctuating rand plays havoc with insured values and risk exposures*, *rm Attorneys*, 27 Aug. 2013, http://www.mlaw.co.za/index.php/publications?sid=783&pid=40 (accessed 12 Nov. 2013).
105. https://tradingeconomics.com/south-africa/inflation-cpi (accessed 20 Apr. 2019).

South Africa, however, also slided on Transparency International's Corruption Index to 73rd position of 180 countries in 2019.[106] The country experienced major corruption within the government sector that also led to the resignation of the then President in 2018.

18. In 2012, government adopted an infrastructure development plan to transform South Africa's economic landscape, create employment opportunities and improve basic service delivery. Under the guidance of the Presidential Infrastructure Coordinating Committee, 18 strategic integrated projects (SIPs) have been developed. By January 2013, work had started on all 18 SIPs.[107] Some of these strategic projects related to the upgrading and expansion of electricity infrastructure.[108] An Infrastructure and Development Act 23 of 2014 was passed through Parliament. The purpose of the Act is to facilitate and coordinate public infrastructure development that is of significant economic and social importance to the Republic. The aim is also to give these types of projects priority in planning, approval and implementation. The Act is supposed to ensure that the developmental goals of the state are promoted, that the management of infrastructure is improved during the life cycle of the operation of the projects.[109] The Act proposes fast track procedures for infrastructure development.[110]

§4. Social and Cultural Characteristics

19. As has been stated before,[111] the people of South Africa have a rich cultural and religious diversity. There is a tendency towards urbanization. However, as a result of the apartheid policy, men moved from the rural areas to the cities in order to obtain work and to provide a livelihood for their families. Men were not allowed to take their families along. Rural households mostly consist of women, children and elderly people. The so-called *trek*-labour system resulted in a break-up of the traditional family system.

20. Various programmes have been introduced to ensure poverty alleviation. A strategy for social assistance has been developed. Treasury budgeted ZAR 567 billion for the payment to social grants in the 2019/2020 budget.[112] The money is mostly given to the elderly, the disabled and families with children. The child support programme reached 10.6 million children in 2011. The grants are, however, not

106. https://www.transparency.org/cpi2018 (accessed 20 Apr. 2019).
107. *SA Yearbook 2012–2013* at 134.
108. Deputy Minister Magwanishe on Infrastructure Development in South Africa at a meeting in Beijing 30 Oct. 2013, http://www.gov.za/deputy-minister-honourable-bulelani-magwanishes-speech-infrastructure-development-south-africa (accessed 24 Jul. 2015).
109. Long title to the Act.
110. The Act came into operation on 10 Jul. 2014 – Proclamation 44 in *Government Gazette* 37824 of 10 Jul. 2014.
111. *See supra,* para. 1.
112. http://www.treasury.gov.za/documents/national%20budget/2019/speech/speech.pdf (accessed 20 Apr. 2019).

high (differ between ZAR 260 and ZAR 1,200 per month in 2012 – approximately USD 26–USD 120). The system of payment is in some areas effective in that it reaches the rural poor, who do not always benefit from government programmes and services. Unfortunately, this is not the general position. In 2010, approximately ZAR 140 million was made available for social relief of distress caused by poverty. The projected budget for social development in 2010 was more than ZAR 93 billion which is set to increase even further to ZAR 122 billion by 2015.[113] The number of people who rely on these social grants increases per year, but due to rising living costs, it is not enough to sustain a poor household.[114]

21. The spreading of HIV/AIDS is a major problem in South Africa. Approximately 7.2 million South Africans were infected in 2017. There is a drop in the number of new infections.[115] Life expectancy for males was 54.9 years in 2012 and 61.1 in 2019. Women's life expectancy was 59.1 years in 2012 and 67.3 years in 2019. Access to antiretroviral treatment raised the life expectancy of those living with HIV/AIDS.[116] In 2015, a total of 90,000 children lived in 50,000 child-headed households.[117] In 2011 the number of child-headed households was 82,000.[118]

22. In 1998 a *Population Policy for South Africa* was published by the then Department of Welfare. It includes the principle that the development must meet the needs of the present generation and improve their quality of life without compromising the ability of future generations to meet their own needs.[119] Three population factors are addressed in the *White Paper*, namely fertility, mortality and migration. It is recognized that rapid population growth puts pressure on natural

---

113. *SA Yearbook 2012–2013* at 529–530. *See also*, StatsSA, Poverty Trends in South Africa An examination of absolute poverty between 2006 and 2011, March 2014 http://beta2.statssa.gov.za/publications/Report-03-10-06/Report-03-10-06Mar.2014.pdf (accessed 15 Jan. 2015).
114. For the government social grant system – *see* http://www.sassa.gov.za/index.php/social-grants (accessed 20 Apr. 2019); Gabrielle Kelly, *Everything you need to know about social grants*, *GroundUp*, 7 Apr. 2017, https://www.groundup.org.za/article/everything-you-need-know-about-social-grants_820/ (accessed 20 Apr. 2019).
115. UNAIDS, Country Reports – South Africa http://aidsinfo.unaids.org/ (accessed 20 Apr. 2019).
116. *SA Yearbook 2012–2013* at 320; https://www.statssa.gov.za/publications/P0302/P03022018.pdf (accessed 20 Apr. 2019).
117. Parliamentary Monitoring Group, *Child and Youth headed households*, https://pmg.org.za/page/Child-%20and%20youth-headed%20households%20%E2%80%8B (accessed 20 Apr. 2019).
118. Children's Institute, University of Cape Town, *Demography – Child-only households*, October 2013, http://www.ci.org.za/depts/ci/pubs/pdf/general/gauge2014/ChildGauge2014_childrencount_demograaphy.pdf (accessed 23 Jul. 2015); R. Dorrington, et al., *The Demographic Impact of HIV /AIDS in South Africa – National Indicators for 2006* (Centre for Actuarial Research, South African Medical Research Council and Actuarial Society of South Africa 2006) www.assa.org.za (accessed 3 Feb. 2011); Aids Foundation South Africa *HIV/Aids in South Africa* www.aids.org.za/hivaids-in-south-africa/ (accessed 9 Nov. 2013).
119. On the future generations and climate change, *see* A. Du Plessis, *Climate change, public trusteeship and the tomorrows of the unborn*, 31(2) South African Journal of Human Rights 269–293 (2015).

resources and limits social and economic development. Alternatives to migration are proposed to relieve the pressure on natural resources and social services in urban areas.[120]

§5. Main Environmental Problems with Regard to Energy Use

I. Types of Energy

23. Various types of energy are used in South Africa, namely coal, nuclear power, liquid fuels, gas, electricity and biomass. Solar, wind and hydropower are becoming more important.[121] As stated above, South Africa is investigating various other possibilities of energy, namely gas by way of hydraulic fracturing, carbon capture and storage, gasification of coal, etc.[122]

South Africa's main energy source is based on coal. Electricity is generated from coal. The country is also the fifth-largest coal producer and the second-largest exporter of steam coal. Fifty-five percent of the coal mining is done underground; the rest is gathered in opencast mines. The production of electricity is among the cheapest in the world.[123] The reason for this is that the environmental cost of coal mining is not calculated as part of the cost. Low-grade coal is used as the better grade coal is exported to Europe and Japan. South Africa supplies two-thirds of Africa's electricity. Eskom built new power stations to meet the high-energy demand for both domestic and commercial use. To cope with the high demand, Eskom has also reopened three decommissioned power stations. Eskom was established ninety-four years ago, was incorporated as a public company in 2002 and

120. *State of the Environment* at 4.

121. *White Paper on the Energy Policy of the Republic of South Africa* – Government Notice 3007 in *Government Gazette* 19606 of 17 Dec. 1998 (hereinafter '*White Paper on Energy*'); National Energy Act 34 of 2008.

122. *See also* DEA, *National Climate Change Response White Paper* of 2011 para. 8.

123. In 2013 85.4% of South Africa's population had access to electricity – *StatsSA, Household Service Delivery Statistics,* http://www.statssa.gov.za/?page_id=739&id=2=1 (accessed 20 Apr. 2019). A total of 90% of households were connected to the grid in 2016 – Eskom, Recent statistics show that nearly 90% of households in SA now have access to electricity, 4 Jun. 2016, http://www.eskom.co.za/news/Pages/Jun4.aspx (accessed 20 Apr. 2019). It is, however, a problem when electricity is provided to communities who cannot afford to pay for it. The electricity then has no benefit for them. Free electricity for lighting, media and basic cooking is provided to poor households, *see* para. 181 *infra*. Municipalities may only disconnect consumers' electricity who make illegal or unlawful electricity connections if they are specifically authorized to do so in terms of their by-laws or other legislation, *see*, for disputes between municipalities and Eskom: *Xhosana v. King Sabata Dalinyebo Municipality and Others; In Re: Mpakati v. King Sabata Dalinyebo Municipality and Others; In Re: Mehlwempi v. King Sabata Dalinyebo Municipality and Others* (1477/2013, 1478/2013, 1482/2013) [2014] ZAECMHC 24 (13 Mar. 2014); *Matjhabeng Local Municipality v Eskom Holdings Soc Ltd and Others* (924/2013) [2015] ZAFSHC 30 (19 Feb. 2015).

supplies more than 95% of electricity in the country (and more than 60% of electricity consumed in the rest of Africa).[124] As indicated above, Eskom is in financial difficulty, due to various reasons, including overspending and corruption.[125]

Koeberg is South Africa's only nuclear power station, supplies approximately 6% of South Africa's electricity and is located in the Western Cape near the sea. Eskom, the electricity company, developed new nuclear technology, namely a pebble-bed modular reactor to produce energy. It was said that this technology was safe and cost-effective. Eskom abandoned the idea of the pebble-bed and is investigating the introduction of more conventional nuclear power stations.

Low and intermediate-level waste from Koeberg should be disposed of in the Northern Cape at Vaalputs. A dry store has also been commissioned at Thabana.[126] Pelindaba is a nuclear and radiation technology industry and is situated near the Hartbeespoort Dam, west of Pretoria. It has a 20 MW Safari Research and Isotope Reactor.[127] Allegations of radiation in the surrounding area of Pelindaba led in early 2005 to the government threatening to 'gag' alarmists with legislation.[128]

Liquid fuels are produced from coal and natural gas, which is obtained locally. Other liquid fuels are refined from imported crude oil.[129] Natural gas is found at Mossel Bay and the Oribi field off the Cape south coast – this gas is condensed into liquid fuel.[130]

In the rural areas, fuelwood, obtained from natural woodlands, is used for cooking and heating. In some areas, the wood source is totally depleted, and in others it is under severe pressure. The sustainable supply of fuelwood in the rural areas is estimated at 12 Mt. Only half of this can be used as fuelwood. The residues of commercial wood (estimated at 4.2 Mt per year), as well as wood cleared for commercial farming, are also used.[131] Dung is used in some areas as fuel and in some areas to create gas.

Before 2005 renewable energy sources, such as solar, wind and hydro had not been exploited to their full potential.[132] Sunshine in most areas of South Africa averages 2,500 hours per year. Radiation levels range between 4.5 and 6.5 kWh/m^2. In

---

124. *SA Yearbook 2012/2013* at 194, 199–200; Eskom, www.eskom.co.za (accessed 9 Nov. 2013).
125. Canny Maphanga, *Eskom was the 'main theatre where corruption and state capture was taking place' – Mabuza, News24* 22 Feb. 2019, https://www.news24.com/SouthAfrica/News/eskom-was-the-main-theatre-where-corruption-and-state-capture-was-taking-place-mabuza-20190222 (accessed 20 Apr. 2019). Government regularly has to bail out Eskom, *see*, for example, Eskom Subordinated Loan Special Appropriation Amendment Act (2008/09–2010/11 Financial Years) 6 of 2015 – *Government Gazette* 38973 of 6 Jul. 2015 – commenced 6 Jul. 2015 and the Eskom Special Appropriation Act 7 of 2015 – *Government Gazette* 38974 of 6 Jul. 2015 – commenced 6 Jul. 2015.
126. D. Burger, *SA Yearbook 2003/04* at 422–423 (Government Printer 2003).
127. *See* Anon., SAFARI-1 Research Reactor, http://www.necsa.co.za/Necsa/SAFARI-1 (accessed 23 Jul. 2015); World Nuclear Association, Nuclear Power in South Africa, http://www.world-nuclear.org/info/Country-Profiles/Countries-O-S/South-Africa/ (accessed 23 Jul. 2015).
128. S. Smillie, *Nuclear Peek Avoids the Dumping Site*, 6 May The Star 3 (2005).
129. *SA Yearbook 2012//2013* at 200–202; *SA Yearbook 2009/10* at 471–473.
130. *Ibid.*
131. *Ibid.*
132. http://www.energy.gov.za/files/esources/renewables/r_solar.html (accessed 13 Nov. 2013). *See also* B. Schaller, *Solar Energy Becomes a Player*, 3 (December) Civil Engineering 14–16 (1995); L.T.N. Dube, *Wind Energy Potential in Maputaland*, 12 Development Southern Africa 625–636 (1995).

the last few years, subsidies and incentives have been provided for the installation of solar geysers in houses and the number of applications to erect smaller and larger solar power plants increased. The first solar PV power station, located in the Northern Cape, became operational in November 2013 and was the first to be connected to the national grid.[133] Solar energy is also used by the Department of Human Settlements, Water and Sanitation to pump underground and surface water in the rural areas. Solar energy is used to a limited extent in the heating of swimming pools, commerce, industry and agriculture. In the housing plan of government, solar passive design techniques are to be included. This is aimed at reducing the high levels of indoor pollution created by indoor heating either by coal or wood fires.[134] Government aimed to instal more than a million solar water heaters by 2014.[135] In December 2014, the National Energy Regulator of South Africa (NERSA) published a *Draft Discussion Document on Small-Scale Renewable Embedded Generation: Regulatory Framework for Distributor*[136] for discussion. The possibility of the connection of private solar roof panels to the national grid is discussed as well as the implications this may have on revenue income for municipalities. Subsequent to 2014, numerous solar farms were developed, bringing to the fore new environmental challenges that were not previously foreseen.[137]

Along the coastline, wind speeds of up to 4 m/s and in some areas up to 6 m/s are recorded. The first experimental wind farm was opened at Klipheuwel in the Western Cape on 21 February 2003. Subsequently, additional wind farms were developed, with wind contributing 52% of the renewable energy mix in South Africa.[138] At present, wind power is also used for water pumping in the rural areas – approximately 300,000 windmills are used to supply water for livestock and communities. Government is promoting increased installation of wind power. A wind atlas was compiled to provide information on possible locations for these types of plants.[139] Wind power generation, however, has a severe impact on birds and bats. Several NGOs have developed strategies to reduce the effect of wind on these species, for example by drafting an *Aviation Wind Farm Sensitivity Map* as well as drafting of *Minimum Requirements for Avifaunal Impact Assessment for Wind Energy Facilities* and *Guidelines for Bat Monitoring at Wind Farms.*[140]

South Africa as a dry country has little perennial hydropower potential. A few of these plants were established at man-made dams, and it produces approximately

---

133. M. Gosling, *First SA Solar 'Farm' Starts Feeding Grid*, IOL SciTech (2013), http://www.iol.co.za/scitech/science/environment/first-sa-solar-farm-starts-feeding-grid-1.1606082#.UoSKPFfO3_Q (accessed 13 Nov. 2013).
134. http://www.energy.gov.za/files/esources/renewables/r_solar.html (accessed 13 Nov. 2013).
135. http://www.energy.gov.za/files/swh_frame.html (accessed 13 Nov. 2013).
136. http://www.nersa.org.za/ (accessed 6 Jan. 2015).
137. *See* in this regard J. Rudman, P. Gauché and K.J. Esler, *Direct environmental impacts of solar power in two arid biomes: An initial investigation.* 113(11/12) S Afr J Sci. 2017, http://dx.doi.org/10.17159/ sajs.2017/20170113.
138. SAWEA, *Stats and Facts SAWEA*, 25 Mar. 2019, https://sawea.org.za/stats-and-facts-sawea/ (accessed 20 Apr. 2019).
139. http://wasadata.csir.co.za/wasa1/WASAData (accessed 13 Nov. 2013).
140. http://www.birdlife.org.za/conservation/birds-and-wind-energy (accessed 13 Nov. 2013). Similar guidelines were drafted for solar plants.

2.3% of South Africa's total energy output.[141] There are only a few areas that have the potential for hydropower. It is estimated that South Africa's hydropower potential is five times more than its current use. In 2016, the Minister of Water and Sanitation published a *Draft Sustainable Hydropower Generation Policy.*[142] South Africa has not really made use of unconventional sources of hydropower in urban and rural areas, such as canals and water supply pipelines.[143] The Draft Policy provides the 'Policy position for the Department of Water and Sanitation on the establishment and development of hydropower on existing DWS infrastructure as well as within the water resources of South Africa as part of long term interventions by the Department to support sustainable power supply in South Africa'. A few small-scale projects have been introduced in rural areas.[144] The mines also developed innovative technology to use hydropower in deep mine shafts as opposed to conventional electricity or compressed air.[145]

II. Demand and Supply Sectors

24. There are various demand sectors for energy, namely households, industry, commerce and mining, transport and agriculture.[146] In the case of households, there is an increased demand for resources due, *inter alia*, to rapid urbanization and migration to urban centres and coastal centres. Despite the relatively cheap production of electricity, many people in rural as well as urban areas in South Africa have no access to electricity. The government embarked on an accelerated and sustainable electrification programme. Communities are involved in the planning and execution of the programme. Since 1994, 3.8 million households have been connected, which exceeds the target set for the period 1994–2003.

141. *See also* Department of Minerals and Energy, *Implementation Strategy for Renewable Energy in South Africa, Draft 2*, www.dme.gove.za/energy/restrategy_index.htm (accessed 7 May 2001). *See also* the Department's *National Energy Efficiency Strategy of the Republic of South Africa 2008* in Government Notice 908 *Government Gazette* 32342 of 26 Jun. 2009.

142. General Notice 436 in Government Gazette 40140 of 15 Jul. 2016.

143. *See* Draft Policy.

144. http://www.microhydropower.net/rsa/ (accessed 13 Nov. 2013). *See also* W. Karanitsch, *South Africa's Hydro Options*, Jul. Energize, 84–87 (2011).

145. R. Cloete, '*Hydropower System Overcomes Underground Mining Challenges*', Mining Weekly (18 Jul. 2008), http://www.miningweekly.com/article/hydropower-system-overcomes-underground-mining-challenges-2008-07-18 (accessed 13 Nov. 2013); C. Kotze, '*Hydropower Increasingly Used as Opposed to Compressed Air in Platinum, Gold Mines*', Mining Weekly (23 Aug. 2013), http://www.miningweekly.com/article/hydropower-increasingly-used-as-opposed-to-compressed-air-in-platinum-gold-mines-2013-08-23 (accessed 13 Nov. 2013).

146. *White Paper on Energy* – Government Notice 3007 in *Government Gazette* 19606 of 17 Dec. 1998 – Part 2, as well as the National Energy Act 34 of 2008. Also *see* Department of Transport, *Green Transport Strategy for South Africa: (2018–2050)*, http://www.transport.gov.za/documents/11623/89294/Green_Transport_Strategy_2018_2050_onlineversion.pdf/71e19f1d-259e-4c55-9b27-30db418f105a (accessed 2 Jul. 2019).

25. In June 2010, government adopted an Electrification Strategy for Informal Settlements. In 2013, the cabinet approved a new Household Electrification Strategy that aims to 'achieve universal access of 97% of households by 2025'.[147] Several households benefitted from government's electrification strategies. In the period 2012/13, 175,473 (166,130 grid and 9,343 non-grid) households received access to electricity through the Integrated National Electrification Programme. The Integrated National Electrification Programme aiming for better service delivery by municipalities provided 47,204 households with electricity.[148] Government also adopted guidelines to implement its policies and programmes in the rural areas of the country, namely the *Non-grid Electrification Policy Guidelines* of 19 March 2012 (solar home system in rural areas), *Policy Guidelines for Electrification of Unproclaimed areas* of 20 January 2011) and *Policy Guidelines for Electrification of Farm Dweller Households* of 2 February 2010.[149]

Government foresees that energy security for low-income households can reduce poverty, increase livelihoods and improve living standards. A minimum standard for basic household energy services will be determined and monitored over time. Cost, access and health should be considered in the provision of these services.[150] Non-payment for services was once the means used during the struggle against apartheid to force change in government. Unfortunately, the culture persisted after the new government was introduced, as people had become used to not paying for services. To educate people to pay for services, the government launched a massive project, Masakhane. In some areas, the project was very successful, in others less so. Non-payment and theft of electricity are still widespread.[151]

26. Industry, commerce and mining are energy-intensive. The pre-1994 regime did not give any regard to energy efficiency in these areas. Greater energy efficiency could save between 10% and 20% of the current consumption. The introduction of international environmental standards was already considered in 1999,[152] and the importance thereof was reiterated in the *National Climate Change Response White Paper* of 2011 where energy efficiency was announced as one of the government's flagship programmes to address climate change adaptation and mitigation.[153] In 2009, the Department of Energy published a National Energy Efficiency Strategy,[154] in 2010 a *Policy to support the Energy Efficiency and Demand Side Management Program for the Electricity Sector through the Standard Offer Incentive Scheme*[155] and in 2011 an *Integrated Resource Plan 2010–2030*,[156] which was

---

147. Department of Energy, *Annual Report 2012/13* at 43, http://www.energy.gov.za/files/Annual%20 Reports/DoE-Annual-Report-2012-13.pdf (accessed 13 Nov. 2013).
148. *Ibid.*
149. http://www.energy.gov.za/files/policies_frame.html (accessed 13 Nov. 2013).
150. *White Paper on Energy* at 129, Part 2. *See also* M.R. Bhagavan & S. Karekezi, *Energy for Rural Development* (Zed Books 1992).
151. Department of Energy, *Annual Report 2012/2013* at 192.
152. *White Paper on Energy* at 129.
153. https://www.environment.gov.za/legislation/whitepapers (accessed 13 Nov. 2013).
154. General Notice 908 in *Government Gazette* 32342 of 26 Jun. 2009.
155. http://www.energy.gov.za/files/policies/Energy_Efficiency_and_Demand_Side_Management_ Policy.pdf (accessed 12 Nov. 2013).
156. Government Notice R400 in *Government Gazette* 34263 of 6 May 2011.

updated in 2016.[157] The *National Energy Efficiency Strategy* set a target of 12% energy savings by 2015. The target was to be achieved by way of 'economic and legislative means, information activities, energy labels, energy performance standards, energy audits, energy management and the promotion of efficient technologies'. The *Policy to support the Energy Efficiency and Demand Side Management Program* introduced an energy conservation scheme. This scheme identified certain key industrial electricity consumers with a monthly consumption above 100 GWh *per annum* per site. These consumers had to submit their 'historical baseline consumption profile ... in GWh points spread over one year over any twelve-month period) to the licencee (Eskom) by June 2010'. The Minister of Energy set reduction targets for each industrial sector, and NERSA determined a tariff on a punitive scale using the baseline information as its point of departure. If less energy than the baseline is consumed a standard rebate is offered. The *Integrated Resource Plan 2013–2030* supported the continuation of this programme.[158] In 2015 a *Draft Post-2015 National Energy Efficiency Strategy*[159] was published for comment. The Draft Strategy indicates energy-efficiency targets for the public, private and transport sectors. In 2015 the Minister of Energy published draft Regulations regarding registration, Reporting on Energy Management and Submission of Energy Management Plans[160] and in 2018 draft Regulations for the Mandatory Display and Submission of Energy Performance Certificates for Buildings for comment strategies of government to promote energy efficiency.[161]

27. A draft Sixth National Greenhouse Gas (GHG) Inventory Report was published for comment to comply with its obligations in terms of United National Framework Convention on Climate in 2018.[162] The Inventory indicates South Africa's emission trends and states, among other things, that 'gross emissions increased by 1.7% (11 738 Gg CO_2e) and a 6.5% (2 573 Gg CO_2e) increase in the emissions from the *Waste* and *IPPU* sectors respectively. The gross *AFOLU* sector showed an increase of 2.97% while the *Energy* sector showed a decline of 0.04% between 2012 and 2015'. The Energy sector is the largest contributor to CO_2 emissions, contributing 60.4% to gross emissions. The National Energy Act 34 of 2008 makes provision for the South African National Development Institute to undertake research and development of energy-efficiency programmes as well as general energy

157. Department of Energy, Integrated Resource Plan Update: Assumptions, Base Case, Results and Observations (October 2016) – Government Notice 1431 in *Government Gazette* 40445 of 25 Nov. 2016.
158. Paragraphs 4.11–4.13.
159. General Notice 948 in *Government Gazette* 40515 of 24 Dec. 2016. By December 2019, a final strategy had not been published yet.
160. Government Notice R259 in *Government Gazette* 38614 of 27 Mar. 2015.
161. General Notice 369 in *Government Gazette* 41754 of 6 Jul. 2018. By December 2019, these regulations have not been finalized yet.
162. General Notice 552 in *Government Gazette* 41903 of 14 Sep. 2018. In February 2019 a notice was published that the DEA is not able to complete its report in terms of its 2017 Regulations (Government Notice 257 in *Government Gazette* 40762 of 3 Apr. 2017) and provided an alternative as to how Category A and B institution should report on their emissions – Government Notice 71 in *Government Gazette* 42203 of 1 Feb. 2019.

research and development.[163] The Act also provides that the Minister of Energy may introduce energy-efficiency measures by way of regulation.[164] Similar measures are included in the Electricity Regulation Act 4 of 2006.[165] The DEA published a concept strategy on low emissions, namely *South Africa's Low-emission Development Strategy 2050* in December 2018.[166] The document cannot be divorced from socio-economic development, and any changes in placing South Africa on a low-carbon trajectory should also ensure job creation and social upliftment. The strategy includes both mitigation and adaptation measures. The document also indicates that transport is the second contributor to greenhouse gas emissions.

28. Transport, however, still needs liquid fuels. Equitable access to affordable transport is necessary. The government wants to increase fuel diversity within the transport sector. Transport, energy, land use, economic development and environmental policies need to be considered and the departments dealing with these policies be consulted in order to formulate fiscal and transport policies to promote energy conservation and efficiency. At agricultural level, most commercial farmers have access to energy, traditional farmers not necessarily. Also in the case of agriculture, energy efficiency is necessary. Energy policies that need to be considered are access to diesel (removal of barriers to the provision of bulk supplies to small-scale farmers), the electrification of farmworker households and the provision of agricultural, forestry and agroforestry products, by-products and residues as raw material for biofuels. Government published a *Biofuels Industrial Strategy for the Republic of South Africa* in 2007.[167] The Strategy set a '2% penetration level of biofuels in the national liquid fuel supply'. Only sugar cane and sugar beet may be used for bioethanol and sunflower and canola and soya beans for biodiesel. Due to concerns raised about food security, maize and Jatropha may not be used for the production of these substances.[168] From 1 October 2015, petroleum and diesel must be blended with biofuel.[169] In 2014, the then Minister of Energy[170] published a Draft Position Paper on the South African Biofuels Regulatory Framework for comment. The document specifies that grain sorghum and soya beans should be the only reference feedstock that could be used for bioethanol and biodiesel. A biofuel levy will form part of the General Fuel Levy of petrol and diesel. The blending of biofuels

---

163. *National Energy Act* 34 of 2008 – ss 7–8.
164. *See* the discussion in paras 46.1–46.5.
165. Section 14. *See* para. 46.4. *See also* Government Notice R74–75 in *Government Gazette* 37288 of 7 Feb. 2014 – Compulsory specification for incandescent lamps and Compulsory specification for energy efficiency and labelling of electronic and electronic apparatus in terms of National Regulator for Compulsory Specifications Act 5 of 2008.
166. DEA, *South Africa's Low-emission Development Strategy 2050*, https://www.environment.gov.za/sites/default/files/strategic_plans/southafricas_lowemission_developmentstrategy_dec2018 draft.pdf (accessed 7 May 2019).
167. http://www.energy.gov.za/files/esources/renewables/biofuels_indus_strat.pdf%282%29.pdf (accessed 13 Nov. 2013).
168. *Ibid.* at 3.
169. Government Notice R719 in *Government Gazette* 36890 of 30 Sep. 2013.
170. Since June 2019, Minister of Mineral Resources and Energy.

with petrol and diesel will occur at a refinery or depot and will have to be transported by road as the existing petroleum pipelines cannot be used for blended products. In 2019, the Department of Transport published a *Green Transport Strategy for South Africa (2018–2050)* committing government to reduce greenhouse gas emissions in the transport sector. The long-term vision of the Strategy is to introduce 'no-car zones' in central business districts, cycle lanes and pedestrian walkways, reintroduce rail freight for long-distance freight. Green corridors will be introduced to reduce road traffic and fossil-fuel-driven vehicles are to be replaced with 'vehicle technologies with low or zero tailpipe emissions, such as electric and fuel cell vehicles'. Waste collection vehicles and municipal buses should, where not already done, be 'retrofitted to enable propulsion with a combination of biogas and biofuels produced from domestic, commercial and agricultural waste'.

29. The supplier of electricity is Eskom, originally a government-funded institution but 'was converted into a limited liability company, wholly owned by government'. Eskom generates 95% of South Africa's electricity – approximately 45% of this electricity is directly distributed to end users. The other 55% is resold by redistributors such as municipalities. Eskom also distributes 45% of the electricity used in Africa. According to its *Integrated Report* 2013 for the financial year 2012/2013, Eskom distributed 216,561 GWh of which 91,386 GWh was transmitted to municipalities.[171] Municipalities may distribute electricity as an income basis but not all of them can afford to do so.[172] The tariff structures within some municipalities also differ substantially. Electrification is not evenly distributed across regions, with some poorer regions being in the greatest need.[173] As indicated above, Eskom is experiencing financial and other constraints.[174]

30. The provision, distribution and control of nuclear energy are regulated by government.[175] A separate control body, the National Nuclear Regulator, has been established in terms of the National Nuclear Regulator Act 47 of 1999. A company named PetroSA does gas and oil exploration along the Southern African coastline. Offshore rights vest in the state.[176]

---

171. Eskom Holdings SOC, Limited *Integrated Report 2013,* 61, https://overendstudio.co.za/online_reports/eskom_ar2013/pdf/book5.pdf (accessed 13 Nov. 2013).
172. In terms of the Constitution (s. 156 read with Schs 4A and 5A) municipalities with executive authority have the right to administer gas and electricity reticulation if they have the capacity to do so.
173. http://www.eskom.co.za/CustomerCare/TariffsAndCharges/Pages/Tariff_History.aspx (accessed 23 Jul. 2015). For a comprehensive discussion of South Africa's electricity law, *see* A. Klees, *Electricity Law in South Africa* (Juta 2014).
174. Also *see* Anon, *Eskom received emergency bailout in early April, The Citizen,* 19 Apr. 2019, https://citizen.co.za/news/south-africa/government/2121001/eskom-received-emergency-bailout-in-early-april/ (accessed 20 Apr. 2019).
175. *See infra* Part I § 1 and Part I Ch. 2 § 2.
176. http://www.petrosa/ (accessed 13 Nov. 2013).

31. Various petroleum companies are operating in South Africa. Sasol, which produces petroleum from coal and gas, is semi-state owned and was established in 1950. It is listed on the Johannesburg Stock Exchange and the New York Stock Exchange.[177]

32. The coal industry is deregulated. The coal mines belong more or less to three major companies. The aim of the government is to reduce the environmental impact of coal with clean coal technologies. The potential of shale gas is being investigated as well the gasification of deep-lying coal.[178]

The use of renewable energy resources is important in non-grid areas. The government will facilitate the sustainable production and management of solar power and non-grid electrification systems (e.g., solar cookers, solar pump water supply systems, solar systems for schools, clinics and homes, as well as hybrid electrification systems and wind power). The development of these energy resources is targeted at rural communities. Research into low-smoke fuels will also be promoted.[179]

III. Environmental Problems

33. Various reasons contributed to the current environmental situation.[180] These reasons include the need to meet the food and energy requirements of the population, the need for economic growth and job creation.[181] The previous government's macroeconomic and sectoral policies included settlement policies, discrimination with regard to access to natural resources and subsidization. Government subsidized energy and water use. This helped industry and commercial farmers to produce their goods cheaply. The environmental costs were not taken into account. As it is stated in the 1999 *State of the Environment in South Africa Report*:[182]

(c)onservation measures were typically to restrict access to protected areas, alienating large sections of the population from environmental issues such as wildlife conservation. The resource use patterns that resulted were exploitative. Industry and agriculture used energy and water wastefully, as there were no incentives to use them wisely, or to recycle waste products. These policies created large distortions in the economy and the distribution of wealth. As a result, large sections of the

---

177. www.sasol.co.za (accessed 13 Nov. 2013).
178. Also *see* the study of R. Scholes et al., eds, *Shale Gas Development in the Central Karoo: A Scientific Assessment of the Opportunities and Risks*, CSIR/IU/021MH/EXP/2016/003/A (CSIR 2016).
179. *White Paper on Renewable Energy*, 2004.
180. *See also* J. Glazewski & L. du Toit, eds, *Environmental Law in South Africa* 1–6–1–7 (2nd edn, LexisNexis 2013); *National Biodiversity Framework* – Government Notice 813 in *Government Gazette* 32474 of 3 Aug. 2009. Also *see* the global issues in L.J. Kotzé, *Global Environmental Constitutionalism in the Anthropocene* (Hart Publishing Co 2016); L.J. Kotzé, *Environmental Law and Governance for the Anthropocene* (Hart Publishing Co. 2017).
181. *See also State of the Environment* at 4.
182. DEAT, *State of the Environment South Africa 1999 – An Overview* 9 (Government Printer 1999).

population were driven to live in settlements which had no formal services such as water supplies and sanitation. Levels of resource use were unsustainable, and environmental degradation was widespread.

In the past few years, the pressures on the environment resulted in the loss of aquatic biodiversity,[183] five plant species became extinct due to urbanization, soil acidification led to reduced productivity and sea-level rise damaging coastal habitats. South Africa was ranked 128th out of 132 countries in the 2012 Environmental Sustainability Index of Yale University, at the World Economic Forum, Davos, Switzerland. South Africa was then regarded as among the 'lowest 10 trend index performers'. The index is compiled taking into account countries' natural resources, past and present pollution levels, environmental management efforts as well as the improvement in performance over a period of time.[184] In 2018, South Africa was ranked as 142nd out of 180 countries worldwide and 21st out of 46 African countries.[185]

34. South Africa's contribution on a global scale to greenhouse gases is relatively small. On a local basis and per capita, however, it exceeds global averages and that of other middle-income developing countries. The reason is that South Africa relies on coal as the primary source of electricity and oil (and coal) for its primary sources for fuel. Mining operations contribute to greenhouse gases with methane and other emissions. Large volumes of sulphur dioxide and nitric oxide released into the air by industrial and agricultural activities are deposited on soil, vegetation and water, where they cause acidification. Large areas of farmland and forests on the Eastern Highveld and Mpumalanga already show reduced productivity. Some pollutants cause respiratory diseases and cancer.[186]

35. South Africa ratified the Montreal Protocol in 1990 and is, therefore, committed to phasing out production of ozone-depleting substances by 2030. Since 1992, chlorofluorocarbons and carbon tetrachloride have been phased out, while others are still in the process of being phased out.[187] Air pollution is also caused by the stockpile of burning coal dumps in the Mpumalanga region. These coal discards have a spontaneous combustion. The emissions from these dumps are not always monitored. The rate of combustion is also unpredictable.[188]

---

183. Twenty-four plant species, twenty-five fish species, six amphibian species, two reptile species, twenty-four bird species and two mammal species are on the endangered list – *see ibid.* at 24–27.
184. *See* Yale Centre for Environmental Lawcll and Policy, Yale University, Centre for International Earth Science Information Network, Columbia University *2012 Environmental Performance Index,* http://epi.yale.edu/sites/default/files/downloads/Summary_Final-%20OnlineV3_1.pdf (accessed 13 Nov. 2013).
185. *See* Yale Centre for Environmental Law and Policy, Yale University, Centre for International Earth Science Information Network, Columbia University *2018 Environmental Performance Index,* https://epi.envirocenter.yale.edu/epi-country-report/ZAF and https://epi.envirocenter.yale.edu/2018-epi-report/executive-summary (accessed 21 Apr. 2019).
186. DEAT, *State of the Environment South Africa 1999 – An Overview* 15, 21 (Government Printer 1999).
187. *Ibid.* at 8.
188. *See* J.D. Wells, et al., *Terrestrial Minerals* in Fuggle and Rabie's Environmental Management in South Africa, 524–526 (H.A. Strydom & N.D, King, eds, 2nd edn, Juta 2009).

36. Coal as such is used by 950,000 households per day, which brings indoor pollution problems with a serious health risk.[189] In some instances, people's exposure to particulate matter exceed the World Health Organization Standards (180 mg/m^3) by factors of six to seven during winter, and two to three in summer. Low-smoke alternatives are being investigated for use especially in townships.

37. Three million households rely on fuelwood.[190] These people experience even a higher level of exposure to particulate matter than coal users – exposure in one instance exceeded the World Health Organization's lowest-observed level effect twenty-six times. The introduction of improved wood stoves, solar cookers and biogas are being investigated to address the pollution problem. The use of paraffin by low-income households as fuel source is even more widely spread in both rural and urban areas. Paraffin is associated with health and safety problems.[191] Higher electricity and paraffin prices lead to a reduction in the use of electricity and the indigent returning to using firewood as their main source of energy.[192]

38. Freshwater was also exploited by industry, mining and other users. Rapid population growth and urbanization put further stress on water resources. It is foreseen that South Africa will experience water stress especially in the main metropolitan areas.[193] In future social and economic equity will play a major role in the allocation of water.[194]

39. More than 42 million cubic metres of solid waste is generated each year, as is an additional 5 million cubic metres of hazardous waste. The country's capacity to store and treat waste is limited and landfill shortages occur. Not all hazardous waste is correctly disposed of. It seems that only 5% of the total amount of waste is treated at hazardous waste disposal sites. This implies that there is illegal dumping, or frequent accidents and spills.[195]

---

189. *See also* C. Crothers, *Levels of Winter Smoke Pollution in South Africa: Establishing a Need for Policy to be Developed*, 5 SAJELP 141–148 (1998); R. Norman, et al., *A Comparative Risk Assessment for South Africa in 2000: Towards Promoting Health and Preventing Disease*, 97 South African Medical Journal 637–641 (2007).
190. C. van Horen & A. Eberhard, *Energy, Environment and the Rural Poor in South Africa*, 12 Development Southern Africa 197–211 (1995); *see also* A. Williams & C.M. Shackleton, *Fuel Wood Use in South Africa: Whereto in the 21st Century*, 196 The Southern African Forestry Journal 1–7 (2002); S.E. Uhunamure, N.S. & A. Musyoki, *Driving forces for fuelwood use in households in the Thulamela municipality, South Africa*, 28 Journal of Energy in Southern Africa (2017) http://dx.doi.org/10.17159/2413-3051/2017/v28i1a1635.
191. R. Norman, et al., *Estimating the Burden of Disease Attributable to Indoor Air Pollution from Household Use of Solid Fuels in South Africa in 2000*, 97 South African Medical Journal 764–771 (2007).
192. DEAT, *Energy, the Millennium Development Goals and the Key Emerging Issues* 9 (2010), http://deat.gov.za/State_of_the_Environment.html accessed under 'emerging issue papers' (accessed 13 Nov. 2013).
193. *State of the Environment.*
194. General Notice 888 in *Government Gazette* 36798 of 30 Aug. 2013.
195. *State of the Environment.*

40. Since 1994, there has been a policy shift towards sustainable development.[196] New legislation includes sustainable development as a principle.[197] Some of the aims included in the *White Paper on Energy* are the improvement of air quality, the introduction of safety standards, the removal of subsidies, the promotion of cleaner technologies and use of renewable energy resources, the introduction of environmental performance auditing and the establishment of emission reductions programmes.

41. In 2004 a *White Paper on Renewable Energy* was also published stating as its vision '(a)n energy economy in which modern renewable energy increases its share of energy consumed and provides affordable access to energy throughout South Africa, thus contributing to sustainable development and environmental conservation'.

The policy shift indicates that government is serious on the one hand to provide energy, but on the other to take the environmental and health consequences into consideration.[198] Several incentives and disincentives have been introduced to promote the use of alternative energy, to become energy efficient or not to pollute water resources.[199] Subsequently, South Africa also became a signatory to the 2030 Agenda for Sustainable Development in 2015.[200]

42. The Department of Trade and Industry promotes spatial development initiatives to ensure that development is concentrated in certain areas. The purpose is to reduce the fragmented approach to development by concentrating it in specified corridors. With these initiatives, strategic environmental assessments are also done, although there is no legal obligation to do so. The environmental opportunities and constraints to policies and development on a regional scale are considered. The potential conflict between projects must be identified, and awareness must be raised with regard to the cumulative impacts from different projects.[201]

---

196. *See also* E. Bray, *Towards Sustainable Development: Are We on the Right Track?* 5 Southern African Journal of Energy Law and Policy 1–16 (1998).
197. *See*, e.g., the NWA 36 of 1998; NEMA 107 of 1998; National Forests Act 84 of 1998; National Energy Act 34 of 2008.
198. *See also National Climate Change Response White Paper* at 137 (2011).
199. *See* in this regard L.J. Kotzé & C. Bosman, *A Legal Analysis of the Proposed Waste Discharge Charge System in Terms of the South African Environmental and Water Law Framework*, 27 Obiter 128–145 (2006); W. Du Plessis, *Recent Developments in the Use of Environmental and Energy Taxes in South Africa* in Critical Issues in Environmental Taxation, 217–237 (K. Deketelaere, ed., Oxford University Press 2007).
200. *See* D. French and L.J. Kotzé, eds, *Sustainable development goals: Law, theory and implementation* (Edward Elgar 2018); W. Fourie, ed, *Implementing Sustainable Development Goals in South Africa: Challenges and Opportunities*, Report, August 2018.
201. *See* DEAT, *State of the Environment South Africa 1999 – An Overview* at 33 (Government Printer 1999).

Chapter 2. Basic Principles of Energy Law

43. In the past, one principle governed energy laws, and that was to ensure government control over this important source and to ensure its exploitation to the fullest in order to expand industry and agriculture. Environmental costs were not taken into account. Subsequent to 2000, new energy legislation introduced a shift towards the protection of safety, health and the environment.[202]

The regulation of energy laws was and still is fragmented[203] and the laws were not really enforced. One of the reasons was that most of the energy-related industries were government-controlled. The energy legislation did not address the full cycle of production, exploitation, transportation, distribution and consumption. These matters were to be found in different legislation if regulated at all. Some of the energy sectors were not regulated at all or were indirectly regulated by other legislation, the main purpose of which was not energy-related.

44. Since the introduction of the Constitution, however, a new dispensation has arrived. Section 24 gives people a right to an environment that is not detrimental to their health or well-being and to have the environment protected against activities which are damaging or degrading. The principle of sustainable development is included in this right, but it is also stated that a balance must be found between the protection of the environment on the one hand and justifiable social and economic development on the other.[204]

45. The new environmental policies and legislation introduced subsequent to 1994[205] all focus on sustainable development.[206] They also acknowledge the importance of improved information and communication technology, access to information,[207] international awareness and pressure towards sustainable development and

202. *See*, e.g., Gas Act 48 of 2001; Petroleum Pipelines Act 60 of 2003; Electricity Regulation Act 4 of 2006.

203. The fragmentation was further exacerbated with the introduction of the so-called homeland system. Six so-called self-governing territories and four so-called independent countries were created. Each of these areas was allowed to legislate on certain matters, which included the environment. Most of the legislation still exists as it has not been repealed or rationalized. *See* in this regard W. Du Plessis, *Integration of Existing Environmental Legislation in the Provinces*, 2 SAJELP 23–36 (1995); M. Kidd, *Environmental Law* 100–101 (2nd edn, Juta 2011).

204. *Fuel Retailers Association of Southern Africa v. Director-General Environmental Management, Department of Agriculture, Conservation and Environment, Mpumalanga Province* 2007 6 SA 4 (CC); E. Couzens & M. Lewis, *South Africa*, in International Encyclopaedia of Laws: Environmental Law, paras 77–79 (K. Deketelaere, et al., ed., Kluwer Law International 2013). *See also infra* para. 130 and E. Snyman, et al., ed., *An Integrated Environmental Management System for the North West Province – Final Report Phase II* (Unpublished 2004).

205. *See* the discussion on legislation Parts I–VI *infra*.

206. *See also* T.P. van Reenen, *Environmental Policy-Making and Effective Environmental Administration*, 1 SAJELP 35–48 (1994).

207. *See infra* Part VI.

a raised public awareness.[208] The National Environmental Management Act (NEMA) 107 of 1998 (NEMA), for example, provides in detail in section 2 for the principle of sustainable development that has to be taken into account by organs of state taking decisions which may impact on the environment.[209]

46. A participatory approach is also followed. Public participation is of the utmost importance, both in the formulation of new legislation,[210] but also in being consulted on matters that may influence their health, lives and the environment.[211] In the case of environmental impact assessments, for example, an extensive public participation process is to be followed.[212]

47. Section 39 of the Constitution contains an extensive *locus standi* provision. Before the new Constitutional dispensation in 1994, a person could only approach the court if he or she experienced harm or if there was a potential for harm. Section 39 of the Constitution provides that persons who may approach the court are (a) 'anyone acting in their own interest; (b) anyone acting on behalf of another person who cannot act in their own name; (c) anyone acting as a member of, or in the interest of a group or class of persons; (d) anyone acting in the public interest; and (e) an association acting in the interest of its members'. NEMA added that a person might also act in the interest of the environment.[213] The Constitution and NEMA broadened the scope of persons who may approach the courts. This resulted in the energy industry taking their environmental responsibilities more seriously.

48. The principle of the polluter pays is, for example, included in NEMA and the National Water Act 36 of 1998 (NWA).[214] It is only since the late 1990s that this principle was formally introduced into South African legislation.[215]

49. The precautionary approach is included in section 2(4)(a)(vii) in NEMA as a risk-averse and cautious approach, which takes into account the limits of current knowledge about the consequences of decisions and actions.[216] It is also included in

208. DEAT, *State of the Environment South Africa 1999 – An Overview*, 28 (Government Printer 1999); DEA, *2nd South Africa Environment Outlook – a report on the state of the environment – Executive Summary* (2016), https://www.environment.gov.za/sites/default/files/reports/environmentoutlook_executivesummary.pdf (accessed 21 Apr. 2019).
209. *See infra* para. 140.
210. *See Doctors for Life International v Speaker of the National Assembly and Others* (2006 (6) SA 416 (CC).
211. *See* in this regard also A. Du Plessis, *Public participation, Good Environmental Governance and fulfilment of Environmental right,* Potchefstroom Electronic Law Journal 12 (2008) https://journals.assaf.org.za/per/article/view/2762 (accessed 21 Apr. 2019).
212. Section 24 of NEMA read with Government Notice R982 in *Government Gazette* 38282 of 4 Dec. 2014.
213. *See infra* para. 245.
214. *See* paras 240 and 255 respectively.
215. In the late 1980s, it was introduced into the previous Water Act 56 of 1954 with s. 22A.
216. *See* in this regard J. Glazewski and L. Plit L, *Towards the application of the precautionary principle in South African law*, Stellenbosch Law Review 190–219 (2015).

the Marine Living Resources Act 18 of 1998.[217] The duty of care principle is, for example, included in section 28(1) of NEMA and section 19(1) of the NWA.

50. A person or company can be held liable if there is a fault and in some instances absolute or strict liability present.[218] Fault or blameworthiness is present when a person acts in a reprehensible state of mind (intent) or with insufficient care (negligence). Intent is a manifestation of the will to the attainment of a certain consequence and the consciousness that the conduct in question is wrongful. A subjective test is applied. 'Conduct is negligent if the actor does not observe that degree of care which the law requires'. The standard of care is that which a reasonable man would exercise in the same situation. The objective standard of care implies that legal blameworthiness can attach to a person or company who, for example, was unable to prevent an act that someone else would have prevented. Absolute or strict liability is an English concept, which was taken over in South African law in some legislation dealing with occupiers of dangerous premises (e.g., initially in the Aviation Act 74 of 1962). The Nuclear Energy Act 131 of 1993 refers to strict environmental liability.[219] The concept was not known to South African common law and is still regarded as the exception rather than the rule.

51. Energy law can be linked to administrative law.[220] Before 1994, the administrative law in South Africa was based on the English law. Since the introduction of the 1993 Constitution, provision was made in section 24 for a right to administrative action that is lawful, reasonable and procedurally fair, as well as to a right to written reasons for administrative action. A similar right was included in the Constitution.[221] This right was given effect by the Promotion of Administrative Justice Act 3 of 2000.[222] Cooperative governance is another important principle that was introduced by the 1996 Constitution.[223] It is also an important issue in the *White Paper on Energy*,[224] as it is foreseen that energy policies must be 'carefully coordinated with other social sectors and also be coordinated between energy subsectors'. The obligation placed on organs of state to cooperate is strengthened by the *Intergovernmental Relations Framework Act*,[225] which establishes a framework for national, provincial and local governments to promote and facilitate intergovernmental relations. One of the objectives of the Act is to facilitate coordination in

---

217. *See also* J. Glazewski & L. du Toit, eds, *Environmental Law in South Africa,* 1–25–1–26, 7–13 (LexisNexis 2013).
218. In the case of *Chief Pule Shadrack VII Bareki NO and Another v. Gencor Limited and Others* (19895/03) [2005] ZAGPHC 109 (19 Oct. 2005) the court, for example, stated that s. 28 refers to strict liability.
219. *See infra* para. 112.
220. Also *see* M. Kidd. *Administrative Law,* 209–261. In Fuggle and Rabie's Environmental Management in South Africa (King, N.D, Strydom, H.A. & F.P. Retief, eds. 3rd edn, Juta 2018).
221. Section 33. *See also* C. Hoexter, *Administrative Law in South Africa* (2nd edn, Juta 2012).
222. *See infra* paras 28, 134, 179.
223. *See infra* para. 135.
224. Government Notice 3007 in *Government Gazette* 19606 of 17 Dec. 1998 – executive summary.
225. 13 of 2005.

the implementation of policy and legislation to ensure the effective provision of services. It was found that non-cooperation hampers development.[226] In some legislation, provision is made for a positive obligation on government departments to draft cooperative agreements, for example in the National Nuclear Regulator Act 47 of 1999.[227]

52. Although government stresses the realization of cooperative governance, it is apparent that some government departments are still in a tug of war regarding decision-making on environmental issues. The Department of Minerals Resources' (DMR)[228] legislation, for example, indicates a strong trend in monopolizing issues regarding the environment within its own departmental sphere, excluding the final decision-making from the other department. The then DEA, on the other hand, introduced legislation (e.g., biodiversity and environmental impact legislation) to ensure that it will have a say in energy and mining issues pertaining to the environment. Despite amendments to the Mineral and Petroleum Resources Development Act 28 of 2002 (MPRDA) and NEMA in 2008 to align environmental decision-making in mining matters, the status quo continues (with the DMR as main decision-maker on environmental affairs relating to mining issues) with the introduction of the National Environmental Laws Amendment Act 25 of 2014[229] and the National Environmental Laws Second Amendment Act 30 of 2013.[230] This tug of war is in contrast with the Constitutional mandate of cooperative governance.

226. Section 3 read with memorandum to Bill.
227. *See* in this regard W. Du Plessis, *Legal Mechanisms for Cooperative Governance in South Africa: Successes and Failures*, 23 South African Public Law 87–110 (2008). Government Notice 712 in *Government Gazette* 37941 of 29 Aug. 2014 is an example of a cooperation agreement between the National Nuclear Regulator and the National Energy Regulator of South Africa.
228. Since June 2019, the Minister of Mineral Resources also obtained the portfolio of energy and is referred to as the Minister of Mineral Resources and Energy.
229. This Act commenced 2 Sep. 2014. The Mineral and Petroleum Resources Development Bill [B15B-2013] that had to support this amendment has by December 2019 not been signed by the President.
230. The Act will commence on a date as set in the *Government Gazette* or 8 Dec. 2014.

Chapter 3. Historical Background

53. The first 'energy' measures were included in legislation regulating air pollution. Energy law developed as the need arose. Initially, air pollution was first regarded to be a national issue, but it became a global issue that transcends the boundaries of countries. Since 1919, limited control measures have been introduced.[231] The Public Health Act 36 of 1919 regarded air pollution as a classifiable nuisance that was to be regulated by local authorities. Air pollution was a criminal offence. It was, however, difficult to prove which industry or chimney was responsible for the pollution. A bill aimed at air pollution control was introduced in 1958 but was read in Parliament only in 1961. The Bill underwent modifications as a result of input from organizations and bodies.

The Atmospheric Pollution Prevention Act 45 of 1965 was promulgated in April 1965.[232] The Act was based on the British Akali Works Regulation Act of 1906 (control of noxious and offensive gases) and the British Clean Air Act of 1956 (control of smoke). The Act was administered by the Department of Health. In 2005 the National Environmental Management: Air Quality Act 39 of 2004 (NEMAQA) was promulgated. The Act was introduced by the then Department of Environmental Affairs and Tourism (DEAT)[233] and was partially implemented on 11 September 2005. The Act conforms to the principles set out in the *White Paper on an Integrated Pollution and Waste Management Policy for South Africa.*[234]

54. In April 2004, a Draft Energy Efficiency Strategy of the Republic of South Africa was published for comment.[235] The strategy links energy sector development with socio-economic development plans. It provides clear and practical guidelines for the implementation of efficient practices. It foresees the implementation of low-cost or no-cost interventions. A national target of energy-efficiency improvement of 12% by 2014 is expected, allowing, however, for current expectations of economic growth. The vision of the strategy is to minimize the effect of energy usage on human health and environment. In the *Draft Post-2015 National Energy Efficiency Strategy*,[236] it is indicated that South Africa has already exceeded the 12% target in 2012 with the overall economy saving 23.7%, industry 34.5% and households 28.2%, among others.[237]

---

231. The following discussion is based on R.F. Fuggle & M.A. Rabie, *Environmental Management in South Africa* 395–396; 411–416; 421–428; 435–437 (Juta 1992).

232. For a discussion of the Act – *see infra* para. 165.

233. The Minister responsible for the environment, since June 2019 known as the Minister of Environment, Forestry and Fisheries.

234. *See also infra* paras 29, 31, 138 and M. Kidd, *Integrated Pollution Control in South Africa – How Easy a Task?* 2 SAJELP 37–54 (1995); R. Stein, *Regulation of Waste Management in South Africa – A Case for Integration*, 4 SAJELP 253–268 (1997).

235. www.energy.gov.za.

236. General Notice 948 in *Government Gazette* 40515 of 24 Dec. 2016. By December 2019, a final strategy had not been published yet.

237. *See also* the study of Stephen Davis and Ian Durbach, *Modelling household responses to energy efficiency interventions via system dynamics and survey data*, 26(2) OriON (2010) at 79–96.

55. Due to sanctions during the previous dispensation and the price of oil and petroleum, South Africa tried to find alternative sources of energy. Soekor (Pty) Ltd, a state-financed but private company was established in 1965. Exploration was initially done by private companies and by 1976 thirteen wells had been drilled (four with Soekor's collaboration). Since 1976, Soekor has taken over the drilling. Until 1991, the search was confined to the continental shelf 200 m isobath on the south and east coasts and landward 500 m isobath on the west coast. In 1980, an F-A condensate gas field was found 90 km south of Mossel Bay. In 2019 it was announced that new offshore gas fields were found.[238] Since 1991 gas and oil has been sent by pipeline to Mossel Bay to be converted to gas and liquid fuel. Other gas fields have subsequently been found. In terms of the Mineral Rights Act 20 of 1967, all rights to natural oil are vested in the state. Soekor has a prospecting lease which lasted until 20 June 2007. The lease did not include the coastal areas of the former Transkei and Ciskei. In 1991, Soekor was granted a mining lease in terms of the same Act. The Mines and Works Act 27 of 1956 initially did not apply to offshore mining, but in 1990 the Regulations issued in terms of the Act were amended to a chapter dealing with offshore installations. In 2002 PetroSA was established – a merger between Soekor, Mossgas (Pty) Ltd and sectors of the Strategic Fuel Fund Association.[239]

South Africa signed a memorandum of understanding with Mozambique in 1996 and with Namibia in 1997 to facilitate cross-border trade in natural gas.[240] Sasol was established in the 1960s to produce petroleum products from coal. Sasol was funded by the government but enjoyed greater autonomy from political control than other purely governmental organizations.[241] Because of its strategic nature, information on South Africa's crude consumption, refinery capacities and product split is regarded as secret in terms of the Petroleum Products Act 120 of 1977.[242] The Gas Act 48 of 2001 regulates the transfer of gas via pipelines and includes the Mozambique-South African agreement.[243]

56. Before 1994, environmental laws were not really enforced against the energy industry, as most of the enterprises were state-owned or funded.[244] In the 1990s, South Africa again became part of the global economy. Industries soon realized that if they wanted to compete in the global market, they would have to comply with environmental legislation.[245] The imperative in the 1996 Constitution to protect the environment as well as the new environmental legislation published after 1994

238. Lauren Isaacs, *SA offshore gas find could yield 1 billion barrels, says Total*, EWN (7 Feb. 2019) https://ewn.co.za/2019/02/07/sa-offshore-gas-find-could-yield-1-billion-barrels-says-total (accessed 21 Apr. 2019).
239. http://www.petrosa.co.za/discover_petroSA/Pages/Historic-Milestones-PetroSA.aspx (accessed 16 Nov. 2013).
240. Republic of South Africa, http://www.gov.za/about-sa/energy (accessed 24 Jul. 2015).
241. *See* R.F. Fuggle & M.A. Rabie, *Environmental Management in South Africa*, 69 (Juta 1992).
242. *See infra* Part III.
243. Section 36 Gas Act 48 of 2001.
244. *See also* P. Kirk, *Stink over SA's Foul Air*, Mail&Guardian (28 Apr. to 4 May 2000) 7.
245. *See also* P. Ngobese & J. Cock, *Development and the Environment* . In Managing Sustainable Development in South Africa, 256–272 (P. Fitzgerald, A. McLennan & B. Munslow, eds, Oxford University Press 1997).

brought about a mind shift. Some industries strive to comply with international standards even if they are not forced to do so by legislation, others apply for ISO 14001 certification, of which one of its components is legal compliance.

57. In 2007, the then Department of Minerals and Energy (DME) published an Energy Security Master Plan for Liquid Fuels.[246] According to the Plan it was already estimated in 2005 'that the economy would, in the case of total fuel supply disruption, lose at least ZAR 925 million a day (at 2005 prices)'. The Master Plan deals, among other things, with 'developing supply chain solutions to South Africa's liquid fuels supply challenges' and 'management of liquid fuels demand and emergency response tactics'. The Plan states that various factors need to be taken into account in the long-term such as supply, demand, macroeconomics, geopolitics and climate change, while the industry should try to minimize its negative impacts on the environment and the economy. South Africa will follow a central planning approach to ensure energy security in the short, medium and long-term. Various proposals are made in this regard. The Plan concluded that the following issues are prerequisites to ensure energy security, namely:

the development of South Africa's ability to develop properly thought-out energy plans, as well as a tool for evaluating proposed energy policies … there is an urgent requirement to develop an integrated energy modelling capability, which would be instrumental in the development of energy plans and evaluation of options that are proposed by policy-makers. This also implies a clear definition of roles for various players. One of the important areas in this regard is the responsibility for managing the data and models that are used in planning. It is recommended that the approach used by the US Department of Energy in the form of the '*energy information administration*' approach be adopted in South Africa.[247]

---

246. Government Notice 859 in *Government Gazette* 30285 of 12 Sep. 2007. The names of the
247. Paragraph 13 of the Master Plan.

Chapter 4. Role of Government Institutions in Shaping and Administration of Energy Law and Policy

§1. THE GOVERNMENTAL INSTITUTIONS AND THEIR COMPETENCIES

58. There are at present more than fifty government departments, of which the Departments of Mineral Resources and Energy, Environmental Affairs, Forestry and Fisheries, Human Settlements, Water and Sanitation, Defence, National Treasury, Agriculture, Land Reform and Rural Development, Transport, Human Settlements, Trade and Industry, Transport, Tourism, Cooperative Governance, Planning, Monitoring and Evaluation and Health are of importance to the energy industry.[248]

Each department is responsible for the implementation and administration of the legislation applicable to them.[249] The Constitution refers to the basic principles governing public administration.[250] First, public administration must be governed according to the values and principles of the Constitution. The principles apply to administration in every sphere of government, organs of state and public enterprises. A list of additional principles is given, namely that (a) a high standard of professional ethics must be promoted and maintained; (b) efficient, economic and effective use of resources must be promoted; (c) public administration must be development orientated; (d) services must be provided impartially, fairly, equitably and without bias; (e) people's needs must be responded to, and the public must be encouraged to participate in policy-making; (f) public administration must be accountable; (g) transparency must be fostered by providing the public with timely, accessible and accurate information; (h) good human-resource management and career-development practices; and (i) the public administration must be broadly representative of the South African people.

A Public Service Commission has been established in terms of section 196 of the Constitution. This commission is *inter alia* responsible for the promotion of the values and principles in the Constitution, the investigation, monitoring and evaluation of the organization and practices of the public service and the proposal of measures to ensure effective and efficient performance in the public service. A policy document, named *Batho Pele* (people first) was published in 1996 – spelling out the responsibilities of the public service.

59. The legislative process in South Africa goes through various stages. In some instances, a policy document, namely a green paper, is generated by the relevant government department. After a consultation process, a white paper is sometimes

248. The names of the Departments changed in June 2019. Approximately 1.2 million people contributed to the government pension fund in 2013 – http://www.gepf.gov.za/index.php/about_us/article/who-is-gepf (accessed 14 Nov. 2013). For a discussion on the administration, implementation and enforcement of environmental law, *see* J. Glazewski & L. du Toit, eds, *Environmental Law in South Africa,* Ch. 6 (LexisNexis 2013); M. Kidd, *Environmental Law,* 266–291 (Juta 2011); M. Kidd, *Alternatives to the Criminal Sanctions in the Enforcement of Environmental Law*, 9 SAJELP 21–59 (2002); M. Kidd, *Liability of Corporate Officers for Environmental Offences*, 18 SA Public Law 277–288 (2003).

249. *See infra* para. II, as well as Parts I–VII, s. 197 of the Constitution.

250. Section 195.

issued, after which a bill is prepared. The Bill can either first be published for public comment or be sent directly to the parliamentary committee dealing with the specific issue. The parliamentary committee may hold public hearings on the Bill. As soon as the parliamentary committee has approved the Bill it is put before Parliament. After the Bill has been approved in Parliament, it must be sent to the Provincial Council of Provinces for its approval.[251] A bill is only final once signed by the President and published in the *Government Gazette*. The Act comes into operation on the date of publication in the *Government Gazette* or, if indicated in the Act, on a future date to be specified in a *Government Gazette.*

60. Several green papers and white papers pertaining to energy and the environment have been issued over the past couple of years. The previous government rarely made use of this process. In the light of the new democratic dispensation this route is frequently used. The green and white papers that are of importance are the *White Paper on Sustainable Coastal Development* of April 2000; *White Paper on a Minerals and Mining Policy for South Africa,*[252] *White Paper on the Conservation and Sustainable Use of South Africa's Biological Diversity,*[253] *White Paper on Environmental Management,*[254] *White Paper on Integrated Pollution and Waste Management,*[255] *White Paper on the Energy Policy of the Republic of South Africa,*[256] the *Green Paper on Development and Planning,*[257] the *White Paper on Spatial Planning and Land Use Management,*[258] the *White Paper on the Renewable Energy Policy of the Republic of South Africa*[259] and the *National Climate Change Response White Paper.*[260] In 2019, the DEA published a guideline on *Mitigation Monitoring and Evaluation.*[261] Local governments and provinces also responded and published their own policy papers with regard to climate change and other energy matters, sometimes even before the national government reacted to international pressure.[262] There has also been an influx of environment-related legislation

---

251. *See supra* para. 4. *See also* A. Rabie, *Green Issues, Blueprints, Green and White Papers*, Tydskrif vir Hedendaags Romeins-Hollandse Reg 650–661 (1996).
252. Government Notice 2359 in *Government Gazette* 19344 of 20 Oct. 1998.
253. Government Notice 1095 in *Government Gazette* 18163 of 28 Jul. 1997.
254. Government Notice 749 in *Government Gazette* 18894 of 15 May 1998.
255. Government Notice 227 in *Government Gazette* 20978 of 17 Mar. 2000.
256. Government Notice 3007 in *Government Gazette* 19606 of 17 Dec. 1998.
257. Government Notice 626 in *Government Gazette* 20071 of 21 May 1999.
258. Issued by the Ministry of Agriculture and Land Affairs in July 2001.
259. Government Notice 513 in *Government Gazette* 26169 of 14 May 2004.
260. On climate change and the law in South Africa, *see* T. Humby, L.J. Kotzé, O. Rumble and A. Gilder Andrew, eds, *Climate Change Law and Governance in South Africa* (Juta 2016).
261. Department of Environmental Affairs, *Guidelines Series of the National Climate Change Response Monitoring and Evaluation System Volume 1* (June 2019).
262. *See*, for example, City of Cape Town, Framework for Adaptation to Climate Change in the City of Cape Town (FAC4T), April 2006; City of Cape Town, Moving Mountains: Cape Town's Action Plan for Energy and Climate Change, November 2011, http://www.capetown.gov.za/en/EnvironmentalResourceManagement/EnergyEfficiency/Pages/PolicyandStrategyDocuments.aspx (accessed 15 Jan. 2015); Department of Environmental Affairs and Development Planning Western Cape, Sustainable Energy Strategy for the Western Cape, May 2007, http://www.westerncape.gov.za/Text/2007/7/ses_july07.pdf (accessed 15 Jan. 2015). On climate change,

in the past decade, i.e. the NEMA; the National Energy Act 34 of 2008; the NEM-AQA; the National Radioactive Waste Disposal Institute Act 53 of 2008 and the National Nuclear Regulator Act 47 of 1999 to name but a few.

§2. The Actual Role of Government Institutions

61. There are various government role players for the regulation of the energy sector. The Department of Mineral Resources and Energy is accountable to the Minister of Mineral Resources and Energy and is responsible for general governance of the energy sector, the formulation of long-term energy policy, communication with stakeholders and the management and investigation of regional and international cooperation. The department must also establish appropriate institutions to achieve the energy policy objectives.[263]

The Minister of Mineral Resources and Energy is responsible for the development and implementation of energy policy. He or she is accountable to cabinet and Parliament. The cabinet must assist with the coordination and implementation of energy policy and ensures its integration with other sector policies.

Cabinet is accountable to Parliament. Parliament is responsible for the approval of energy-related legislation and is accountable to the electorate. Parliamentary committees must consider new or amended legislation and supervise the actions of the Minister and the department, especially through the budget. Provincial and local governments play a minor role in energy governance. They are responsible for economic and physical planning and must take the supply and use of energy into account.[264]

The Department of Energy has to evaluate the effect of energy activities on the environment and evaluate the effect of environmental legislation and standards on the supply and cost of energy. These evaluations are done on local, regional and global levels. The local level includes the use of coal and cheap paraffin stoves, the regional level the impact of power stations and chemical plants, and the global level the global climate change.[265]

The Constitution creates a few institutions to support constitutional democracy, namely the Public Protector, the South African Human Rights Commission, the Commission for the Promotion and Protection of the Rights of Cultural, Religious and Linguistic Communities, the Commission for Gender Equality, the Auditor

---

public trusteeship and the unborn, *see* A. Du Plessis, *Climate change, public trusteeship and the tomorrows of the unborn*, 31(2) South African Journal of Human Rights 269–293 (2015).

263. www.energy.gov.za (accessed 11 Nov. 2013).

264. *White Paper on Energy* – Government Notice 3007 in *Government Gazette* 19606 of 17 Dec. 1998. Also *see* T. Humby, *Hands on or hands off? The constitutional court's denial of a provincial municipal planning role*, Journal of South African Law 178–188 (2015); A. Du Plessis, ed. *Environmental Law and Local Government* (Juta 2015).

265. http://www.energy.gov.za/files/au_frame.html (accessed 11 Nov. 2013); *see* also Provincial Government of the Western Cape: Department of Environmental Affairs and Development Planning, *A Status quo, Vulnerability and Adaptation Assessment of the Physical and Socio-Economic Effects of Climate Change in the Western Cape*, June 2005.

General and the Electoral Commission.[266] The function of the Public Protector is to investigate any conduct in state affairs or in the public administration regardless of the sphere of government. The Public Protector is accessible to all persons and communities, and the reports of the Protector are open for public inspection except if there are special circumstances (to be determined in legislation) preventing it. The Public Protector is appointed for seven years, and his or her term cannot be renewed.

The South African Human Rights Commission must promote respect for human rights and a culture of human rights, promote the protection, development and attainment of human rights and monitor and assess the observance of human rights in the Republic. The commission may investigate and report on the observance of human rights, take steps to secure appropriate redress where human rights have been violated, carry out research and educate. The commission must require the relevant organs of state to provide it with information on the measures they have taken to realize the fundamental rights concerning housing, health care, food, water, social security, education and the environment. In 2004, the commission published a report on 'The right to a healthy environment'.[267]

There are various government-controlled energy institutions whose functions are defined in legislation. These institutions include the National Nuclear Regulator and the National Energy Regulator.[268] In terms of NEMA, a Committee for Environmental Cooperation had been established.[269]

The *White Paper on Energy*[270] stresses the importance of interdepartmental coordination. This is of the utmost importance in the energy sector due to the multisectoral impacts thereof. Improved communication between the provinces and local governments and the Department of Mineral Resources and Energy is, however, of the utmost importance.

Government departments of importance for the energy sector are, for example, the Departments of Mineral Resources and Energy, Health, Environmental Affairs, Forestry and Fisheries Cooperative Governance, Human Settlements, Water and Sanitation, Trade and Industry and Science and Technology. Although each of these departments has its own functions, they all have some functions relating to energy.[271]

266. Sections 181–192.
267. South African Human Rights Commission *The Right to a Healthy Environment*, 21 Jun. 2004.
268. *See infra* paras 38, 49, 108 and 141 respectively. The National Energy Regulator Act 40 of 2004 came into force on 15 Sep. 2005.
269. *See infra* para. 141.
270. Government Notice 3007 in *Government Gazette* 19606 of 17 Dec. 1998.
271. *See supra* para. 28 and *infra* Parts I–VII.

Chapter 5. Sources of Energy Law

62. The most important sources of the energy law are the common law, legislation and international law.[272] A wide range of topics (e.g., prevention, control and disposal) is addressed by these sources.

When a matter is not specifically governed by legislation, common law usually applies. South Africa's modern common law is based on the seventeenth and eighteenth-century Roman-Dutch law that was transplanted to the Cape in 1652. English law influenced some parts of South African law. Subsequently, South African law was influenced by the African indigenous and religious systems.[273] South Africa has therefore a unique mixed legal jurisdiction.

The common law has binding authority. The modern interpretation of common law can be found in case law. Sometimes old authorities are consulted to solve a particular problem where no precedent or legislation exists, when it is suspected that the existing precedent was wrongly decided or where there is general uncertainty regarding a common-law matter.

Books and articles written by academics and lawyers are useful sources to find the law. The easiest way to find the law is to consult a textbook on the matter. These books and articles have only persuasive authority.

Custom is unwritten law – it is fixed practices introduced over a long period of time that are acceptable to all, reasonable, certain and clear. Custom does not play such an important role in common law, but it does in international law, African customary law and religion-based systems. (The latter can, however, be left out of this discussion of energy law.)

The most important branches of the common law pertaining to environmental liability are the law of delict, the law of contract and procedural law, especially the interdict as remedy. If a company or person does not exercise proper control, it can be held liable for actual damages as well as for imminent danger.[274] In view of the fact that South African private law focuses on private relationships, businesses were in principle only liable to individual persons and not to the public in general. Section 38 of the 1996 Constitution changes this rule with regard to the enforcement of human rights and section 32 of NEMA the enforcement of matters in relation to the environment.[275] The courts have, subsequent to these provisions, relaxed the legal standing rule in some cases.[276]

---

272. *See also* J. Glazewski & L. du Toit, eds, *Environmental Law in South Africa,* 1–13–1–14 (LexisNexis 2013); Strydom, H.A. & E. Cairncross, *Energy*, 459–517. In Fuggle and Rabie's Environmental Management in South Africa (King, N.D, Strydom, H.A. & Retief F.P., eds,, 3rd edn, Juta 2018).
273. T. Humby, et al., *Introduction to Law and Legal Skills in South Africa*, 46 (Oxford University Press 2012).
274. R. Summers, *Common-Law Remedies for Environmental Protection* in Environmental Compliance and Enforcement in South Africa, 339–369 (A. Paterson & L.J. Kotzé, eds, Juta 2009).
275. *See supra* para. 7.
276. *See* J. Glazewski & L. du Toit, eds, *Environmental Law in South Africa,* 7–32–7.35 (LexisNexis 2013); M. Kidd, *Environmental Law,* 283–286 (Juta 2009).

The purpose of neighbour law or the law of nuisance (branch of the law of property) is to harmonize the interests of neighbours by weighing their rights and obligations in the exercising of their rights and to resolve conflicting interests. A neighbour must exercise his or her entitlements to this land reasonably on the one hand, and on the other hand the neighbouring owners should endure this within reason. If an owner exercised his or her rights in such a way that the neighbour sustained damages or was hindered in the enjoyment of his land, he or she would be committing a delict. He or she may then either claim patrimonial loss (damages) or institute an interdict.[277]

An interdict is available where use of possession has been disturbed or where an imminent danger of such infringement exists. An interdict can be final (e.g., all operations must stop) or temporary (e.g., operations must stop for three months).

63. Legislation as one of the sources of South African law can be confusing not only to laypersons but also to lawyers. An understanding of the hierarchy and network of legislation is, therefore, necessary.

The main distinction is drawn between original and subordinate legislation. Original legislation is passed by a legislator who has the primary capacity granted to it in legislation. Examples of such legislation are the laws passed by Parliament and the nine provinces. Subordinate legislation is dependent on original legislation and derives its authority therefrom. For example, regulations may be issued in terms of the NEMA. The NEMA is primary legislation and the Regulations are subordinate legislation.

To be subordinate legislation, it has to comply with the Constitution; it should not be in conflict with the original legislation; it should not be vague, it should be reasonably clear and comprehensible; it should remain in the framework of the legislative powers granted by the primary legislation; it may not be unjust, unreasonable, discriminatory or retrospective and subdelegation is not permitted (e.g., a subordinate legislator cannot authorize another person to promulgate subordinate legislation).

The highest authority of legislation is the Constitution, then parliamentary and provincial legislation, and on the lowest level local by-laws issued by local authorities. (Provincial legislation was called ordinances before 1986 and proclamations from 1986–1994.) The hierarchy of environmental legislation will, for example, be the Constitution; NEMA and its policies and regulations; parliamentary legislation falling outside Schedules 4 and 5; concurrent national and Schedules 4 and 5 provincial legislation and by-laws.[278]

Legislation is the main source of energy law. Energy law cannot be divorced from environmental law and, therefore, the sources of environmental law must also be considered.

---

277. *See also* R. Summers, *Common-Law Remedies for Environmental Protection*. In Environmental Compliance and Enforcement in South Africa, 342–344 (A. Paterson & L.J. Kotzé, eds, Juta 2009); M. Kidd, *ibid.* at 145–148; A.J. van der Walt, *The Law of Neighbours* (Juta 2010).

278. A. Du Plessis, *Understanding the Legal Context*. In *Environmental Compliance and Enforcement in South Africa Legal Perspectives*, 11–40 (A. Paterson & L.J. Kotzé, eds, Juta 2009).

64. Customary international law is law in South Africa except if it is in conflict with the Constitution or an Act of Parliament.[279] The national executive negotiates and signs all international agreements. Such an agreement is only binding after it has been approved by resolution in both the National Assembly and the National Council of Provinces.[280] International agreements become law when they are enacted into legislation. However, a self-executing provision of an agreement that has been approved by Parliament is law unless it is inconsistent with the Constitution or an Act of Parliament.[281] International agreements of 'a technical, administrative or executive nature, or an agreement which does not require either ratification or accession, entered into by the national executive', are binding without the approval of the National Assembly and Council of Provinces.[282] Courts, when interpreting legislation 'must prefer any reasonable interpretation of the legislation that is consistent with international law over any alternative interpretation that is inconsistent, therewith'.[283] The courts must also take international law into account when interpreting the Bill of Rights in Chapter 2 of the Constitution.[284] South Africa is signatory to various treaties and conventions, some of which have been enacted into legislation.[285]

65. The following South African primary legislation is important sources of energy law:

Electricity

- Electricity Regulation Act 4 of 2006
- Eskom Conversion Act 13 of 2001
- National Energy Regulator Act 40 of 2004
- National Energy Act 34 of 2008
- Environmental legislation listed *infra*

Gas

- Gas Act 48 of 2001
- National Energy Regulator Act 40 of 2004
- Gas Regulator Levies Act 75 of 2002
- Marine Pollution (Control and Civil Liability) Act 6 of 1981
- Mineral and Petroleum Resources Development Act (MPRDA) 28 of 2002
- National Environmental Management: Integrated Coastal Management Act (NEMICMA) 24 of 2008

279. Section 232 of the Constitution.
280. Section 231(1)–(2).
281. Section 231(4).
282. Section 231(3).
283. Section 233.
284. Section 39(1)(b).
285. J. Glazewski & L. du Toit, eds, *Environmental Law*, 2-1-2-62 (2nd edn, LexisNexis 2014 Service Issue 2).

– Environmental legislation listed *infra*

Petrol and Liquid Fuels

– Minerals and Petroleum Resources Development Act 28 of 2002
– Petroleum Pipelines Act 60 of 2003
– Petroleum Products Act 120 of 1977
– Fire Brigade Services Act 99 of 1987
– Hazardous Substances Act 15 of 1973
– National Energy Regulator Act 40 of 2004
– National Energy Act 34 of 2008
– National Road Traffic Act 93 of 1996
– Occupational Health and Safety Act 85 of 1993
– Environmental legislation referred to *infra*

Coal

– Minerals and Petroleum Resources Development Act 28 of 2002
– National Road Traffic Act 93 of 1996
– Road Transportation Act 74 of 1977
– National Energy Act 34 of 2008
– Environmental legislation listed *infra*

Nuclear Energy

– Minerals and Petroleum Resources Development Act 28 of 2002
– National Nuclear Energy Act 46 of 1999
– National Nuclear Regulator Act 47 of 1999
– National Energy Act 34 of 2008
– National Environmental Management: Waste Act (NEMWA) 59 of 2008
– National Nuclear Regulator Act 47 of 1999
– National Radioactive Waste Disposal Institute Act 53 of 2008
– Non-Proliferation of Weapons of Weapons of Mass Destruction Act 87 of 1993
– Environmental legislation listed *infra*

Renewable Energy

– Conservation of Agricultural Resources Act 43 of 1983
– National Energy Act 34 of 2008
– Lake Areas Development Act 39 of 1975
– National Forests Act 84 of 1998
– National Parks Act 57 of 1976
– Environmental legislation *infra*

The following sources of environmental law are of importance to energy law:

- Advertising on Roads and Ribbon Development Act 21 of 1940
- Antarctic Treaties Act 60 of 1996
- Constitution of the Republic of South Africa, 1996
- Dumping at Sea Control Act 73 of 1980
- Environment Conservation Act (ECA) 73 of 1989
- Explosives Act 26 of 1956
- Fencing Act 31 of 1963
- Fertilizers, Farm Feeds, Agricultural Remedies and Stock Remedies Act 36 of 1947
- Health Act 63 of 1977
- Housing Act 107 of 1997
- International Convention for the Prevention of Pollution from Ships Act 2 of 1986
- Lake Areas Development Act 39 of 1975
- Land Survey Act 8 of 1997
- Marine Living Resources Act 18 of 1998
- Marine Pollution (Control and Civil Liability) Act 6 of 1981
- Marine Traffic Act 2 of 1981
- Maritime Zones Act 15 of 1994
- Merchant Shipping Act 57 of 1951
- Merchant Shipping (Civil Liability Compensation) 25 of 2013
- Mine Health and Safety Act 29 of 1996
- Mountain Catchment Areas Act 63 of 1970
- National Environmental Management Act (NEMA) 107 of 1998
- National Environmental Management: Air Quality Act (NEMAQA) 39 of 2004
- National Environmental Management: Biodiversity Act (NEMBA) 10 of 2004
- National Environmental Management: Integrated Coastal Management Act (NEMICMA) 24 of 2008
- National Environmental Management: Protected Areas Act 57 of 2003
- National Environmental Management: Waste Act (NEMWA) 59 of 2008
- National Health Act 61 of 2003
- National Heritage Resources Act 25 of 1999
- National Veld and Forest Fire Act 101 of 1998
- National Water Act (NWA) 36 of 1998
- Occupational Diseases in Mines and Works Act 78 of 1973
- Occupational Health and Safety Act 85 of 1993
- Seabirds and Seals Protection Act 46 of 1973
- Sea Fishery Act 12 of 1988
- Sea-Shore Act 21 of 1935
- Spatial Planning and Land Use Management Act 16 of 2013
- Water Services Act 108 of 1997
- World Heritage Convention Act 49 of 1999
- Wreck and Salvage Act 94 of 1996

Other legislation impacting on energy law:

- Broad-Based Black Economic Empowerment Act 53 of 2003
- Carbon Tax Act 15 of 2019
- Climate Change Bill, 2018
- Competition Act 89 of 1998
- Intergovernmental Relations Framework Act 13 of 2005
- Local Government: Municipal Demarcation Act 27 of 1998
- Local Government: Municipal Structures Act 117 of 1998
- Local Government: Municipal Systems Act 32 of 2000
- Promotion of Access to Information Act 2 of 2000
- Promotion of Administrative Justice Act 3 of 2000
- Protected Disclosures Act 26 of 2000
- Skills Development Act 97 of 1998
- Traditional Leadership and Governance Framework Act 41 of 2003

Part I. Regulatory Framework concerning Electricity

Chapter 1. Overview of Regulatory Framework

§1. Electricity

66. Electricity is supplied mainly by Eskom Holdings Ltd, a public company, with the state as sole or majority shareholder.[286] In some instances, local authorities provide electricity. Eskom is in the process of building two huge coal-fired power stations, Medupi near Lephalale and Kusile near Emalahleni. It is foreseen that these two power stations will be completed by 2020. The first power was delivered mid-2014 when some of the units will go into operation. The final Medupi and Kusile would produce 4800 MW electricity and is built at a cost of an initial ZAR 219 milliard, increasing as the construction is delayed.[287] The building and expansion of coal-fired power stations as well as the reopening of existing power stations to provide in South Africa's demand for energy is controversial as the fact that the projects are supported by the World Bank.[288] What the critics sometimes overlooked, is the fact that the cost involved is due to the environmental protection measures that have to be complied with.[289] In 2013, the construction at the power stations was delayed due to substandard technical support and technology provided by Hitachi, and striking workers.[290]

Nuclear energy and renewable energy also contribute to the electricity grid.[291] Although nuclear energy is well regulated, renewable energy is still in its infancy

286. J. Glazewski & L. du Toit, eds, *Environmental Law*, 18–13 (3rd edn, LexisNexis 2013). Section 4 Eskom Conversion Act 13 of 2001. Eskom is exempted from payment of certain taxes in terms of s. 10(1)(cA) of the Income Tax Act 58 of 1962 – s. 8 of the Act. *See* A. Klees, *Electricity Law in South Africa*, 265–271 (Juta 2014). *See also infra* para. 44.

287. J-B. Styan, *Kragplan dalk gouer*, 11 September, Beeld 2 (2012).

288. J. Blignaut, *Climate Change: The Opportunity Cost of Medupi and Kusile Power Stations*, 23 South African Journal of Energy 67–75 (2012).

289. Eskom, *Kusile and Medupi Coal-Fired Power Stations under Constructions*, COP17 Fact Sheet (2011) http://www.eskom.co.za/AboutElectricity/FactsFigures/Documents/Kusile_and_Medupi.pdf (accessed 18 Dec. 2013).

290. SAPA, *Eskom: Medupi and Kusile stations to be active by 2014*, 30 October Mail&Guardian (2013) http://mg.co.za/article/2013-10-30-eskom-medupi-and-kusile-stations-to-be-active-by-2014 (accessed 18 Dec. 2013).

291. In 2016 the Minister of Energy determined that nuclear energy should contribute 9600 megawatts to the grid and that tender processes should commence in this regard – Eskom would have been the procurer – Government Notice R1557 in *Government Notice* 40494 of 14 Dec. 2016.

and there is no legislation focusing on renewable energy only. As has been stated before, people in the rural areas rely on biomass as their source of energy.

67. The Electricity Regulation Act 4 of 2006 regulates the generation, transmission, distribution, reticulation, trading, import and export of electricity. The objectives of the Act are, among others, to 'achieve the efficient, effective, sustainable and orderly development and operation of electricity supply infrastructure in South Africa, ensure that the interests and needs of present and future electricity customers and end users are safeguarded and met, having regarded to the governance, efficiency, effectiveness, and long-term sustainability of the electricity supply industry, promote the use of diverse energy sources and energy ... efficiency [and] facilitate universal access to energy'.[292]

68. The NERSA/the Regulator is the custodian and enforcer of the national energy regulatory framework.[293] NERSA is a juristic person and its members were appointed by the then Minister of Energy.[294] The members must have adequate legal, technical, business, economic or other experience relevant to the electricity, piped gas and petroleum pipelines industries and should be broadly representative of South Africa as a whole. They must also be able to demonstrate impartiality and objectivity.[295] The duties of the members of NERSA include that they should act in a 'justifiable and transparent manner, act in the interests of the Regulator and not their own or sector interests, recuse themselves from matters in which they may have a direct or indirect personal interest and act in a manner that is required and expected from someone holding a public office and most importantly act in the public interest'.[296] All decisions of NERSA must be in writing and consistent with the Constitution and all other laws. The decision should be procedurally fair, all parties (including affected parties) should be given an opportunity to be heard, the decision should be taken on facts and the evidence must be summarized and recorded. All decisions and reasons of NERSA are available to the public except if it is protected in terms of the Promotion of Access to Information Act 2 of 2000.[297] All administrative actions of NERSA may on request be subjected to review by a High Court. If a person is affected by a decision of NERSA sitting as a tribunal, such a person may appeal against that decision to the High Court.[298] In *National Energy Regulator of South Africa and Another v. Borbet SA (Pty) Ltd and Others, Eskom Holdings*

292. Section 2 Electricity Regulation Act 4 of 2006. *See also* D.C. Moloi, *Access to Electricity under the Power Conservation Programme in South Africa* (LLM Dissertation, University of the Witwatersrand 2010).
293. Section 3 Electricity Regulation Act 4 of 2006 read with National Energy Regulator Act 40 of 2004.
294. Sections 3 and 4 National Energy Regulator Act 40 of 2004.
295. Section 6 National Energy Regulator Act 40 of 2004. Meetings are determined by the chairperson – s. 8. Additional personnel may be appointed – s. 11.
296. Section 9 National Energy Regulator Act 40 of 2004.
297. *See also* the NERSA, *Manual on Electricity Regulation of April 2012*, http://www.nersa.org.za/Admin/Document/Editor/file/Electricity/Licences/Licence%20under%20procedure/Electricity%20Filing%20and%20Archiving%20procedure.pdf (accessed 20 Dec. 2013) and s. 13 of the Electricity Regulation Act 4 of 2006.
298. Section 10 National Energy Regulator Act 40 of 2004.

Soc Limited and Another v Borbet SA (Pty) Ltd and Others,[299] Eskom's application for a tariff adjustment[300] was disputed. The court found that it has jurisdiction to review NERSA's decision as well as Eskom's application.

NERSA's electricity mandate is funded by money appropriated by Parliament, funds collected under section 5B of the Electricity Act and levies imposed by NERSA or mandated by other legislation.[301] NERSA must publish an annual report including information on the licences granted, amended or withdrawn, regulations made and directives issued by the Minister, access to network infrastructure and approved tariffs and tariff structures.[302]

69. NERSA regulates electricity prices and tariffs, issues rules to implement the national electricity policy framework and integrated resource plan and enforces performance and compliance of the Act.[303] NERSA may also mediate disputes between generators, transmitters, distributors, customers or end users or undertake investigations or enquiries into activities of licensees.[304] If a dispute is between licensees, the Regulator may act as mediator if the parties would request it to do so. If the dispute is between a customer or end user and a licensee, a registered person who trades, generates, transmits or distributes electricity, the dispute may be settled in a matter as is deemed fit by the Regulator.[305] NERSA may also appoint advisory forums and establish customer and end-user forums to advise it on any matter.[306]

NERSA may, after consultation with licensees, municipalities that reticulate electricity and other interested person, publish in the *Government Gazette* guidelines,

299. [2017] 3 All SA 559 (SCA). *See also* the court a quo decision: *National Energy Regulator of South Africa and Another v Borbet SA (Pty) Ltd and Others* (24364/2016) [2016] ZAGPPHC 945 (17 Nov. 2016); W. Du Plessis, *Energy efficiency: The progress of policy, legislation, and the role of the courts in South Africa,* 111 South African Journal of Environmental Law and Policy (2015); W. Du Plessis, *Energy efficiency: The progress of policy, legislation, and the role of the courts in South Africa*, 24 South African Journal of Environmental Law and Policy, 175–204 (2019).

300. *See*, for example, Gen Notice 449 in *Government Gazette* 38803 of 22 May 2015 – NERSA's Notice of invitation for public comments on Eskom's Selective Reopener of MYPD3 application for Open Gas Cycle Turbines (OCGT) and Short Term Power Purchase Programme (STPPP) and impact of increase in Environmental Levy; Gen Notice 228 in *Government Gazette* 39938 of 19 Apr. 2016 – NERSA: Invitation for public comments on the revision of the Multi-Year Price Determination (MYPD) methodology and notice on the NERSA decision on the Municipal Tariff Guideline for the 2016/17 Financial Year; General Notice 587 in *Government Gazette* 40273 of 13 Sep. 2016 – NERSA extending the consultative process and invitation for further public comment on the revision of the Multi-Year Price Determination (MYPD) methodology.

301. Section 12 National Energy Regulator Act 40 of 2004. NERSA is subject to the Public Finance Management Act 1 of 1999 and must keep separate accounts for their work on electricity, piped gas and petroleum pipelines. The Auditor General audits the financial records of NERSA – *see* s. 13 National Energy Regulator Act 40 of 2004.

302. Section 14 National Energy Regulator Act 40 of 2004. *See also* http://www.nersa.org.za/ for previous annual and other reports (accessed 20 Dec. 2013).

303. Section 4(a) Electricity Regulation Act 4 of 2006. *See*, for example, General Notice 562 in *Government Gazette* 37805 of 11 Jul. 2014 – Notice of a public hearing on guidelines for the electricity reseller tariffs.

304. Section 4(b) Electricity Regulation Act 4 of 2006.

305. Section 30 Electricity Regulation Act 4 of 2006. The Regulator may appoint a suitable person to act as mediator who must follow the procedure as prescribed by the Minister of Energy.

306. Sections 5–6 Electricity Regulation Act 4 of 2006.

rules and codes of conduct.[307] The following guidelines have been published: *Non-Grid Households Electrification Policy Guidelines*; *Policy Guidelines for the Electrification of Unproclaimed Areas*, *Schools and Clinics Electrification Policy Guidelines*; *Policy Guidelines for the Electrification of Farm Dweller Houses*; and a suite of *Supply Policy Guidelines for the Integrated National Electrification Programme* (INEP).[308]

The Regulator may further investigate complaints or hold enquiries relating to generation, transmission, distribution or trading. They may investigate complaints pertaining to discrimination regarding tariffs or conditions of access or failures to abide to licence conditions.[309] After investigating the complaint, a report must be compiled. A formal investigation is then conducted, and the chair of the investigations committee may summon witnesses and conduct a proper investigation. After the investigation, he or she must submit a report to the Regulator who may then refer the report to the National Prosecuting Authority or sat as a tribunal if a licensee is involved.[310] The Regulator, as a tribunal, decides on any contraventions of the Act. The Regulator will serve a notice on the licensee to comply with the licence condition within a prescribed period. If the licensee fails to comply within the prescribed period, the tribunal may impose a penalty of 10% of the annual turnover of the licensee or ZAR 2 million (whichever is the higher amount) per day commencing on the day of receipt of the notice. The Regulator must take the extent of the contravention into account.[311] Over and above this mandate, the Regulator may authorize inspectors to enter any property on which an activity relating to the supply of electricity is taking place to inspect that facility, equipment, machinery, any books or accounts or documents relating to electricity. The inspectors may require any person to furnish them with information as required. The Regulator may further require that the information is verified under oath or by way of a solemn declaration. The inspector must provide his or her authorization on request.[312]

§2. Nuclear Energy

70. The regulatory framework pertaining to nuclear energy and radioactivity is fragmented. Initially, the Nuclear Energy Act 131 of 1993 was the principal Act dealing with nuclear energy. This Act was repealed in February 2000 and replaced by the National Nuclear Energy Act 46 of 1999 and the National Nuclear Regulator

307. Section 35(1). *See also* http://www.nersa.org.za/ (accessed 20 Dec. 2013) for guideline documents and rules dealing with electricity. Section 35(2) indicates what the guidelines, rules and codes of conduct may deal with.
308. These guidelines are available at http://www.energy.gov.za/files/policies_frame.html (accessed 28 Dec. 2013).
309. Section 32(1) Electricity Regulation Act 4 of 2006.
310. Section 32(2).
311. Section 18(1)-(5). The Minister may by notice in the *Government Gazette* amend the amount to counter the effect of inflation – s. 18(6).
312. Section 33.

Act 47 of 1999.[313] All activities in terms of the 1993 Act are deemed to be approved in terms of the National Nuclear Regulator Act 47 of 1999.[314] Radioactivity is regulated by different laws.

71. In 2008, the then DME tabled a *Nuclear Energy Policy for the Republic of South Africa* as a policy framework within which 'prospecting, mining, milling, use of nuclear materials as well as the development and utilization of nuclear energy shall take place'.[315] It is foreseen that nuclear energy will contribute to the energy mix in South Africa as it is regarded as a 'greener option' than fossil fuels. Since 2008, various Ministers of Energy and the President mentioned nuclear energy as a feasible option for South Africa, despite the objections worldwide (and in South Africa[316]) against the use of nuclear energy. In his end of the year address (2015), former President Zuma stated: 'Government has also entered into several negotiations with nuclear vendor countries and has recently signed Inter-Governmental Framework Agreements with the Russian Federation, the French Republic, the People's Republic of China, the United States of America and South Korea as part of the nuclear exploratory process.'[317]

72. In the case of *Earthlife Africa Johannesburg and Another v Minister of Energy and Others*,[318] the applicants challenged the Minister of Energy's determination of the contribution of nuclear energy as part of South Africa's new energy generation capacity. This determination had to be made before government could embark on a nuclear procurement programme. Subsequently, government concluded various international agreements (intergovernmental agreements) with regard to the possible procurement of nuclear plants in South Africa (United States of America, South Korea and Russia). The applicants challenged these agreements on procedural aspects. With regard to the determination of nuclear energy's contribution to the energy mix of South Africa and NERSA's endorsement of the Minister's determination, the court found that there was insufficient public input: The court stated further that NERSA did not indicate that 'it acted in the public interest' and that it did not take 'any steps to ascertain the views of the public or any interested or affected party'. The court accordingly found that the NERSA decision did not satisfy the test for rationality.[319] The court on the basis of separation of powers did not make a decision on the Russian IGA. However, the court found that the other two agreements did not follow the Constitutional process and had to be set aside.[320]

---

313. These acts came into operation on 24 Feb. 2000.
314. Section 54(2) of the National Nuclear Regulator Act 47 of 1999.
315. Government Notice 1347 of *Government Gazette* 31695 of 12 Dec. 2008.
316. *See*, e.g., website of the Koeberg Alert Alliance, http://koebergalert.org/home/ (accessed 7 Jan. 2015); *Thyspunt nuclear concerns*, Environment, 23 May 2010, http://www.environment.co.za/nuclear-energy-debate/thyspunt-nuclear-concerns.html (accessed 7 Jan. 2015).
317. *See*, e.g., J. Zuma, *End of the Year Statement by President Zuma*, 19 Dec. 2014, http://www.gov.za/president-jacob-zuma-end-year-statement (accessed 7 Jan. 2015).
318. [2017] 3 All SA 187 (WCC); 2017 (5) SA 227 (WCC).
319. *Ibid.* para. 51. Also *see* paras 71–75.
320. *Ibid.* paras 121 and 129.

73. The 1993 Act made provision for an Atomic Energy Corporation, whose main task was the control of research on nuclear energy and the Council of Nuclear Safety that was responsible for the issuing of licences for, *inter alia*, the construction or use of a nuclear installation, the use, production, storage, processing, enriching, conveyance or disposal of radioactive material, as well as the discarding of radioactive waste, the storage of irradiated nuclear fuel or any other activity involving radioactive material. The South African Nuclear Energy Corporation and the National Nuclear Regulator are the legal successors to the Atomic Energy Corporation and the Council of Nuclear Safety respectively. Various regulations that were issued in terms of the 1993 Act still apply.[321]

The Act made no reference to environmental issues. In terms of the ECA, an environmental impact assessment had to be approved before an installation could be built or extended.[322]

Information concerning the operations, transactions, projects, work or activities of the Corporation with regard to or in respect of restricted matter, and activities that were not public knowledge, could not have been disclosed without the written permission of the chief executive officer of the Corporation's board.[323]

74. The purpose of the Nuclear Energy Act of 1999 is to establish the South African Nuclear Corporation, to implement the Nuclear Non-Proliferation Treaty,[324] as well as to regulate the functions of the Corporation. The Act also regulates the acquisition, possession and storage of nuclear fuel and equipment as well as their import and export, the discarding of radioactive waste and the storage of irradiated nuclear fuel. 'Nuclear fuel' is defined as 'any material capable of undergoing a nuclear fission or nuclear fission process on its own or in combination with some other material and which is produced in a nuclear fuel assembly or other configuration'.[325]

The state is the only member and shareholder in the South African Nuclear Energy Corporation[326] whose main functions are to undertake and promote research and development in the field of nuclear energy and radiation sciences and technology; to process source material, special nuclear material and restricted material; and to reprocess and enrich source material and nuclear material, as well as to cooperate

---

321. Government Notices 848–849 in *Government Gazette* 15670 of 23 Apr. 1994 (determination of the levels of specific and total activity of radioactive material and the radiation dose); Government Notice 740 in *Government Gazette* 15648 of 16 Apr. 1994 (declaration of substances, materials and equipment as source material, special nuclear material, nuclear-related equipment and material); Government Notice R1132 in *Government Gazette* 10270 of 13 Jun. 1986 (record-keeping of nuclear accidents, description of incident, names of persons involved); Government Notice 849 in *Government Gazette* 15670 of 23 Apr. 1994 (regulations in respect of nuclear licences).
322. *See infra* para. 137. *See also* G.N. Barrie, *South Africa and Nuclear Energy – National and International Legal Aspects*, Tydskrif vir Suid-Afrikaanse Reg 153–174 (1988).
323. Section 31. *See infra* paras 147 and 178.
324. *See also* G.N. Barrie, *The Nuclear Non-Proliferation Treaty on the Eve of the Fourth Review Conference*, Tydskrif vir Suid-Afrikaanse Reg 100–112 (1991).
325. Section 1.
326. Sections 3–4. The Corporation is controlled by a board of directors which consists of a chairperson, appointed by the Minister, five to seven suitably qualified directors, a chief executive officer, an official of the Department of Energy and an official of the Department of International Relations and Cooperation – s. 16.

with persons and institutions in matters falling within these functions. Such cooperation is subject to the approval of the Minister.[327] The Corporation has various ancillary powers, including to conclude agreements for the production and delivery of source material, to cede or assign all the rights and obligations to the Corporation, to promote prospecting and mining of source and restricted materials, to manufacture, produce, acquire, dispose of,[328] process and possess uranium hexafluoride. The Corporation may also process and sell minerals, produce and process metals, chemicals and related products.[329]

The installations, sites, premises and land belonging to or under the control of the Corporation are regarded as restricted areas and no unauthorized person is allowed on the premises. Persons visiting these areas and their vehicles may be searched.[330] Information concerning the operations, transactions, projects, work or activities of the Corporation with regard to or in respect of restricted matter and activities that are not yet public knowledge may not be disclosed without written permission of the chief executive officer of the Corporation's board.[331] The question is how this secrecy clause relates to the Promotion of Access to Information Act 2 of 2000,[332] which provides for a right of access to information in general. In terms of section 5 of the Promotion of Access to Information Act, the Act applies to other legislation that restricts or prohibits the disclosure of a record of a public body or private body that is materially inconsistent with an object or provision of this Act.

The Minister may also appoint inspectors and may also determine the qualifications of these inspectors.[333] The inspectors may, among others, enter on any premise to monitor compliance with the Act, have powers of search, seizure, inspection and questioning and is entitled to information regarding safety. The inspector may only enter on land with a warrant duly issued by a judge or magistrate. He or she may only in exceptional circumstances act without a warrant.

75. The Minister of Energy may by notice in the *Government Gazette* declare any substance with a degree of purity as restricted material,[334] any substance containing uranium or thorium with a mass and concentration higher than specified to be source material,[335] substances as special nuclear material,[336] any facility, installation, plant, structure designed, adapted, involved with any process within the nuclear fuel cycle involving radioactive material to be a nuclear installation, and may declare equipment and material as nuclear-related equipment and material.[337]

327. Section 13.
328. Section 14(1)(f)–(t).
329. Section 14(2).
330. Section 29.
331. Section 31.
332. *See infra* para. 178.
333. Sections 37–40 and 53, read with Government Notice 177 in *Government Gazette* 36226 of 15 Mar. 2013.
334. Section 2(a) read with definition of 'restricted material' in s. 1: 'means beryllium and zirconium and any other substance declared under s. 2(a) to be restricted material'.
335. Section 2(b).
336. Section 2(c) – plutonium-239; uranium-233; uranium enriched in its 235 or 233 isotope; transuranium elements or a composition of such materials – s. 2(c)(i)–(v).
337. Section 2(d).

However, the Minister may determine the levels of specific or total activity of nuclear material below which the sections of the Act do not apply or may exempt any radioactive material from the provisions of the Act.[338] The Minister made such declarations, determinations and exemptions in 2009.[339]

76. South Africa is a signatory to the Convention on the Non-Proliferation of Weapons of Mass Destruction, which was enacted into legislation by the Non-Proliferation of Weapons of Mass Destruction Act 87 of 1993. Some sections of the Convention dealing with nuclear energy are enacted into the Nuclear Energy Act.[340] Under the international obligation, the Minister of Energy is the national authority for the purposes of the implementation and application of the Safeguards Agreement and other protocols to detect and identify nuclear material intended to be used for peaceful nuclear activities timeously. He or she must also deter the diversion of such material to the manufacture of nuclear weapons or explosives.[341] He or she must also authorize the possession, acquisition, use, disposal, export, import and processing of source material as well as the acquiring of restricted material and the production of nuclear energy.[342] The Minister's responsibilities further include the acquisition by the state of source material and special nuclear material, the management of radioactive waste and the storage of irradiated nuclear fuel.[343] The Act is not applicable to class IV hazardous substances[344] and radioactive materials exempted in terms of sections 2(e) and (g).[345]

In terms of the Non-Proliferation of Weapons of Mass Destruction Act 87 of 1993, notices were published indicating that certain goods, technologies and chemicals are to be controlled and have to be registered to ensure that they are used for peaceful purposes.[346]

The Act is silent on health and safety issues as well as on the protection of the environment.

§3. Renewable Energy

77. As has been stated above,[347] renewable energy is an important source of energy in South Africa. Ten per cent of the primary energy supply in South Africa

---

338. Section 2(e)–(g).
339. Government Notice 207 in *Government Gazette* 31954 of 27 Feb. 2009.
340. *See also* Anon, *Report by South Africa for the Convention on Nuclear Safety*, September 1998, www.nnr.co.za/web%20attachment/Report88.htm (accessed 7 May 2001).
341. Section 33.
342. Sections 33–43.
343. Sections 44–50.
344. *See infra* para. 117.
345. Section 49.
346. *See* in this regard Government Notice 491 in *Government Gazette* 42337 of 29 Mar. 2019 (chemical goods and technologies); Government Notice 492 in *Government Gazette* 42337 of 29 Mar. 2019; Government Notice 493 in *Government Gazette* 42337 of 29 Mar. 2019 (nuclear-related dual use equipment).
347. *See supra* para. 17.

is renewable. The renewable sources include biomass harvested from natural woodlands as fuelwood or waste from commercial forestry and sugar industries. People in the domestic rural areas are especially dependent on fuelwood as their only source of energy. This results in the over-exploitation of natural woodlands and harvesting practices that are unsustainable, which result in scarcity of fuelwood, leading to negative social and environmental impacts.[348]

South Africa has a target of 10,000 GWh of Renewable Energy. Renewable energy will have to contribute at least 3725 MW to ensure the uninterrupted supply of electricity according to the *Integrated Resource Plan 2010–2030*.[349] As indicated above,[350] there is tremendous growth in the number of solar and wind farms in South Africa and more households make use of solar panels as an alternative source of energy. In 2016, the Minister of Energy determined that gas (from whatever source, including shale gas) should contribute 600 MW to the energy mix.[351] The Minister also determined that solar power should be generated and procured from Solar Park Farms in the Northern Cape.[352]

The development of other renewable energy sources is, however, still a new concept in the energy industry and government discussions. The 2004 *White Paper on Renewable Energy*[353] indicates that South Africa relies on coal as it is an attractive cheap source of energy. There is, however, a serious problem with greenhouse gases and alternative sustainable resources need to be tapped. In order to ensure this, financial incentives need to be introduced. The vision of the then DME regarding renewable energy is set out as follows: 'An energy economy in which modern renewable energy increases its share of energy consumed and provides affordable access to energy throughout SA, thus contributing to sustainable development and environmental conservation.'

In order to achieve this, certain essential elements have to be taken into account, namely sustainable development, the creation of an enabling environment, the provision of institutional arrangements (regulators) and the development of renewable energy technologies.[354] Financial instruments, legal instruments, technology development and awareness raising and education need to be explored as incentives for the development and implementation of renewable energy.[355]

---

348. *See*, e.g., M. Madubansi & C.M. Shackleton, *Changes in Fuelwood Use and Selection Following Electrification in the Bushbuckridge Lowveld, South Africa*, 83 Journal of Environmental Management 416–426 (2007); General Notice 382 in *Government Gazette* 32122 of 17 Apr. 2009.
349. Government Notice R400 in *Government Gazette* 34263 of 6 May 2011 read with the *Integrated Resource Plan for Electricity (IRP) 2010–2030* Update Report 2013, 21 Nov. 2013, http://www.doe-irp.co.za/content/IRP2010_updatea.pdf (accessed 8 Jan. 2015).
350. *Supra*, paras 17 and 43.
351. Government Notice 602 in *Government Gazette* 40023 of 27 May 2016.
352. Government Notice 603 in *Government Gazette* 40023 of 27 May 2016.
353. General Notice 513 in *Government Gazette* 26169 of 14 May 2004.
354. *See also* M. Barnard, *The Role of International Sustainable Development Law Principles in Enabling Effective Renewable Energy Policy – a South African Perspective*, 15 PELJ 207–243 (2012).
355. Also *see*, R. Mauger and M. Barnard, *Addressing Fragmentation in the South African Renewable Energy Governance Effort – French lessons to be learned* 29(1) Journal of Energy in Southern Africa (2018).

78. The National Energy Act 34 of 2008 aims to ensure an uninterrupted supply of energy in South Africa. One way to achieve this is to promote a diversity of supply of energy resources in sustainable quantities at affordable prices.[356] The Act must also provide for safety, health and environmental matters that pertain to energy and matters not contemplated in other legislation (e.g., renewable energy) and contribute to the sustainable development of South Africa's economy.[357]

Renewable energy is defined in the Act as 'energy generated from natural non-depleting resources including solar energy, wind energy, biomass energy, biological waste energy, hydro energy, geothermal energy and ocean and tidal energy'.[358]

The Act does not specifically regulate renewable energy but makes provision that the Minister of Energy may issue regulations pertaining to 'minimum contributions to the national energy supply from renewable energy sources', the nature of the resources that may be used for renewable energy as well as measures and incentives to promote the introduction and use of renewable energy.[359] The Minister of Energy may further request from any person to provide information or data with regard to renewable energy (or any other energy), and access to this information will be considered in terms of the Promotion of Access to Information Act 2 of 2000.[360] The National Energy Act establishes the South African National Energy Development Institute to, among others, undertake energy research and development in all fields of energy (excluding nuclear energy) and to advise the Minister on research in the field of energy technology.[361] It seems as if the Institute is to be the main driver of the implementation of the movement towards new energy sources such as renewable energy. One of the ways to obtain financing for renewable projects is via the CDM processes that have been established in terms of the NEMA.

79. The CDM of 2005 gives effect to Article 12 of the Kyoto Protocol and establishes a national intra-governmental steering committee.[362] The Director General of the Department of Energy is the Designated National Authority, and he or she has to consider applications of project proponents, facilitate the effective and beneficial participation of South Africa in the activities of the CDM and report to the Minister on CDM projects and activities.[363] The intra-governmental steering committee monitors the activities of the Designated National Authority. South Africa has introduced several CDM projects – some of them are renewable energy projects.[364]

80. The National Energy Act provides for Integrated Energy Planning. In 2013, the Minister of Energy published a Draft 2012 Integrated Energy Planning Report

356. Section 5.
357. Section 5.
358. Section 1.
359. Section 19(1)(d)-(f).
360. Section 3.
361. Section 7.
362. Government Notice R721 in *Government Gazette* 2799 of 22 Jul. 2005 (hereinafter 'GN R721'). *See also* http://www.energy.gov.za/files/esources/kyoto/kyoto_frame.html (accessed 8 Jan. 2015).
363. Regulations 2 and 3 of GN R721.
364. For a list of the projects, *see* http://www.energy.gov.za/files/esources/kyoto/kyoto_frame.html (accessed 8 Jan. 2015).

for public consultation.[365] A final Integrated Energy Plan was published in 2016.[366] The aim of the planning is to guide the development of new energy policies, to serve as a guideline for energy regulations and for the selection of technology, to guide investment in energy infrastructure in South Africa and to propose alternative energy strategies. It also aims to serve as an overarching policy for specific sector policies. The 2016 Integrated Energy Plan has eight objectives[367] and sets out different scenarios[368] in long-term energy planning.[369]

81. The Electricity Regulation Act 4 of 2006 allows the National Energy Regulator to place conditions in a licence dealing with the types of energy sources from which electricity may be generated, bought or sold and also to determine tariffs.[370] In 2009, the NERSA published the South Africa Renewable Energy Feed-In Tariff (REFIT) Regulatory Guidelines.[371] The purpose of the Guidelines is, among others, to 'set out the regulatory framework for initiating tariffs and licensing conditions for a self-sustaining market for grid connected renewables in South Africa, in accordance with Government policy, through a Renewable Energy Feed-In Tariff' (REFIT) as well as the rules and requirements for licences that have to be obtained to qualify for REFIT.[372] In addition, REFIT aims to create 'an enabling environment for renewable electricity power generation', establish a guaranteed price for such electricity, to 'level the playing field with conventional electricity generation' and to 'create a critical mass of renewable energy investment and support the establishment of a self-sustaining market'.[373] Municipalities may develop their own projects and need to comply with these Guidelines.[374] The NERSA published a *Draft Discussion Document on Small Scale Renewable Generation – Regulatory Framework for Distributions* on 10 December 2014.[375] The idea is to integrate embedded solar energy (e.g., rooftop solar panels) into the national grid system.

---

365. Government Notice 512 in *Government Gazette* 36690 of 24 Jul. 2013.
366. Government Notice 1430 in *Government Gazette* 40445 of 25 Nov. 2016.
367. These objectives include, for example, energy security, reduction in the cost of energy, creation of jobs, addressing environmental concerns, conservation of water, diversification of the energy supply, promotion of energy efficiency and access to modern energy.
368. A base case, environmental awareness, resource constraint and a green shoots scenario. A sensitivity analysis was conducted for big water solar heaters, a no shale gas option and increased nuclear energy, for example.
369. Government Notice 1430 in *Government Gazette* 40445 of 25 Nov. 2016.
370. Sections 14(1)(r) and 15. *See also* para. 39 *supra* with regard to licence applications for electricity generation.
371. General Notice 382 in *Government Gazette* 32122 of 17 Apr. 2009.
372. Paragraphs 2.1 and 3.1 of Government Notice 382.
373. Paragraph 3.5.
374. On municipalities and energy, *see* W. Du Plessis & T. Murombo, *Energy*. In Local government and environmental law in South Africa (A. dD Plessis, ed., Juta 2015).
375. http://www.nersa.org.za/ (accessed 8 Jan. 2015).

82. Biota is seen as one of the sources of renewable energy.[376] Biodiversity and protected area legislation as well as various laws protecting plant species indirectly regulate the use of biomass as an energy source in South Africa.[377]

376. *See infra* para. 125.
377. *See* H. Strydom & N.D. King, eds, *Fuggle and Rabie's Environmental Management in South Africa*, 97–125, 342–393 (2nd edn, Juta 2009).

Chapter 2. Authorizations and Licences

§1. ELECTRICITY

83. The Electricity Regulation Act 4 of 2006 provides for licences that may be issued with conditions,[378] the registration of activities that are not subject to licensing,[379] and the provision of electricity by municipalities.[380] A person that operates a generation, transmission or distribution facility, import or export electricity or trade in electricity must obtain a licence from NERSA.[381] Persons who are involved in Schedule II item 1 activities are exempted from the obligation to apply for or hold a licence but must register their activities.[382] These activities include, for example, the operation of a generation facility, generation plants that are connected to the grid but that generates less than 1 MW of electricity or that supply a single customer or the owner of the facility. Generation facilities also include those that are constructed and operated for demonstration purposes only and that are or are not connected to the national grid and 'generation facilities' where electricity is produced 'from a co-product, by-product, waste product or residual product underlying an industrial process, supplying the owner of the facility with electricity, a person related to the owner or a consumer on the same premises where the electricity is generated'. Back generation facilities are also excluded if their function is to supply energy during service interruptions.[383] A potential licensee may approach the Regulator and ask whether it needs to file an application at NERSA. NERSA must assist the potential applicant. These actions may, however, not be construed as conferring a right or raise an expectation with the potential licensee.[384] The application must be made on the prescribed form and against payment of an application fee. The application must include, among others, a description of the application and all its horizontal and vertical relationships with other persons involved in the operation of electricity activities, documentary evidence of the administrative, financial and technical ability of the applicant, description of the proposed facility including maps and diagrams, description of the customers and proposed tariffs, detailed specification of the services that will be rendered, compliance with integrated resource plans and the ability to comply with applicable labour, health, safety and environmental legislation, subordinate legislation and any other requirements that may be applicable.[385] The Regulator, therefore, places an onus on the applicant to demonstrate that he or she is legally compliant or has the ability to become legally compliant before the licence will be issued. It saves the Regulator time and effort to determine

378. Section 7.
379. Section 9.
380. Sections 27–29.
381. Section 7(1).
382. Schedule II was substituted by Government Notice 1231 in *Government Gazette* 41237 of 10 Nov. 2017. Proposed amendments to this Schedule were published for comment in Government Notice 563 in *Government Gazette* 41685 of 8 Jun. 2018. By December 2019, the final notice has not been published yet.
383. Section 7(2) read with Sch. II.
384. Section 7(3)-(5).
385. Section 10(2).

whether the applicant is indeed in compliance with other laws. The Regulator may also require the applicant to advertise that it has lodged an application.[386] The Regulator must provide all substantiated objections to the applicant to allow him or her to respond thereto and may request additional information if necessary.[387] Separate licences are issued for (a) the operation of generation, transmission and distribution facilities, (b) the import and export of electricity and (c) trading. The Regulator may also decide not to issue a licence.[388] Generation and transmission licences are issued for a period of fifteen years or for a period as determined by the Regulator. Distribution and trading licences are also subject to the time period set out in the licence. All licences are renewable but new licence conditions may be added. Licences are not transferable.[389]

84. Licences may be issued subject to certain conditions which may include the setting, approving and meeting of performance improvement targets, the quality of electricity supply and service, the area of electricity supply to which a licensee is entitled or bound, the classes of customers and end users to whom the electricity may or must be applied, the type of energy sources from which electricity must or may be generated, compliance with health, safety and environmental standards and requirements and compliance with energy-efficiency measures and demand-side management.[390]

The licence may at any time be amended, varied, suspended or a condition be removed. This may be done on request of the licensee, upon non-compliance or if it is necessary to give effect to the Electricity Regulation Act.[391] A licensee must give the Regulator at least twelve months' notice of his or her intention to cease the activities.[392] The Regulator will revoke a licence if the facility or activity is no longer required or not economically viable, another person is willing to assume the rights and responsibilities of the existing licensee (a new licence will have to be issued) or if the conditions of the licence are not met. If it is necessary, the Regulator may apply to the High Court for an order to suspend or revoke a licence.[393]

85. The 1987 Electricity Act was silent on environmental matters. Environmental impact assessments (EIA) had to be done in terms of the now-repealed measures of the ECA.[394] New electricity generation facilities have to comply with section 24 of the NEMA, as well as its environmental impact assessment regulations.[395] The

386. Section 11.
387. Section 12.
388. Section 13.
389. Section 20.
390. Section 14.
391. Section 16.
392. Section 17.
393. Section 19.
394. Read with Government Notices R1182–1184 in *Government Gazette* 18261 of 5 Sep. 1997.
395. Government Notices R983–985 in *Government Gazette* 38282 of 4 Dec. 2014, as amended by Government Notices 324–327 in *Government Gazette* 40772 of 7 Apr. 2017 and Government Notice 706 in *Government Gazette* 41766 of 13 Jul. 2018. *See also* E. Couzens & M. Lewis, *South Africa* . In International Encyclopaedia of Laws Part IV Ch. 4 (K. Deketelaere et al., eds, Kluwer Law International 2013).

DEA conducted a strategic environmental assessment and indicated 'five Strategic Transmission Corridors that are of strategic importance for the rollout of the supporting large scale electricity transmission and distribution infrastructure in terms of Strategic Integrated Project 10: Electricity Transmission and Distribution' and prescribed specific procedures for applications for such large scale projects.[396] In 2019, the then DEA further published a generic environmental management programme that may be used for applications for environmental authorizations for substation and overhead electricity transmission and distribution infrastructure.[397] The aims of these documents are to ease burdensome bureaucratic procedures and to give effect to the government's ideal to provide access to energy for all.

86. Ash waste dumps, created due to electricity generation by coal, were excluded from the definition of waste in terms of the now-repealed section 20 of the ECA.[398] They were also not regarded as mine tailings that should be rehabilitated in terms of the repealed Minerals Act 50 of 1991. Eskom has, however, always been committed to working towards environmental conservation as set out in its environmental policy.[399] The company and its affiliates voluntarily worked towards ISO 14001 certification.[400] Ash dumps were also rehabilitated, although it was not legally enforceable.

Ash waste dumps are now regulated in terms of the NEMWA.[401] The potential of groundwater pollution also necessitates a water use licence.[402] The definition of 'pollution' in section 1 of the NEMA is worded in such a manner that any pollution derived from the ash dump or fly ash may be regarded as 'pollution', which implies that Eskom may be held liable in terms of the duty of care principle as well as the polluter pays principle.[403] Eskom must also comply with the measures of the NEM-AQA to control its fly ash emissions. An EIA must be undertaken in terms of the NEMA.[404]

---

396. Government Notice 113 in *Government Gazette* 41445 of 16 Feb. 2018.
397. Government Notice 435 in *Government Gazette* 42323 of 22 Mar. 2019. A generic environmental management programme for applications for environmental authorizations for substation infrastructure for the transmission and distribution was published for comment – Government Notice 163 in *Government Gazette* 41473 of 2 Mar. 2018.
398. Government Notice 1986 in *Government Gazette* 12703 of 24 Aug. 1990.
399. Eskom, *Environmental Policy*, 2006 http://www.eskom.co.za/OurCompany/SustainableDevelopment/EnvironmentalImpactAssessments/Documents/AppDEnvPolicy.pdf (accessed 20 Dec. 2013).
400. *See also* J. Glazewski, *Environmental Law*, 499 (2nd edn, LexisNexis 2005). He also mentions that Eskom introduced Environmental Key Performance Indicators into its environmental management system.
401. Section 19 read with Government Notices 634–635 in *Government Gazette* 36784 of 23 Aug. 2013 (waste classification and management regulations). *See also* E. Couzens & M. Lewis, *South Africa*. In International Encyclopaedia of Laws Part II Ch. 3 (K. Deketelaere, et al., eds, Kluwer Law International 2013).
402. Section 21(g) NWA 36 of 1998.
403. Section 28. *See infra* para. 240.
404. Section 24 read with Government Notices R983–985 in *Government Gazette* 38282 of 4 Dec. 2014. *See also* E. Couzens & M. Lewis, *South Africa*. In International Encyclopaedia of Laws Part IV Ch. 4 (K. Deketelaere et al., eds, Kluwer Law International 2013).

87. In terms of the repealed Electricity Act 41 of 1987, an undertaker, whether or not a riparian owner, would have to apply for permission to use a defined quantity of the normal flow of a stream or to abstract or impound or store a definite quantity of surplus water of a public stream within or outside the channel. The position changed with the introduction of the NWA 36 of 1998. As a natural resource, all water is regarded as a national asset[405] and authorizations are granted by the Department of Human Settlements, Water and Sanitation. The definition of 'water use' in the NWA[406] includes the activities mentioned in the repealed Electricity Act. Electricity suppliers also had to reregister their existing rights if the activities fell under section 43 or 48 of the NWA.

88. Polychlorinated biphenyl (PCB) has been used to prevent fires in transformers and various other electricity installation equipment. However, due to its carcinogenic nature it has been banned. The DEA proposed new regulations to phase out the use of PCBs, PCB materials and PCB-contaminated materials.[407]

89. The Minister of Environmental Affairs declared certain areas where power stations are found as priority areas for purposes of the NEMAQA.[408] She also published air quality management plans and in some areas implementation and enforcement regulations.[409] The power stations fall within all three of the areas that were proclaimed priority areas, namely the Highveld Priority Area, the Vaal Triangle Air-Shed Priority Area and the Waterberg-Bojanala National Priority Area.[410]

90. It is possible to offset air emissions in these priority areas, and in 2016 an Air Quality Offsets Guideline was published.[411] The Guideline regards offsets as an additional tool to the regulatory tools to improve the ambient air quality as well as to address the complex ambient air quality issues relating to non-industrial pollution. The Guideline's definition of offsets in the air quality context is 'an intervention, or interventions, specifically implemented to counterbalance the adverse and residual environmental impact of atmospheric emissions in order to deliver a net ambient air quality benefit within, but not limited to, the affected airshed where ambient air quality standards are being or have the potential to be exceeded and whereby opportunities and need for offsetting exist'. Electricity generators may therefore offset some of their emissions in terms of these Guidelines.

---

405. Previously, a distinction was drawn between private and public water, and the rights of private owners of water were respected – one of the reasons why s. 18 was built into the Electricity Regulation Act.
406. Section 21.
407. General Notice 849 in *Government Gazette* 36749 of 15 Aug. 2013.
408. Section 18.
409. Section 19.
410. *See*, e.g., Government Notice 144 in *Government Gazette* 35072 of 2 Mar. 2012 (Highveld Priority Area Air Quality Management Plan), Government Notice R614 in *Government Gazette* 32254 of 29 May 2009 (Regulations for implementing and enforcing the Vaal Triangle Air-Shed Priority Area Air Quality Management Plan); Government Notice 154 in *Government Gazette* 36207 of 8 Mar. 2013 (Declaring Waterberg-Bojanala National Priority Area, amending Government Notice 495 in *Government Gazette* 35435 of 15 Jun. 2012).
411. Government Notice 333 in *Government Gazette* 39833 of 18 Mar. 2016.

91. The Minister may after consultation with the Regulator and stakeholders in the advisory forum determine that certain activities no longer need licensing. This must be done by notice in the *Government Gazette*.[412] The Minister may also after consultation with the Regulator and by notice in the *Government Gazette* determine that these or other activities need to register with the Regulator. Registration must be done on the prescribed form and after payment of a registration fee.[413]

§2. Nuclear Energy

92. In addition to the above regulation for electricity generation, a nuclear installation will need additional authorizations and is regulated in terms of a different set of legislation. The purpose of the National Nuclear Regulator Act 47 of 1999 is to provide for the establishment of a National Nuclear Regulator,[414] to regulate nuclear activities, to provide safety standards and regulatory practices for the protection of persons, property and the environment against nuclear damage. This Act introduces a shift in emphasis from the mere production of nuclear energy towards the protection of people and the environment.[415] Cooperative governance was one of the principles embedded in the Constitution[416] and the NEMA.[417]

The function of the Regulator is to grant or amend nuclear authorizations and certificates of registration,[418] advise the Minister on the possibility of nuclear damage and to submit a yearly report on the safety and health of workers, the public and the

412. Section 8.

413. Section 9(1)-(2). The Regulator must register the activity on receipt of the form – however, it may refuse to register if the application is not made within the prescribed period or the application is contrary to the objects of the Act. The registration may also be made subject to conditions – s. 9(3)-(4).

414. The National Nuclear Regulator (hereinafter 'Regulator') is the legal successor to the Council for Nuclear Safety – s. 55.

415. Section 5. *See also* the investigation into claims by former employees of the Pelindaba nuclear facility that they possibly suffered from exposure to radiation – S. Smillie, *Disease stalks workers at nuke plant*, 2 May, The Star 1 (2005).

416. Sections 40–41.

417. Sections 2(l) of NEMA and section 6 of the National Nuclear Regulator Act.. The cooperative agreements deal with the effective monitoring and control of nuclear hazards, the coordination of such functions, the minimizing and duplication of functions and procedures and the promotion of consistency in the exercise of these functions. The cooperative agreements must be published for comment. *See*, e.g., General Notice 712 in *Government Gazette* 37941 of 29 Aug. 2014 (between the National Nuclear Regulator and the NERSA); Government Notice 759 in *Government Gazette* 21232 of 7 Jul. 2008 (between National Nuclear Regulator and then DEAT, Government Notice 1015 in *Government Gazette* 30407 of 2 Nov. 2007 and Government Notice 1014 in *Government Gazette* 30406 of 2 Nov. 2007 (various other cooperative agreements).

418. Regulations for a nuclear installation licence – Government Notice R479 in *Government Gazette* 21171 of 12 May 2000. Section 22 deals with certificates of registration. *See also* Government Notice R38 in *Government Gazette* 37262 of 31 Jan. 2014 that deals with application and authorization fees and General Notice 590 in *Government Gazette* 40279 of 16 Sep. 2016 whereby Eskom (Pty) SOC applied to the National Nuclear Regulator (NNR) for Nuclear Installation Site Licences for Thyspunt and Duynefontyn – this notice was published for comment.

environment.[419] The Regulator is governed and controlled by a board of directors, which consists of one representative of organized labour, one from organized business, one person representing communities that may be affected by nuclear activities, an official from the Department of Energy, an official from the DEA, the Chief Executive Officer[420] and seven other qualified directors.[421]

93. The Act applies to the siting, design, construction, operation, decommissioning and closure of nuclear installations as well as to vessels propelled by nuclear power or having radioactive material on board.[422] However, the Act does not apply to exposure to cosmic radiation or to potassium-40 in the body or any other radioactive material or actions determined by the Minister, where the radioactivity concentrations of individual radioactive nuclides are below the exclusion levels provided for in the safety standards,[423] Group IV hazardous substances, and exposure to ionizing radiation emitted from equipment declared to be Group III hazardous substances.[424] The Minister may after consultation with the Board of the Regulator declare any facility, installation, plant or structure, including a mine or ore-processing facility, to be a nuclear installation.[425]

94. A nuclear licence is necessary to site, construct, operate, decontaminate or decommission a nuclear installation. A vessel entering, anchoring or sojourning in the territorial waters or a port of the Republic also requires a licence.[426] An application must be made in the prescribed format.[427] The applicant may be directed to furnish certain information and to serve a copy of the application upon each municipality affected by the application or any other person identified by the chief executive officer. A copy of the application must also be published in the *Government Gazette* and two newspapers circulating in the area of each municipality.

Any person who may be directly affected by the granting of a nuclear installation or vessel licence may make representations to the board of the Regulator relating to health, safety and environmental issues. The objections must be lodged thirty days

---

419. Section 7. *See also* Anon, *Organizational Profile*, nnr.co.za/documents/organisation_profile.htm (accessed 7 May 2001).
420. Appointed in terms of s. 15. The person must have suitable qualifications and is appointed for a period of three years with the possibility of reappointment.
421. Section 8.
422. Section 2(1).
423. Published in terms of s. 36 read with s. 41(4) – Government Notice R388 in *Government Gazette* 28755 of 28 Apr. 2006. *See also* Anon, *Safety Standards*, nnr.co.za/documents/Power_Reactors/safety_standards_and_development.htm (accessed 7 May 2001).
424. *See infra* para. 117.
425. Section 2(3).
426. Sections 20–28. Government Notice 581 in *Government Gazette* 26327 of 7 May 2004 categorized the South African nuclear installations as follows: Category 1 – Koeberg; Category 2 – SAFARI-1 Research Reactor; Category 3 – Vaalputs and installations at Pelindaba for purposes of the levelling of financial security that has to be provided by holders of licences. The Regulations also prescribed the manner in which the financial security is to be provided. In 2017, draft regulations in this regard were published for comment – *see* Government Notice R773 in *Government Gazette* 41023 of 4 Aug. 2017.
427. Section 21 read with Government Notice R910 in *Government Gazette* 30102 of 27 Jul. 2007. *See also* www.nnr.co.za for more information on how to apply for a licence.

after publication in the *Government Gazette*. If the board is of the opinion that further debate is necessary, it may arrange for hearings.[428] If an application is refused, the applicant must receive written reasons. An approval may also be made subject to certain conditions.[429]

A nuclear installation or vessel licence and a certificate of registration may be made subject to conditions if they are necessary for the protection of persons, property or the environment and may provide for rehabilitation of the site. The conditions may be amended at any time in which case the licensee or holder of the registration certificate must be notified in writing. The amendments must also be put to the board for ratification.[430] A nuclear authorization is not transferable[431] but may be revoked at any time.[432]

95. If the proposed action may cause nuclear damage,[433] an applicant may apply in the prescribed format for a certificate of registration or a certificate of exemption. All necessary information must be furnished.[434] To determine when an applicant has to apply for a registration certificate, the definitions in section 1 of the Act needs to be examined. 'Nuclear damage' is defined as '(a) any injury to or the death or any sickness or disease of a person; (b) other damage, including any damage to or any loss of the use of property or damage to the environment, which arises out of, or results from, or is attributable to, the ionizing radiation associated with a nuclear installation, nuclear vessel or action'. 'Action' is then defined as '(a) the use, possession, production, storage, enrichment, processing, reprocessing, conveying or disposal of, or causing to be conveyed, radioactive material; (b) any action, the performance of which may result in persons accumulating a radiation dose resulting from exposure to ionizing radiation; or (c) any other action involving radioactive material'. It is, however, still not clear exactly who will have to apply for a registration certificate, and the Regulator will have to be contacted to determine whether an application for a certificate of registration or an exemption should be made.

96. The responsibilities of holders of nuclear authorizations are set out in section 26. In terms of the section, they must display copies of the authorizations at specified places and in the languages determined by the chief executive officer to ensure public access to the conditions. The holder of the authorization must implement an inspection programme and must provide information to the executive officer on a monthly basis. A public safety forum must also be established to inform the public of the emergency plans established in terms of section 38.[435] Section 37

428. Section 21(1)–(4).
429. Section 21(5).
430. *See* s. 23. Special conditions can be added to nuclear vessel licences – *see* s. 24.
431. Section 25.
432. Section 27.
433. In terms of s. 2(1)(c).
434. Section 22(1). More or less the same procedure is followed as described in the case of a s. 21 application.
435. In terms of Government Notice R299 in *Government Gazette* 26112 of 12 Mar. 2004 (regulation 3), the holder of licence must establish public safety forum where an emergency plan has been drawn up. The licence holder must also provide the venue and facilities for meetings and provide

describes the duties of the holder of a nuclear authorization with regard to nuclear accidents and incidents. The holder of a nuclear authorization must provide financial security.[436]

§3. Renewable Energy

I. Renewable Energy: Wind and Solar

97. A renewable energy project may trigger one of the listed activities for which a basic assessment or environmental impact assessment may be required in terms of section 24 of the NEMA.[437] In 2015, the DEA published an *EIA Guideline for Renewable Energy Projects*.[438] The Guideline describes the different renewable energy sources and indicates their environmental impacts. It also indicates which legislation will be applicable to a specific project and for which activities additional authorizations may be necessary. These laws include but are not limited to the NEMWA; the NEMAQA; the NWA; the Hazardous Substances Act 15 of 1973 and planning authorizations.[439] In 2018, the then DEA indicated that although large scale solar and wind farms may trigger an environmental impact assessment, a basic assessment would suffice if the development is undertaken in specified geographic areas of strategic importance.[440]

II. Biomass

98. In the Preamble to the National Forests Act, it is *inter alia* stated that the economic, social and environmental benefits of forests have been distributed

---

a secretariat for the functioning of the forum. Information on nuclear and radiation matters and also nuclear accidents must be provided to the forum. The holder must cover all reasonable costs. 'Nuclear safety' (regulation 1) is defined as the 'achievement of safe operating conditions, prevention of nuclear accidents or mitigation of nuclear accident consequences, resulting in the protection of workers, the public and the environment against the potential harmful effects of ionizing radiation or radioactive material', and 'radiation safety' is defined as 'to protect against the harmful effects of ionizing radiation or radioactive material'. On the establishing of public safety forums in municipal areas for which an emergency plan exists, *see* Government Notice 968 in *Government Gazette* 31403 of 12 Sep. 2008.

436. Government Notice R773 in *Government Gazette* 41023 of 4 Aug. 2017 published regulations pertaining to financial security for comment. By December 2019, the final regulations have not been published yet.

437. Listing Notice 1 item 1– Government Notice R983 in *Government Gazette* 38282 of 4 Dec. 2014; Listing Notice 2 item 1– Government Notice R983 in *Government Gazette* 38282 of 4 Dec. 2014.

438. General Notice 989 in *Government Gazette* 39297 of 16 Oct. 2015.

439. For a discussion of the South African environmental legislation, *see* E. Couzens & M. Lewis, *South Africa*. In International Encyclopaedia of Laws: Environmental Law (K. Deketelaere, ed., Kluwer Law International 2013).

440. Government Notice 114 in *Government Gazette* 41445 of 16 Feb. 2018. *See also* the earlier Government Notice 350 in *Government Gazette* 40785 of 13 Apr. 2017 that was published for comment and dealt with the procedure to be followed in applying for an environmental authorization for large scale wind and solar photovoltaic development activities occurring in a renewable energy development zone (REDZ) or associated strategic transmission corridor.

unfairly in the past. The principles to guide decisions affecting forests include that natural forests should not be destroyed save in exceptional circumstances where the new proposed land use is preferable in terms of its economic, social or environmental benefits and that forests should be developed and managed to conserve biological diversity, ecosystems and habitats, but, on the other hand, promote the fair distribution of their economic, social and environmental benefits.[441] Sustainable forest management and use must on the one hand benefit, therefore, the environment and on the other hand contribute to economic development, for example mining.

The National Forests Act controls use of land in state forests for commercial purposes,[442] as well as provides for special measures to protect natural forests and trees.[443]

Indigenous trees in a declared natural forest[444] may only be cut, disturbed, damaged or destroyed in terms of a licence[445] or if an exemption was received from the Minister of Human Settlements, Water and Sanitation. The Minister may declare certain forests as protected forest areas, which will result in total protection of such forests.[446] In the same manner, a particular tree or species of trees, group of trees or particular woodland can be declared to be protected.[447]

In terms of Chapter 4 of the Act, the Minister may publish a national list of ecosystems that are threatened or in need of protection. The following categories may be identified: critically endangered ecosystems, endangered ecosystems, vulnerable ecosystems and protected ecosystems.[448] The Minister may also identify any process or activity as a threatening process.[449] Similarly, a list of critically endangered species, endangered species, vulnerable species and protected species may be listed in terms of section 56 as well as restricted activities with regard to these species in terms of section 57. A restricted activity includes among others the gathering, collecting or plucking of listed, threatened or protected species, the chopping off, uprooting, damaging or destroying of the same.[450] In some instances, permits may be issued authorizing restricted activities with regard to species.[451]

99. In some of the National parks or protected areas, the surrounding communities and the National Parks Board came to an agreement that communities may

441. Section 3(3).
442. Sections 4 and 17.
443. Sections 7 and 12.
444. Section 7(3).
445. Issued in terms of ss 7(4) or 23.
446. Sections 8–11. *See*, e.g., Government Notice 650 in *Government Gazette* 37941 of 29 Aug. 2014.
447. Sections 12–15. The Minister may request the Registrar of Deeds to register the fact that a forest has been declared a natural forest or that a tree, group of trees or a woodland have been declared to be protected – s. 16. *See*, e.g., also Government Notice 673 in *Government Gazette* 36827 of 13 Sep. 2013.
448. Section 52. Government Notice 1002 in *Government Gazette* 34809 of 9 Dec. 2011.
449. Section 53.
450. Section 1. *See also* lists of threatened and protected species – Government Notice R152 in *Government Gazette* 29657, of 23 Feb. 2007.
451. Section 87. The procedure for applications is set out in s. 88. It may be required of the applicant to do a risk assessment in terms of s. 89. Permits may be integrated with other authorizations that are to be obtained in terms of other legislation – s. 92. Appeals are regulated by ss 94–96.

gather firewood in these parks under the supervision of a game ranger. These agreements are voluntary and no legal provision exists for them. In terms of the NEMBA, permits would now have to be obtained if the species are listed in terms of the Act. Agreements may also be concluded with communities in terms of the National Environmental Management: Protected Areas Act 57 of 2003.[452]

There are no legal provisions with regard to the collection of dung or other not listed biomass in order to create energy, except for one provision of the Gas Act.[453] The national government embarked on a programme to determine how affordable alternative energy can be provided to rural communities.

---

452. *See*, e.g., A. Paterson, *Co-managing South Africa's Conservation and Land Reform Agendas: Evaluating Recent Initiatives to Resolve the Unruly Interface Thrust Upon South Africa's Protected Areas*, 17 SAJELP 97–137 (2010); A. Paterson & J. Glazewski, *Protected Areas and Community-Based Conservation*, 321–362. In Environmental Law in South Africa (J. Glazewski & L. du Toit, eds, LexisNexis 2013).

453. *See infra* para. 138.

Chapter 3. Exploitation

§1. Coal-based Electricity

100. The MPRDA regulates the exploitation of coal. *See* in this regard Part IV of this book. Coal mines have to obtain a mining licence, environmental authorization as well as draft an environmental management programme indicating how the mine will address the environmental issues during the life cycle of the mine.

§2. Nuclear Energy

101. Similar to coal mines, uranium mines have to apply for a mining licence and an environmental authorization in terms of the NEMA and prepare an environmental management programme.[454] The mines will further have to address any radioactivity issues in the environmental management programme.[455]

One of the issues that will have to be addressed will be radioactivity and the handling of radioactive waste. Provision is also made that the Minister may take remedial steps where pollution or environmental damage occurs or if a public safety risk exists. Before the closure of a mine, an environmental risk report has to be completed which will include an investigation into the possibility of radioactivity.[456]

§3. Renewable Energy

102. The use of biomass as such is not regulated; however, certain activities in state forests can be licensed, namely the felling of trees and the removal of timber, the cutting, disturbance, damage or destruction of any forest produce, the use of the land for agriculture or other purposes, the grazing or herding of animals, hunting and fishing.[457] Section 24(9) of the National Forest Act provides that the right to prospect or mine or dispose of minerals as defined in the MPRDA or any source material as defined in the nuclear legislation may be granted, but the holder of such a right has to obtain a licence in terms of section 23 of the National Forest Act. The granting of the licence is subject to the principles set out in section 3(3) of this Act.[458]

103. The National Forest Act further provides for the possibility to enter into community forestry agreements. The Minister and a defined community can enter into an agreement to do anything in a state forest for which a licence is required or

454. *See* Part VI of the book.
455. Section 24 NEMA read with item 17 Government Notice R984 in *Government Gazette* 38283 of 4 Dec. 2014.
456. *See also* regulations 57 and 60 of Government Notice R527 in *Government Gazette* 26275 of 23 Apr. 2004.
457. Section 23 National Forest Act.
458. *See supra* para. 123.

to manage the forest jointly.[459] The Minister may provide information, training, material or financial assistance to the community.[460] Such forestry community agreements must regulate the use and management of the forest in a manner that is sustainable. The forest can, for example, be used to collect firewood if necessary.[461]

104. Plants are also protected by the Mountain Catchment Areas Act 64 of 1970, the Lake Areas Development Act 39 of 1975, the Conservation of Agricultural Resources Act 43 of 1983, provincial legislation such as the Limpopo Environmental Management Act 7 of 2003 and various older provincial ordinances such as the Transvaal Nature Conservation Ordinance 12 of 1983, the Orange Free State (OFS) Nature Conservation Ordinance 9 of 1969, the Natal Nature Conservation Ordinance 14 of 1974, the Cape Nature and Environmental Conservation Ordinance 19 of 1974, the North West Nature Conservation Ordinance 12 van 1983[462] as well as legislation issued by the former so-called homelands that were created during the apartheid system.[463]

105. In 2004, the National Environmental Management: Protected Areas Act 47 of 2003 came into operation.[464] The Act provides for the protection and conservation of ecologically viable areas representative of South Africa's biodiversity and its natural landscapes and seascapes, including former national parks established in terms of the National Parks Act 57 of 1996 and new national parks established in terms of the 2003 Act.[465] This allows for community-based natural resource management, the use of biological resources in the area and the development of economic opportunities within land adjacent to the protected area.[466] A local community may be allowed to use in a sustainable manner biological resources in a natural reserve or world heritage site.[467]

Commercial and mining activities are only allowed in a protected area if written permission from the Minister of Environmental Affairs, Forestry and Fisheries or a responsible cabinet member is obtained. The Minister must review all mining activities which were lawfully conducted with the cabinet member responsible for minerals and energy. Conditions may be placed on the mining operations. The Minister

459. Section 29.
460. Section 32.
461. Section 31(1)(e).
462. For a discussion of this legislation *see* R.F. Fuggle & M.A. Rabie, *Environmental Management in South Africa*, 224–242 (Juta 1992); J. Glazewski, *Environmental Law*, 374–397 (2nd edn, Butterworths 2005).
463. *See* in this regard W. Du Plessis, *Integration of Existing Environmental Legislation in the Provinces*, 2 South African Journal of Environmental Law and Policy, 23–36 (1995).
464. Proclamation 52 in *Government Gazette* 26960 of 2 Nov. 2004.
465. National Environmental Management: Protected Areas Amendment Act 31 of 2004.
466. Sections 41–42. *See also* Government Notice R 1061 in *Government Gazette* 28181 of 28 Oct. 2005 that published regulations regarding the proper administration of special nature reserves, national parks and world heritage sites. The Regulations deal extensively with the use of biological resources (regulations 5, 31–32, 45) and mining (regulations 39–40). Activities that may have an adverse effect on the environment are dealt with in regulations 38–43.
467. Section 50. *See* J. van Wyk, *Development in Protected Areas*, 17 SA Public Law 163–177 (2002); R. Peart & K. Govender, *Natural Resources Policies for the New Millennium: is South Africa Moving towards a More Sustainable Path?*, 8 SAJELP 39–76 (2001).

may also cancel or acquire a mineral right by way of expropriation.[468] In the case of *Mpumalanga Tourism and Parks Agency and Another v Baberton Mines (Pty) Ltd and Others*,[469] the appellant appealed against a finding of the High Court that the granting of a prospecting right was not in a protected area and therefore valid. The SCA upheld the appeal.

106. The objectives of the NEMBA include, among others, the management and conservation of biological diversity, the use of indigenous biological resources in a sustainable manner and the fair and equitable sharing among stakeholders of benefits arising from bioprospecting of indigenous biological resources. 'Sustainable use' of a biological resource is defined in section 1 of the Act as 'the use of such resource in a way and at a rate that – (a) would not lead to its long-term decline, (b) would not disrupt the ecological integrity of the ecosystem in which it occurs, and (c) would ensure its continued use to meet the needs and aspirations of present and future generations of people'.[470]

468. Section 48 read with s. 84.
469. [2017] 2 All SA 376 (SCA); 2017 (5) SA 62 (SCA).
470. *See* in this regard A. Paterson, *Biological Diversity,* 519–572. In Fuggle and Rabie's Environmental Management in South Africa (King, N.D, H.A Strydom & F.P Retief, eds, 3rd edn, Juta 2018).

Chapter 4. Generation

107. The generation of electricity is regulated in terms of the Electricity Regulation Act, regardless of the source of the energy (excluding small-scale projects).[471]

108. The Minister of Energy in consultation with the Regulator may determine that new generation capacity is needed to ensure an uninterrupted supply of electricity. He or she may also determine the types of energy sources from which electricity must be generated as well as the percentages that each source of energy should contribute. He or she must also determine the manner of selling and purchasing of these types of energy. The new type of generation capacity is to be effected by a tendering process and must provide for private sector participation.[472] In 2011, the Minister issued regulations on new generation capacity. The new generation capacity includes energy derived from co-generation with renewable energy, 'base load, mid-merit load and peak load new generation capacity; and cross-border projects'. The new generation capacity does not refer to nuclear energy as an energy source.[473]

109. The Minister may further by notice in the *Government Gazette* make regulations pertaining, among others, to activities that may be licensed or registered, norms and standards relating to the quality of supply, compulsory national norms and standards for reticulation services, inspections, types of energy sources from which electricity must be generated as well as the percentage and the setting of standards relating to health, safety and the environment and their incorporation into licences.[474] In 2008, the Minister of Energy issued regulations, for example, to minimize load-shedding, blackouts and to improve the quality of electricity supply.[475] In these regulations, certain practices were prescribed. It was determined that energy-efficiency fittings must be used in all buildings except if a specific fitting is required for business purposes. All users who used more than 1000 kWh must instal smart systems. Street and highway lighting had to be energy efficient and switched off during daytime. All streetlights also had to be fitted with energy-efficiency systems to allow remote reduction of power.[476] In 2010, the Minister of Energy published an

471. Exclusions are listed in the Sch. 2 to the Act.
472. Section 34 Electricity Regulation Act 4 of 2006.
473. Government Notice R399 in *Government Gazette* 34262 of 4 May 2011 – Electricity Regulations on New Generation Capacity, as amended by Government Notice 1366 in *Government Gazette* 40401 of 4 Nov. 2016.
474. Section 35 Electricity Regulation Act 4 of 2006. *See also* Government Notice R148 in *Government Gazette* 30755 of 8 Feb. 2008 – Electricity regulations for the prohibition of certain practices in the electricity supply and compulsory norms and standards for reticulation services.
475. Government Notice R773 in *Government Gazette* 31250 of 18 Jul. 2008 as amended by General Notice 1190 in *Government Gazette* 31436 of 17 Sep. 2008.
476. *See also* Government Notice R26 in *Government Gazette* 31793 of 16 Jan. 2009 – Electricity regulations on deviation from set or approved tariff.

Integrated Resource Plan.[477] According to the plan, renewable energy should contribute 4% of the energy mix by 2013, the installation of 1 million solar water heaters and the institution of financial incentives for demand-side management and energy efficiency. The 2016 Integrated Resource Plan provides a contribution of 18.85% coal, 24.96% nuclear energy, 26.15% gas, 11.61% solar, 22.31% wind energy and 3% hydropower. Subsequent to the publication of the Integrated Resource Plan, the nuclear option became less viable.[478] Non-governmental organizations also resist the introduction of nuclear energy.[479] In 2018, the National Planning Commission added an additional response addressing the challenges and new changes pertaining to the energy mix.[480]

477. Government Notice 25 in *Government Gazette* 32898 of 29 Jan. 2010.

478. Anon., *South Africa drops nuclear energy plan,* Business Insider, 27 Aug. 2018 https://businesstech.co.za/news/energy/267581/south-africa-drops-nuclear-energy-plan/ (accessed 25 Apr. 2019). Also *see* GiZ, *Assessing the impact of increasing shares of variable generation on system operations in South Africa* (September 2017).

479. *See*, e.g., *Earthlife Africa Johannesburg and Another v Minister of Energy and Others* [2017] 3 All SA 187 (WCC); 2017 (5) SA 227 (WCC) (26 Apr. 2017).

480. National Planning Commission, *Energy*, NPC Economy Series Version 1.0 (January 2018). In Government Notice 454 in *Government Gazette* 39940 of 20 Apr. 2016 the Minister determined the contribution of coal from cross-border projects.

Chapter 5. Transmission

110. Eskom transmits electricity and would be regarded as a licensee in terms of the Act. The licensee must exercise his or her powers or performs his or her duties in terms of the conditions set out in the licence and the Electricity Regulation Act 4 of 2006. A licensee may not discriminate between its customers or classes of customers regarding access, tariffs, prices, etc. except if they are approved by the Regulator. The licensee must provide non-discriminatory access to the transmission and distribution power systems to third parties. The licensee may not reduce or terminate the supply of electricity to a customer except if the customer is insolvent, failed to honour an agreement or has contravened the payment conditions.[481]

111. Any person authorized by the licensee has the right to enter any premises to which electricity has been supplied in order to inspect the lines meters, fittings, works and apparatus. This person has to make the necessary arrangements with the occupier of the premises before entering and must exhibit his or her authorization.[482]

112. If any damage is caused by an inspection, entry by a person authorized by the licensee or removal of any equipment, the licensee must repair the damage or compensate the licensee.[483] Where damage or injury is caused by induction, electrolysis or any other matter by means of which electricity is generated or transmitted or distributed negligence on the side of the licensee is presumed.[484] The licensee will have to prove that the damage or injury was not due to his or her negligence. The reason for the inclusion of such a presumption is that the generation of electricity is a high-risk business and, therefore, it is deemed that an undertaker should carry the burden of proof.

481. Section 21.
482. Section 22(1)–(2).
483. Section 22(3).
484. Section 25.

Chapter 6. Distribution

113. Eskom distributes electricity, for example, to rural areas or municipalities that do not have the capacity to reticulate electricity.[485] Municipalities, however in principle, reticulate electricity to its communities as part of its service delivery function.[486] They may enter into service delivery agreements with service providers, following the correct procedures.[487] The Electricity Regulation Act 4 of 2006 places certain duties on municipalities.[488] A municipality must comply with all technical and operational requirements for electricity networks as determined by NERSA. A municipality must refer to its reticulation services in its integrated development plans.[489] Municipalities must also progressively ensure access to at least basic reticulation services by investing in its electricity infrastructure and must provide such services free of charge or a minimum cost to certain classes of end users within its available resources.[490]

The municipality must adhere to national norms and standards and must ensure sustainable, effective and efficient distribution of energy. The Regulator must prescribe key performance indicators for technical issues that may differ depending on the type of municipality.[491] Electricity reticulated and sold by a local authority is, therefore, under the control of that authority, except if the supplier has lawfully acquired the right of supply within a specific area. The provision of electricity services provides revenue to municipalities.[492]

114. The Act further provides for the possibility of expropriation of land and interests in land,[493] appeals from decisions of the Regulator,[494] breaking up of

485. *See*, e.g., *J R Properties CC v Eskom Holdings Limited* (1514/2013) [2016] ZANWHC 76 (15 Dec. 2016) where there was a dispute between a new housing developer applying for an electricity connection in a municipal area and Eskom.
486. Schedule 4B of the Constitution.
487. Section 28. *See*, for example, the case of *City Power (Pty) Ltd v Grinpal Energy Management Services (Pty) Ltd and Others* [2015] ZACC 9 where such a service agreement is explained – the case however deals with a labour dispute.
488. Section 27.
489. An integrated development plan is a strategic plan of a municipality. Each municipality must develop an integrated development plan in terms of s. 25 of the Local Government: Municipal Systems Act 12 of 2000. The integrated development plan remains in force for five years (the elected term of a municipal council).
490. In 2015 NERSA published a document dealing with the *Cost of Supply Framework for Licensed Electricity Distributors* in South Africa for comment.
491. Section 29. On municipalities and their responsibilities in terms of energy, *see* Willemien Du Plessis and Tumai Murombo, *Energy*, 877–907, In Environmental Law and Local Government in South Africa, Cape Town (A.A. Du Plessis, ed., Juta 2015).
492. *See also* para. 45.
493. Section 26. *See also* Government Notice R147 in *Government Gazette* 30754 of 8 Feb. 2008 – Electricity Regulations for expropriation on behalf of a licensee; E. Witbooi, *Restrictive Environmental Measures: (when) Do They Justify Compensation for the Property Owner?* 8 South African Journal of Environmental Law and Policy, 215–245 (2001). *See* A.J. van der Walt, *Constitutional Property Law*, 334–520 (3rd edn, Juta 2011); P.J. Badenhorst, J.M. Pienaar & H. Mostert, *Silberberg and Schoeman's The Law of Property*, 558–578 (5th edn, Butterworths 2006).
494. Section 31.

streets,[495] offences and penalties.[496] All electricity infrastructures, whether regarded as movable or immovable property, remain the property of the licensee and may not be attached or taken in execution of any liquidation proceedings against the occupier of a premise; They may also not be subject to a landlord's hypothec for rent and may only dealt with as set out in an agreement with the licensee.[497] The reason for inclusion of this section is that in terms of property law, such items might be regarded as fixtures and, therefore, the ownership passes to the owner of the land and they cannot be removed.[498]

115. In 2001, the Eskom Conversion Act 13 of 2001 was enacted.[499] Eskom was converted from a commission into a public company.[500] Eskom operates since as Eskom Holdings Ltd. having share capital.[501] The state is the sole or majority shareholder.[502] The Electricity Council and Management Board of Eskom ceased to exist and was replaced by a board of directors.[503] Although Eskom became a company rather than a commission, it is in effect still government-controlled. A question to be asked is what the environmental regulatory implications would be.[504]

116. At some stage, government tried to establish regional energy distributors that would have taken the mandate away from municipalities. This idea was met with fierce criticism and has for the time being been abandoned. Approximately twelve cities use 80% of the electricity distributed to municipalities. Municipalities, however, do not always maintain or refurbish their electricity infrastructure and serious backlogs may endanger energy security in South Africa, and government realizes that urgent attention is needed to address the matter.[505]

---

495. Section 24.
496. Sections 18, 19 and 25.
497. Section 23.
498. P.J. Badenhorst, J.M. Pienaar & H. Mostert, *Silberberg and Schoeman's The Law of Property*, 147–154 (5th edn, Butterworths 2006).
499. The Act came into operation on 1 Jul. 2002.
500. According to s. 8 Eskom Conversion Act 13 of 2001, Eskom may enter upon any land to make plans or survey the land but must give prior notice to the landowner. Eskom must also pay any damage caused by its officers or employees in the performance of their duties.
501. Section 3.
502. Section 4(2).
503. Section 11(6)–(7).
504. J. Glazewski, *Environmental Law*, 498–499 (2nd edn, LexisNexis 2005).
505. A. Eberhard, *The Reds are dead*, 17 August, Engineering News (2012) http://www.engineeringnews.co.za/article/the-reds-are-dead-2012-08-17 (accessed 20 Dec. 2013). In 2012, the backlog was ZAR 35 billion. *See also* J. Mettler & K. Smith, *Bulk Electricity Prices, Exemptions and the Demise of Local Democracy*, 10 Local Government Bulletin 4–7 (2008).

Chapter 7. Consumption

§1. Electricity

117. South Africa has different consumers of electricity as well as poor households that must receive free basic energy. Even before the Electricity Regulation Act was implemented, a policy dealing with access to free basic electricity was published.[506] According to a cabinet decision, all poor households will receive 50 kWh free electricity. It is enough for an indigent household to have access to lighting, media, limited ironing and water heating. However, not all households are connected to the grid. In 2007, a *Free Basic Alternative Energy Policy* was published.[507] According to this policy, municipalities in remote un-electrified areas must provide free basic alternative energy to its indigent households. The municipality may choose the energy carriers. The municipality must provide as a minimum energy to the value of ZAR 55 which has to be increased on an annual basis by the inflation rate plus 1.5%.[508] The municipality must ensure that the indigent benefits from the policy and must put fraud prevention measures into place. In 2008, the then DME published an *Electricity Pricing Policy*.[509]

Sometimes municipalities that reticulate energy in their jurisdictions do not pay Eskom. Eskom threatens to disconnect the electricity supply of these municipalities. However, the consumers of electricity pay the municipality directly. There are many reasons for municipalities to default payment, one of it that some of their consumers do not pay their electricity bills. This lead to conflict between the paid-up and default consumers vis-à-vis the municipality. In the case of *Cape Gate (Pty) Ltd and others v Eskom Holdings Soc Ltd and others*,[510] the Emfuleni Municipality owed Eskom more than ZAR 1 billion. Eskom threatened to interrupt the electricity supply to Emfuleni. This interruption will also affect paid-up consumers and businesses. The court referred the dispute back to NERSA, Eskom and Emfuleni to draft a payment plan and also not to interrupt the electricity supply to paid-up consumers. In another case, consumers approached the court to pay Eskom directly, rather

506. DME Electricity Basic Services Support Tariff Policy – General Notice 1693 in *Government Gazette* 25088 of 4 Jul. 2003. Also *see* General Notice 356 in *Government Gazette* 40088 of 24 Jun. 2016 where a draft strategy to address air pollution in dense low-income settlements was published for comment.

507. General Notice 391 in *Government Gazette* 2976 of 2 Apr. 2007.

508. Also *see*, for example, City of Cape Town, *State of Energy Report 2015*, http://www.cityenergy.org.za/uploads/resource_335.pdf (accessed 12 May 2015); WWF Report 'Potential for integration of distributed solar photovoltaic systems in Drakenstein municipality' (2015) https://www.crses.sun.ac.za/files/research/publications/technical-reports/RE%20Drakenstein%20Report%20Thursday%2027%20Sep.pdf (accessed 12 May 2019).

509. General Notice 1398 in *Government Gazette* 31741 of 19 Dec. 2008.

510. [2019] 1 All SA 141 (GJ) para. 5. Also *see* M. Mathenjwa, *The constitutional obligations imposed on a provincial government in instances where a municipality cannot provide basic services as a result of a crisis in its financial affairs*, Journal of South African Law 59–75 (2015).

than the defaulting municipality.[511] An agreement was reached between the consumers and Eskom for direct payment and this was made an order of the court. The court refers to the dire situation of non-payment of municipalities as follows:[512]

> Because of widespread delinquency, it has become necessary for Eskom to take extraordinary steps to collect substantial outstanding debts from various municipalities across South Africa. In the period March 2016 to November 2016, total municipal debt owed to Eskom increased from ZAR 6 billion to ZAR 10.2 billion. As at the end of November 2016, twenty defaulting municipalities owed Eskom approximately ZAR 7.476 billion of which ten owed approximately ZAR 6.032 billion. Seventy-four municipalities were overdue in respect of debts exceeding ZAR 10 million, and ninety-nine municipalities were overdue in respect of debts exceeding ZAR 500 000.

118. In the case of *Eskom Holdings Limited v Halstead-Cleak*,[513] the SCA held that Eskom could not be held strictly liable in terms of the Consumer Protection Act 68 of 2008[514] for damages that may occur from contact with transmission lines as being the 'alleged supply of unsafe goods and/or defective good'. In this instance, the defendant came into contact with a low-hanging powerline while cycling on a footpath. The powerlines were vandalized due to theft. The court found that the cyclist could not be regarded as a consumer in terms of the Act and that accordingly Eskom cannot be held liable.[515] In the case of *A v Blue Crane Route Municipality*,[516] the court held that the applicants had to prove negligence on the part of municipality in order to be held liable for a delictual action.

119. In *Mercedes Benz South Africa v Buffalo City Municipality*,[517] the plaintiff sued the municipality for damage that was caused by voltage fluctuations. The machinery was damaged and had to be replaced – the factory lost three working days. Mercedes Benz received its electricity from a substation that the municipality specifically erected to supply electricity to the factory. There was a dispute as to who was responsible for the fluctuation. The court, however, found that the defendant, the municipality, was responsible for the damage.

---

511. *Afriform NPC and Others v Eskom Holdings Soc Limited and Others* (99984/2015) [2017] ZAGPPHC 199; [2017] 3 All SA 663 (GP) (24 May 2017). Also *see NCP Chlorchem (Pty) Ltd v National Energy Regulator and Others* [2017] 1 All SA 950 (GJ); 2017 (6) SA 158 (GJ) that dealt with electricity tariffs.
512. Para. 15.
513. ZASCA 150 (30 Sep. 2016).
514. Section 16.
515. Para. 25. The court *a quo* found that Eskom was 100% liable – *see* in this regard *Halstead-Cleak v Eskom Holdings Limited* (26360/14) [2015] ZAGPPHC 736 (1 Jun. 2015).
516. (4784/2015) [2017] ZAECGHC 86 (11 Jul. 2017).
517. (EL1123/2011, ECD1956/2011) [2015] ZAECELLC 17 (11 Dec. 2015). Also *see* the case of *Sabie Chamber of Commerce and Tourism and Others v Thaba Chweu Local Municipality and Others; Resilient Properties Proprietary Limited and Others v Eskom Holdings Soc Ltd and Others* (2295/2017, 83581/2017) [2019] ZAGPPHC 112 (7 Mar. 2019) where the court allowed an interdict to prevent Eskom to interrupt the power supply to customers as a result of the municipality's default payment.

In the case of *Eskom Holdings Soc Ltd v Sidoyi and Others*,[518] Eskom disconnected unlawful connections and apparatus to its grid. The affected persons challenged the disconnection and ask the court to order reconnection for their electricity supply. The court did not make a decision as it found that the question of whether the electricity was connected lawfully or not was a dispute of fact that has to be proven before the court. The court date was set for oral evidence on the matter. In a similar case, *Eskom Holdings Soc Ltd v Masinda*,[519] the SCA held that a *mandament van spolie* order could not be granted to the respondent in that she did not prove the elements of the action. The court also remarked that it would be problematic to order to restore an illegal connection to the grid but did not make an order in this regard as its based its finding on purely on the *mandament.*

120. Consumers are also urged to use energy efficiently, while industry and producers are urged to use energy economically and efficiently. Energy efficiency is defined in section 1 of the National Energy Act 34 of 2008 as 'the economical and efficient production and utilization of an energy carrier or resource'. The definition in the Act does not necessarily correspond with scientific definitions dealing with the matter.[520]

121. The concept of energy efficiency was initially mentioned in policy papers, such as the *White Paper on Energy*, 1998 and the *White Paper on the Renewable Energy Policy*, 2004 only. In May 2010, however, the Department of Energy published a *Policy to Support the Energy Efficiency and Demand Side Management Programme for the Electricity Sector through the Standard Offer Incentive Scheme.* The policy introduced an energy conservation scheme. The idea was that certain industries with high-energy consumption (above 100 GWh per annum) would have to negotiate a baseline with the National Energy Regulator. If they exceed this baseline, the prize for their electricity usage will increase. The Minister simultaneously set a reduction target for the different industries. The *Climate Change Response White Paper* introduced so-called Near-Term Flagship Programmes as part of government strategy to introduce adaptation and mitigation measures. One of the programmes relates to energy efficiency. It is foreseen that government will, among others, introduce energy-efficiency targets and standards.

In 2011, an *Integrated Resource Plan*[521] (IRP2) introduced, among others, an energy-efficiency and demand-side management financial incentive scheme (standard offer).[522] The draft update of IRP2 foresees that the market will drive the introduction of energy efficiency. However, other than original IPR2010 it also

518. (1207/2018) [2019] ZASCA 65 (28 May 2019).
519. (1225/2018) [2019] ZASCA 98 (18 Jun. 2019).
520. *See* W. Du Plessis, *Energy Efficiency and the Law: A Multidisciplinary Approach*, 111 South African Journal of Science (2015).
521. Government Notice R400 in *Government Gazette* 34263 of 6 May 2011. The *Integrated Resource Plan* is to be updated every two years. In 2018 a draft Integrated Resources Plan was published – Government Notice 897 in *Government Gazette* 41865 of 27 Aug. 2018. By July 2019, the Plan was not finalized yet.
522. *See also* A. Klees, *Electricity Law in South Africa*, 31–32 (Juta 2014).

recognizes that additional measures such as standards, incentives and education will be necessary to drive energy efficiency.[523]

122. The National Energy Act 34 of 2008 does not regulate energy efficiency per se but allows the Minister of Energy to issue regulations pertaining to energy efficiency.[524] His or her mandate includes regulations relating to the minimum levels of energy efficiency in each sector of the economy, the steps and procedures necessary for the application of energy-efficiency technologies and procedures, labelling for energy-efficiency purposes (household and motor vehicles), the prohibition of the manufacture, or importation or sale of electrical and electronic products and fuel-burning appliances for reasons of poor energy efficiency, and 'standards and specifications for energy carriers and energy efficiency standards for specific technologies, processes, appliances, devices, motor vehicles and buildings'.[525] At the end of 2019, the Minister has not issued any regulations in this regard yet, but a Draft Policy has been published.[526]

123. One of the aims of the Electricity Regulation Act 4 of 2006 is to promote energy efficiency.[527] The Act does not regulate energy efficiency extensively but allows the Minister of Energy some discretion in the matter. NERSA may, for example, place conditions in electricity licences dealing with energy-efficiency standards and demand-side management amend them from time to time to adapt to national energy priorities as set out in policies.[528] Although the Act does not specifically mandate the Minister to make regulations with regard to energy efficiency, it may be regarded as incidental to his or her mandate.[529]

124. National Treasury introduced some tax incentives to entice industry to introduce energy-efficiency measures. These measures are discussed in Part VI.

§2. Nuclear Energy

125. The Act introduces strict liability in the case of nuclear damage in section 30. Radioactive material or material contaminated by radioactivity which is being conveyed on behalf of the licence holder is regarded to be under the control and in the possession of the licence holder. The liability for nuclear damage by holders of nuclear authorizations is limited to the amounts determined by the procedure set out

523. *Integrated Resource Plan for Electricity 2010–2030*, Update Report 2013, 21 Nov. 2013, para. 10. In the case of any developments in relation to the Integrated Resource Plan, the Minister of Environmental Affairs will be the competent authority – General Notice 779 in *Government Gazette* 40110 of 1 Jul. 2016 – Identification of the Minister as competent authority for the consideration of environmental authorizations and amendments thereto for activities related to the Integrated Resource Plan (IRP) 2010–2030 – the notice was published for comment.
524. Section 19(1).
525. Section 19(1)(g)-(l).
526. *See infra* para 26.
527. Section 2(e).
528. Section 14(1)(u) read with s. 16.
529. Section 35(4)(s).

in section 27. The liability ends upon the relevant material coming onto a site for which a nuclear authorization has been issued or a site in possession or under the control of a person authorized in terms of section 3A of the Hazardous Substances Act 15 of 1973.

126. The licence holder is not liable to any person for nuclear damage if the damage is attributable to the presence of an unauthorized person on his or her property on the site, or if such a person intentionally caused or contributed to the damage. If the executive officer did not determine any conditions for liability in the case of a vessel, the provisions of section 31 apply.

127. The Regulator must keep records of nuclear accidents for a period of forty years and must make the information available on request.[530] Disclosure of information is restricted in terms of section 51 of the Act. The disclosure is made subject to the provisions of the Promotion of Access to Information Act 2 of 2000.[531] The National Nuclear Regulator must submit an annual public report to the Minister of Energy on the safety and health of works, the public and the environment on sites with nuclear installations or sites where nuclear damage may be caused.[532]

128. The Minister may issue regulations in terms of section 47. In 2004, regulations[533] were issued on developments surrounding nuclear installations to ensure the effective implementation of nuclear emergency plans. The Minister may lay down requirements relating to the control or monitoring of developments within the formal emergency planning zone. He or she has to consult with local and provincial authorities on the effective implementation of emergency plans. A report must be sent to the Regulator in this regard.[534] Regulations dealing with safety standards and regulatory practices were also published in 2006.[535]

129. The use of nuclear energy is a point of dispute between industry and the general public. Although few, if any, nuclear accidents have been reported in South Africa,[536] any proposal involving nuclear energy has been met with disapproval. The dispute is not on existing problems but on the potential danger of nuclear facilities. Due to the nature of nuclear energy and South Africa's history, all information regarding nuclear energy was kept secret. It is only under the new government that information in this regard has been released. It is difficult to establish what the extent of pollution by the creation of nuclear energy is. The nuclear energy industry

530. Sections 39–40. *See also* Government Notice 778 in *Government Gazette* 29078 of 4 Aug. 2006 for details of the information that needs to be provided.
531. *See Earthlife Africa (Cape Town Branch) v. Eskom Holdings Ltd* (04/27514) [2005] ZAGPHC 129 (15 Dec. 2005); *Earthlife Africa (Cape Town) v. Director General Department of Environmental Affairs and Tourism and Another* 2005 3 SA 156 (C); *Earthlife Africa (Cape Town) v. Director-General: Department of Environmental Affairs and Tourism and Another* 2005 3 SA 156 (C).
532. Section 7(1)(j) read with Government Notice 716 in *Government Gazette* 29050 of 28 Jul. 2006.
533. Government Notice 287 in *Government Gazette* 26121 of 2004–05-05. *See also McDonald & Others v. Minister of Minerals and Energy & Others* (CPD) (Case No. 3626/06) (Unreported case).
534. Compiled in terms of s. 38 of the Act.
535. Government Notice R388 in *Government Gazette* 28755 of 28 Apr. 2006.
536. *See also* Council for Nuclear Safety, *Annual Report 1998/1999*.

must, however, comply with all South African environmental legislation and most probably also with international law in this regard.

130. In 2003, the then Department of Mining and Energy published a *National Radioactive Waste Management Strategy* for comment, indicating its commitment to safe nuclear management. In the same year, the Chamber of Mines commenced with a ZAR 6 million clean-up of 38 sites where mines dumped radioactive material in Gauteng and the Free State. The materials were dumped on scrap yards or in the veld in the gold mine areas. Priority was given to areas where a public health risk existed.[537]

131. In 2005 Earthlife Africa approached the Cape High Court to set aside a record of decision to allow the construction of a demonstration pebble-bed modular reactor at Koeberg, by the then Director General of Environmental Affairs and Tourism. Their argument was based on the fact that not all information was revealed during the public participation process and that new information was added to the final documents sent to the director general. They also indicated that they did not have the opportunity to comment on the new information. The court indicated that nuclear issues are sensitive and controversial and, therefore, set aside the decision of the director general to allow for an additional period for comments on the new information. The court, however, indicated that except for the final decision the process followed was fair and procedurally correct.[538]

---

537. *Green clippings* No. 42 of 3 Nov. 2003.

538. *Earthlife Africa (Cape Town) v. Director-General: and Another* 2005 3 SA 156 (C); *see also Earthlife Africa (Cape Town Branch) v. Eskom Holdings Ltd* (04/27514) [2005] ZAGPHC 129 (15 Dec. 2005); *Earthlife Africa (Cape Town) v. Director General DEAT and Another* 2005 3 SA 156 (C).

Part II. Regulatory Framework Concerning Gas

Chapter 1. General Introduction

132. South Africa makes use of different gas resources, namely imported gas from its neighbours via pipelines, gas fields in the ocean and gas produced from coal by way of industrial processes. The possibility of coal-bed methane and shale gas exploration is investigated.[539] Coal mines in the Waterberg District in South Africa already exploit coal-bed methane as a precautionary mine health and safety measure.[540] The economic and environmental feasibility of such projects is still a major concern.[541] As indicated the exploration of shale gas by way of hydraulic fracturing is also being explored in South Africa. The then Department of Mineral Resources appointed a task team to investigate the possible environmental risks of exploration of shale gas, as well as the negative social and economic impacts of such activities in the Karoo area of South Africa in 2012.[542] The report compiled by the task team indicated that shale gas would have to be exploited by way of horizontal drilling and hydraulic fracturing. The major concern will be the use of large quantities of water in a dry area.[543] This means that water will have to be transported to the area. The disposal of water and the contamination of groundwater are also major concerns. The existence of kimberlite and dolerite dykes or intrusions also complicates

539. Also *see* ASSAf, *The Shale Gas Industry in South Africa: Toward a Science Action Plan*, Proceedings Report, 31 Aug. – 1 Sep. 2017.

540. Anglo American and Golder Associates, *Draft EIA and EMPR: Proposed 37-Spot Coalbed Methane Bulk Yield Test, Lephalale*, April 2011, Report No. 12016–10525-12 www.golder.co.za/public (accessed 9 Dec. 2013); Umbono Coalbed Methane Springbok Flats (Pty) Ltd., *Exploration for Coalbed Methane in the Springbok Flats West Area Limpopo Province, South Africa Petroleum Agency South Africa*, Reference Number: 12/3/226/1 Dec. 2011.

541. L. Jeffrey, *Challenges Associated with Further Development of the Waterberg Coalfield*, 106 July, The Journal of the South African Institute of Mining and Metallurgy, 453–457 (2005).

542. Department of Mineral Resources, *Investigation of Hydraulic Fracturing in the Karoo Basin of South Africa*, http://www.dmr.gov.za/publications/viewcategory/182-report-on-hydraulic-fracturing.htmlhttp://www.dmr.gov.za/publications/viewcategory/182-report-on-hydraulic-fracturing.html (accessed 9 Dec. 2013); also *see* H. Lerm, *Fracking: an energy dream come true or an environmental nightmare?*, 36 Obiter 41–56 (2015).

543. Sasol, South Africa's gas and oil company, indicated that the cost of a gas well in the Karoo will be six times higher than one in the United States of America and that they would, therefore, not continue with exploration in this area in the Karoo – D. van Rensburg, *Sasol gee gas met goeie wins*, 11 September, Beeld 16 (2012).

the matter. The task team also indicated that extensive hydrological and geohydrological studies would have to be undertaken to determine the effect of hydraulic fracturing on other water users and especially farmers in the area.[544] The report, however, also indicates the possible revenue income and job creation potential of the exploration of shale gas in the area as well as the fact that it may lessen South Africa's dependency on fossil fuels. The task team recommended that limited exploration be allowed but that activities be monitored and that research into the matter be further undertaken. The report finally concluded that:[545]

> South Africa's regulatory framework must be robust enough to ensure that, if hydraulic fracturing associated with shale gas exploration and exploitation were approved, any resultant negative impacts would be mitigated. This will require a comprehensive review of the adequacy of the existing framework in order to identify any shortfalls or omissions and to ensure that it is sufficiently detailed and specific. The use of existing regulations from mature regulatory environments to inform the development of South African regulations in this matter is recommended.

The Karoo area is also well known as an astronomy area. The possibility of hydraulic fracturing operations in the area is regarded as a possible obstacle to these activities. Certain areas of the Karoo have been declared astronomy advantage areas and the notices were published for public comment. The declaration of the areas as such may affect future planned development (in terms of shale gas activities) in the area.[546]

544. *See also* F. Williams, *Shell, Agri SA sit koppe bymekaar oor protokolle vir eksplorasie*, 10 September, Beeld 17 (2012).
545. Department of Minerals and Energy, *Investigation of Hydraulic Fracturing in the Karoo Basin of South Africa* – Executive Summary, 4.
546. Government Notice 872 in *Government Gazette* 37035 of 15 Nov. 2013; General Notice 198 in *Government Gazette* 37434 of 12 Mar. 2014 – issued in terms of the Astronomy Geographic Advantage Act 21 of 2007. *See also* E. Tempelhoff, *Pandor moet sê oor hidrobreking*, 13 September, Beeld 9 (2012). In 2018, the Minister published a notice that she does find it necessary to have public hearings on declaring the Sutherland area an astronomy advantaged area or to disallow mining in the area – Government Notice 1299 in *Government Gazette* 42054 of 22 Nov. 2018; Government Notice 1261 in *Government Gazette* 42049 of 21 Nov. 2018.

Chapter 2. Overview of Regulatory Framework

133. In 2001, the Gas Act 48 of 2001 was promulgated.[547] The purpose of the Act is to promote the orderly development of the piped gas industry. 'Gas' is defined as 'all hydrocarbon gases transported by pipeline, including natural gas, artificial gas, hydrogen-rich gas, rich gas, synthetic gas, coal bed methane gas, liquefied natural gas, compressed natural gas, re-gasified liquefied natural gas, liquefied petroleum gas or a combination thereof'. 'Production' is defined as 'recovery, processing, treating, gathering of gas from wells in the earth up to the boundary of the mine, or the manufacture of synthetic or artificial gas, or the manufacturing of any gases in the refining process up to the boundary of a factory, or any activity incidental thereto',[548] while 'reticulation' is defined as 'the division of bulk gas supplies and the transportation of bulk gas by pipelines with a general operating pressure of no more than 2 bar gauge to points of ultimate consumption, and any other activity incidental thereto'.[549] 'Re-gasification' is defined as the conversion of 'liquefied natural gas to a gaseous state at a re-gasification plant' – the draft Gas Amendment Bill, 2013 specifies where the regasification plant may be situated – either land-based or on a floating device within South Africa's territorial waters or a South African port.[550]

134. The objectives of the Gas Act are among others to[551] (a) promote the efficient, effective, sustainable and orderly development and operation of gas transmission, storage and distribution, liquefaction and regasification facilities and the provision of efficient, effective and sustainable gas transmission, storage, distribution, liquefaction, regasification and trading services; (b) facilitate investment in the gas industry; (c) ensure the safe, efficient, economic and environmentally responsible transmission, distribution, storage, liquefaction and regasification of gas; (d) facilitate investment in the gas industry; (e) promote companies in the gas industry that are owned or controlled by historically disadvantaged South Africans by means of licence conditions to become competitive; (f) ensure that gas transmission, storage, distribution and trading services are provided on an equitable basis and that the interests and needs of all parties are taken into consideration; (g) promote the development of competitive markets for gas and gas services; (h) facilitate the gas trade between the Republic of South Africa and other countries; and (i) promote access to gas in an affordable and safe manner.

---

547. Commenced on 1 Nov. 2005.
548. In terms of a draft Gas Amendment Bill, 2013 – General Notice 443 in *Government Gazette* 36425 of 2 May 2013 – the definition of 'gas' is to be amended to delete the phrase referring to 'transported by pipeline' and excluding liquefied petroleum gas that is stored within the ambit to the Petroleum Products Act 120 of 1977 and the Petroleum Pipelines Act 60 of 2003.
549. Section 1. The Gas Amendment Bill, 2013 proposes an amendment to add the words 'with or without the intervention of a distributor'. Previously Sasol mostly distributed the gas but is now transferring the distribution of gas to other subsidiaries or private companies – the amendment will ensure that the Gas Act covers all possible liabilities.
550. Section 1.
551. Section 2.

135. The legislation does not address the full circle of gas, namely production, exploitation, transportation, distribution and consumption, but rather deals with these topics piecemeal if at all.

Chapter 3. Licensing and Authorization Regime

136. The National Energy Regulator[552] is responsible for the issuing of licences for the (a) construction; (b) conversion of infrastructure; (c) operation of gas transmission, storage, distribution, liquefaction and regasification facilities; and (d) the trading of gas.[553] The Regulator is also responsible for approving prices, tariffs and charges to ensure that they are applied in a non-discriminatory manner.[554]

137. An applicant must apply for a licence in the prescribed manner. The application must include *inter alia* a description of the proposed facility, the type of customers and the plans and ability to comply with all applicable health, safety and environmental legislation.[555] The Regulator may request additional information or propose to the applicant to amend his or her application to comply with legislation or to provide access to third parties.[556] The applicant must also publish a notice in at least two newspapers (one must be English) circulating in the area of the proposed activity of the intention to construct or operate a gas facility and must indicate where objections to the proposed activity may be lodged.[557]

In considering the application, the Regulator must satisfy itself that the application meets criteria set by the Minister – the criteria of the Minister must reflect the national interest, the promotion of regional growth and social objectives.[558] The Gas Amendment Bill, 2013 proposes a new Clause 17A that prescribes how the Regulator should deal with objections from the public.[559]

552. Established in terms of the National Energy Regulator Act 40 of 2004. The Gas Amendment Bill, 2013 proposes amendments to the Gas Act 48 of 2001 (s. 4) to further expand the mandate of the National Energy Regulator.
553. Section 15. The Gas Amendment Bill, 2013 proposes amendments to the wording of s. 15, referring to gas infrastructure rather than the details of the nature of the gas infrastructure. The amended s. 4 will include the details of what types of licences may be issued by the National Energy Regulator – the new Act will also refer to the compression of gas. If the new Act comes into operation, all persons who are not in possession of licences for new activities that are listed in terms of the amended Act will have six months to apply for a licence – *see* Clause 31 inserting s. 32. *See also* the Gas Regulator Levies Act 75 of 2002 discussed in para. 181 *infra*.
554. Section 4(g)–(h) read with ss 21(1)(p) and 22.
555. Section 16. The applicant may request that commercially sensitive information contained in the application should be treated confidentially – s. 16(3). This section is also to be amended to refer to the Promotion of Access of Information Act 2 of 2000 – Clause 7 of Gas Amendment Bill, 2013. *See also* the proposed s. 29A of the Gas Amendment Bill, 2013 (Clause 22) that prescribes how the Regulator should deal with confidential information. How to apply the rules are to be found in Government Notice R1251 in *Government Gazette* 32849 of 31 Dec. 2009. *See also* www.nersa.org (accessed 18 Dec. 2013).
556. Section 18.
557. Section 17.
558. Section 19. *See also* the new proposed s. 19(5) of the Gas Amendment Bill, 2013 stating that a licence must be issued if the applicant complies with all the necessary criteria and the proposed infrastructure is suitable for the proposed site (Clause 11). Separate licences are issued for the construction or conversion of infrastructure in facilities as described *supra*, the operation of such facilities and the trading in gas.
559. By December 2019, this Bill has not been passed in Parliament yet.

The Regulator may impose licence conditions within a specific framework as set out in the Act.[560] There should, for example, be no limitations on ownership of vertically integrated companies, as these companies' gas transmission, storage, distribution and trading activities must be managed separately with no cross-subsidization. Non-discriminatory third-party access to uncommitted capacity in transmission pipelines should be allowed. Interested parties may negotiate changes with transmission companies in the routing, size and capacity of the proposed pipelines and may negotiate for increases in the compression of existing transmission pipelines to benefit equitably from reduced costs resulting from the increased volume. The term of the licence is as specified in the licence.[561] The licence may be renewed, amended or revoked at any time.[562] Licensees may not discriminate between customers or classes of customers regarding access, tariffs, prices, conditions or services except if there are objectively justifiable and identifiable differences, for example regarding quantity, transmission distance and load profile.[563] Certain persons are exempted from applying for a licence, namely persons transmitting gas for their own exclusive use and small biogas projects in rural communities not connected to the national grid as determined by the Regulator.[564] They must, however, register with the Regulator.[565]

Persons owning or operating gas facilities or trading in gas prior to the commencement of the Act must apply for a licence within six months after the Act is put into operation. The Mozambique Gas Pipeline Agreement between the then Minister of Minerals and Energy, Minister of Trade and Industry and Sasol regarding the introduction of natural gas by pipeline from Mozambique into South Africa initially bound the National Energy Regulator for a period of ten years after natural gas has been received from Mozambique.[566] This agreement has been renewed with consent from the National Energy Regulator.[567] The conflict between the agreement and the Gas Act led to court disputes.[568]

---

560. Section 21.
561. Section 21. The rights of the licensee are set out in s. 33.
562. Sections 24–27. *See also* the proposed insertion of s. 25(2A) in the Gas Amendment Bill, 2013 especially as to the reasons why a licence may be revoked (Clause 16). Section 27 dealing with revocation of licences is to be repealed according to the Gas Amendment Bill, 2013 (Clause 18).
563. Section 22. The Regulator is to determine the prices and tariffs – *see* the to be inserted s. 28A – Clause 29 Gas Amendment Bill, 2013.
564. Section 15(2) read with Sch. A.
565. Section 28.
566. Section 36. *See also* W. Du Plessis, *Cross-Border Gas Pipelines and Sustainability in Southern Africa*, 10. In Environmental law and sustainability after Rio, 279–296 (J. Benidickson, et al., eds Edward Elgar 2011) for a more detailed discussion of the *Gas Act* in comparison with Mozambican legislation.
567. The agreement is available at http://www.nersa.org.za/Admin/Document/Editor/file/Legislation/Piped%20Gas/Agreements/Mozambique%20Gas%20Pipeline%20Agreement%20and%20Schedule%20One%20%282%29.pdf and http://www.energy.gov.za/files/policies/treaty_gas_sasol_2001.pdf (accessed 15 Dec. 2013).
568. *See*, for example, *PG Group & others v NERSA* (150/2017) [2018] ZASCA 56 (10 May 2018). The case is referred to in Ch. 6 Consumption *infra*.

138. Before a facility can be erected for the transmission of gas, an environmental impact assessment must be approved.[569] Public participation plays a major role in South Africa and is becoming more important.[570] Various projects received a setback because of public outrage at the prospect of a gas line in their area. The Act also provides that an applicant must indicate that he or she complies with all health, safety and environmental legislation and that the Minister may make similar legislation applicable by referral.[571]

139. Several municipalities commenced to recover landfill gas either as a precautionary measure to prevent the release of methane gas or explosions or to generate energy for various projects. In November 2013, the Minister of Environmental Affairs issued national standards for the extraction, flaring or recovery of landfill gas.[572] The aim of the standards is to control these activities to 'prevent or minimize the negative impacts on the bio-physical and socio-economic environment'.[573] The standard prescribes technical requirements during the planning, operational and decommissioning phases.

140. When a landfill site includes a landfill gas project, the applicants must identify and list all environmental aspects or hazards to the proposed projects either biological or socio-economic, and they must evaluate the level of significance of such impacts or risk and develop an environmental management plan to deal with the impacts and risks. The applicant must conduct studies or develop models to determine the depth of the landfill site and lining system before digging any wells. The environmental management plan must be implemented during the construction, operation and decommissioning phases of the project.[574] The standard prescribes specific technical requirements for the landfill gas extraction system, the landfill gas flaring system, the landfill gas to energy system and general construction requirements.[575] When landfill gas is used to generate electricity, an electricity generation plan must be completed, the terrain must be fenced off with limited access for operational staff, spark-ignition engines and generators must be enclosed in units and containers and gas combustion and power-generating systems must be designed complying with specific specifications. The facility must also instal lightning conductors to prevent and minimize potential damage to the facility.[576]

---

569. General Notice R982 in *Government Gazette* 38282 of 4 Dec. 2014 and item 59 General Notice R983 in *Government Gazette* 38282 of 4 Dec. 2014 deal with the expansion of exploration and production operations.
570. *See also* M. Kidd, *The National Environmental Management Act and Public Participation*, 6 SAJELP 21–32 (1999); M. Kidd, *Of Gas Pipelines and Sour Judicial Air: Merebank Environmental Action Committee v. Executive Member of KwaZulu-Natal Council for Agricultural and Environmental Affairs*, 8 SAJELP 135–138 (2001).
571. For example, by making provincial legislation from another province applicable to the specific company.
572. Government Notice 924 in *Government Gazette* 37086 of 29 Nov. 2013, issued in terms of s. 19(3)(a) of the NEMWA 59 of 2008.
573. Regulation 2.
574. Regulation 5.
575. Regulation 6.
576. Regulation 6(3).

141. The regulatory framework initially did not provide for the exploration of shale gas and coal-bed methane. At the end of 2013, the then Minister of Mineral Resources issued a moratorium on shale gas exploration applications.[577] In terms of the MPRDA,[578] the definition of 'petroleum', however, refers to 'any liquid, solid hydrocarbon, or combustible gas exiting in a natural condition in the earth's crust and includes any such liquid or solid hydrocarbon or combustible gas, which gas has in any manner been returned to such natural condition, but does not include coal, bituminous shale or other stratified deposits from which oil can be obtained by destructive distillation or gas arising from a marsh or other surface deposit'.[579] This implies that Chapter 6 of the MPRDA dealing with petroleum exploration and production will be applicable to the exploitation of coal-bed methane and shale gas. Various permits may be applied for, namely technical cooperation permits, reconnaissance permits,[580] exploration rights and production rights.[581] A technical cooperation permit allows the applicant to do a desktop study and acquire seismic data from other sources; it also gives the holder thereof the exclusive right to apply for an exploration right.[582] A reconnaissance permit allows the holder 'to carry out operations for or in connection with the exploration for ... [gas] by geological geophysical and photo-geological surveys and may include any remote sensing techniques'.[583] In order to obtain a reconnaissance permit, the applicant must indicate that his or her actions 'will not result in unacceptable pollution, ecological degradation or damage to the environment and that the environmental authorization is issued'.[584] The Mineral and Petroleum Resources Development Amendment Bill (B15-2013), however, proposes that the environmental obligations as well as the

577. In 2012, the then Minister of Mineral Resources placed a moratorium on the granting of any new applications for reconnaissance permits, technical cooperation permits, exploration rights and production rights in certain geographical areas until she has issued regulations to deal with hydraulic fracturing. *See* Government Notice 932 in *Government Gazette* 35866 of 16 Nov. 2012. The restriction was not applicable to applications received before 1 Feb. 2011 – however, the applicants, if they were in possession of any permit or right would not have been able to commence with their activities.

578. The MPRDA has been amended by the Mineral and Petroleum Resources Development Amendment Act 49 of 2008 that came into operation on 7 Jun. 2013. The Minister was praised by the environmental faction and condemned by the economic sector – *see* F. Williams, *Verbod sal ekonomiese kanse knel*, 12 September, Beeld 21 (2012).

579. Section 1 MPRDA.

580. A reconnaissance permit allows the holder thereof to, after consultation with the owner of the land, enter upon the land and to conduct reconnaissance operations. He or she may not conduct exploration or production operations – *see* s. 15.

581. Section 69 MPRDA.

582. Sections 77–78 MPRDA. This right is valid for one year and is not transferable or renewable.

583. L. Oberholzer, *Getting the deal through – Oil regulation – South Africa*, 159 (Bowman Gilfillan Attorneys 2012) www.gettingthedealthrough.comwww.gettingthedealthrough.com (accessed 9 Dec. 2013).

584. Section 76(2)(c) Mineral and Petroleum Resources Development Amendment Act 49 of 2008. The Mineral and Petroleum Resources Development Amendment Bill [B15-2013] proposes the introduction of s. 74(2A) that will allow the regional manager to grant reconnaissance permits to an applicant even if he or she had already granted technical cooperation permits, exploration and production rights in the same area. He or she may only do so with the written permission of such permit or right holders – Clause 48. The Bill was approved in Parliament in 2013. The President did not sign the Bill but refer it back to the National Assembly for revision in 2015 as he was of the

newly proposed consultation obligation with the landowner will not be applicable if the reconnaissance involves space-borne or air-borne instruments operating at altitudes greater than 100 metres.[585] A reconnaissance permit is granted for one year and is not transferable or renewable. However, the 2013 Bill proposes that reconnaissance permits be granted for a period of seven years.[586] An exploration right provides the applicant the right to 're-process the existing seismic data, acquisition and processing of new seismic data or any other related activity to define a trap to be tested by drilling, logging and testing, including extended well testing, of a well with the intention of locating a discovery'.[587] The holder of an exploration right has the exclusive right to apply for a production right as well as a renewal of this right. He or she also has the exclusive right to remove and dispose of any gas samples found during the course of the exploration.[588] The court in *Normandien Farms (Pty) Limited v South African Agency for Promotion of Petroleum and Exploitation Soc Ltd*[589] set aside a decision of Petroleum Association of South Africa (PASA) to issue an exploration right as not all the owners were notified of the intended exploration. They did not have sufficient time to raise their objections.

142. The holder of the right must continuously and actively conduct his or her exploration operations in accordance with an exploration work programme, comply with the conditions in the exploration authorization and commence with his or her activities within ninety days after the right has been granted.[590] The holder of an exploration right or any other person may apply for a production right.[591] A production right allows the holder of the right to exploit the resource, remove and dispose

---

opinion that some clauses might be unconstitutional. *See also* Government Notice 619 in *Government Gazette* 40041 of 10 Jun. 2016 setting out the Requirements – Information for submission of an environmental authorization application related to shale gas.

585. Clause 48(e) amending s. 74(4) MPRDA.
586. Clause 49. The reconnaissance right will be an exclusive right but only in relation to other reconnaissance permits – proposed s. 75(3)(b)-(c).
587. Impact Oil & Gas, Impact licences, https://www.impactoilandgas.co.uk/Locations.aspx?id=7 (accessed 9 Dec. 2013). In the case of *Normandien Farms (Pty) Limited v South African Agency for Promotion of Petroleum and Exploitation Soc Ltd* (24294/2016) [2017] ZAWCHC 53 (3 May 2017), the court set aside a decision to grant an exploration right due to insufficient compliance with the procedural requirements.
588. Section 82(1) MPRDA.
589. (24294/2016) [2017] ZAWCHC 53 (3 May 2017).
590. Section 82(2) MPRDA. The Minerals and Petroleum Resources Development Amendment Bill (B15-2013) proposes that s. 82(2)(g) and (h) be inserted. The holder of the right will have to relinquish a contiguous portion of the area when he or she apply for renewal of the exploration right except if the holder can prove that he or she is able to explore the whole area or has made a discovery in respect of the whole area. In terms of s. 82(2)(h), the holder will have to pay royalties in terms of any gas removed or disposed of during exploration operations. An additional subs. (3) is added – if the holder made a discovery in the area during exploration, then he or she must notify the Minister of the discovery, submit a reappraisal programme and apply for an environmental authorization in terms of the NEMA. Section 82A is also inserted (Clause 57) indicating that the holder of the exploration right may only remove and dispose 'petroleum' (i.e., also gas) in such quantities that are necessary to conduct tests, to identify or analyse. He or she needs the permission of the Minister to dispose of it – again an environmental authorization will be needed before any such resource is removed or disposed of.
591. Section 83 MPRDA.

of any gas found during the course of production. He or she must continuously and actively conduct production operations in accordance with its approved work programme and in accordance with the conditions in the authorization and the environmental authorization as well as the prescribed social and labour plan.[592] A production right is granted for thirty years and may be renewed for additional period of thirty years.[593] Communities, who want to obtain a preferential right to any resource that is on their land, must lodge an application to the Minister of Mineral Resources and Energy in the prescribed manner. The community must indicate that the right will be used for development and social upliftment of the community and the community must submit a development plan in this regard – it must also be clear that the community will be the beneficiary of the mining project and not individuals within the community.[594]

Before operation of exploration or production may commence, the holder of such a right must make financial provision as a guarantee that he or she has the ability to fulfil all obligations in terms of the exploration or production work programmes.[595]

Permits, rights, programmes, plans and environmental authorizations may only be amended with the permission of the Minister of Mineral Resources and Energy. The Minister will not give permission if the amendment or variation will extend the area or a portion of an area or add shares of the mineralized body.[596]

In some instances, the Minister may publish a notice in the *Government Gazette* to exempt certain organs of state from the provision of sections of the Act with regard to any activity they have to fulfil – however, the exemption may not be with regard to the obtainment of an environmental authorization.[597]

143. On 3 June 2015, the Minister of Mineral Resources published regulations to regulate onshore petroleum exploration and production.[598] The Regulations are

592. Section 86, as amended by the Mineral and Petroleum Resources Development Amendment Act 49 of 2008.
593. Section. 84 MPRDA. In case of an application for renewal, the applicant will in future have to submit a detailed report indicating that he or she complies with the requirements of the environmental authorization and that the rehabilitation has been completed and what the expenditure in this regard was – *see* the to be amended s. 85(1)(c) Minerals and Petroleum Resources Amendment Bill [B15-2013].
594. Section 104. *See also* H. Kloppers & W. Du Plessis, *To be Destitute or to Benefit – Corporate Social Responsibility and Mining in South Africa* . . In Community Futures, Legal Architecture: Foundations for Indigenous Peoples in the Global Mining Boom, 269–283 (M. Langton & J. Longbottom, eds, Routledge 2012).
595. Section 89 MPRDA.
596. Section 102, as amended by the Mineral and Petroleum Resources Development Amendment Act 49 of 2008.
597. Section 106, as amended by the Mineral and Petroleum Resources Amendment Act 49 of 2008.
598. Government Notice R466 in Government Gazette 38855 of 3 Jun. 2015 (hereinafter 'GN R466') – the Regulations were issued in terms of the Mineral and Petroleum Resources Development Act 28 of 2002 (MPRDA) and amends the existing MPRDA regulations. For a discussion of these Regulations, see W. Du Plessis, Regulation of Hydraulic Fracturing in South Africa: A Project Life-Cycle approach? 18(5) Potchefstroom Electronic Law Journal, 1440–1478 (2015). The Regulations have been declared unconstitutional in one province while in another province it was upheld. *See*, e.g., *Stern NO and Others v Minister of Mineral Resources* (5762/2015) [2017] ZAECGHC 109 (17 Oct. 2017); *Treasure Karoo Action Group and Another v Department of Mineral Resources and*

applicable to all gas, including casinghead gas, coal-bed methane and shale gas.[599] All holders of rights will have to complete an environmental impact assessment in terms of NEMA before embarking on their exploration or exploitation activities.[600] The applicant must determine the geology and geohydrology of the area and submit a geological report to the authorities.[601] In addition an independent specialist will have to conduct a hydrocensus study within three kilometres radius from the place where horizontal drilling may take place.[602] The risk of potential hydraulic fracturing related seismicity must be determined, and the applicant must submit a risk assessment report as well as proposed mitigation measures to the relevant authority. The Council for Geoscience must also endorse the report.[603] The holder will further have to ensure that all radio and optical astronomy advantage areas are protected.[604]

144. The site must be prepared in terms of the environmental management programme that accompanies the environmental authorization and must be designed to prevent pollution.[605] Chapter 8 of the GN R466 prescribed detail requirements for well design and construction taking into account the eventual decommissioning of the well. Chapter 9 deals with the operational phase of the hydraulic fracturing process, while Chapter 10 deals with decommissioning. The operational phase refers among others to the management of water-related issues, waste as well as fracturing fluids. The holder of the right may not use the fluids listed in Schedule 1 to the Regulations and must disclose his or her use of fluids to the relevant authority.[606]

145. The Regulations were contested in two different divisions of the High Court. The court in the Eastern Cape found the Regulations to be unfair in that not all the procedures were followed,[607] while the other court did not make such a finding. The challenge in the Eastern Cape was that the 'Minister of Mineral Resources did not have the authority to make the Petroleum Regulations' as he was not

---

Others (95261/15) [2018] ZAGPPHC 334 (16 May 2018). The SCA confirmed the unconstitutionality of the regulations – *Minister of Mineral Resources v Stern and Others; Treasure the Karoo Action Group and Another v Department of Mineral Resources and Others* [2019] 3 All SA 684 (SCA). The Constitutional Court have not pronounced judgment in this regard. The 2015 regulations differ from the draft regulations that were published in 2013 – General Notice 1032 in *Government Gazette* 36938 of 15 Oct. 2013.

599. Regulation 84 (Definitions) GN R466.
600. Regulation 86 GN R466.
601. Regulation 87 GN R466.
602. Regulation 88 GN R466.
603. Regulation 89 GN R466.
604. Regulations 92 and 93 GN R466.
605. Regulations 90–91 GN R466.
606. Regulation 113 GN R466.
607. *Stern NO and Others v Minister of Mineral Resources* (5762/2015) [2017] ZAECGHC 109 (17 Oct. 2017). In *Minister of Mineral Resources v Stern and Others; Treasure the Karoo Action Group and Another v Department of Mineral Resources and Others* [2019] 3 All SA 684 (SCA) (4 Jul. 2019), the SCA also declared the environmental sections relating to gas exploration and production unconstitutional. Subsequently, new draft regulations were issued to amend the Petroleum Regulations, deleting the chapter on environmental regulations – Government Notice R1554 in *Government Gazette* 42870 of 28 Nov. 2019. The Minister of Environmental Affairs, Forestry and Fisheries will now have to issue regulations pertaining to gas exploration and production in terms of the NEMA.

empowered to do so in terms of the MPRDA and that the process of making the Regulations was procedurally unfair. In the alternative, it was argued that 'the aim or purpose of the Petroleum Regulations was to regulate the environmental consequences of deep drilling and hydraulic fracturing' and that he was similarly not empowered to do so in terms of the main Act.[608] The court found, among others, that the necessary procedures were not followed and that the public, for example, did not have an opportunity to comment on the Schedule to the Regulations listing the hydraulic fluids that will be excluded. As the rights of the public were affected, the Regulations were declared procedurally unfair and set aside.[609] In a similar application to the Gauteng High Court, the application to review and set aside the Regulations was rejected.[610] The SCA, subsequently, declared the environmental regulations for gas exploration unconstitutional as they were issued by the then Minister of Mineral Resources, while the then Minister of Environmental Affairs had the mandate to regulate environmental matters.[611]

146. One of the reasons that the High Court felt that the then Department of Water and Sanitation and the DEA will not be prejudiced if the above Regulations were set aside is that an application for hydraulic fracturing will in any case have to obtain other authorizations. These include, among others, a water use licence in terms of the NWA and the waste licence in terms of the NEMWA.[612] The then Minister of Water and Sanitation issued a notice declaring the 'exploration and or production of onshore naturally occurring hydrocarbons that requires stimulation, including but not limited to hydraulic fracturing and or underground gasification, to extract, and any activity incidental thereto that may impact detrimentally on the water resource' as a controlled activity in terms of the NWA.[613] Once an activity is declared as a controlled activity, a water use licence will have to be obtained.

147. Section 99 of the MPRDA deals with offences and penalties. Currently the penalties differ between ZAR 100,000 and ZAR 500,000. The Mineral and Petroleum Resources Development Amendment Bill (B15 of 2013) proposes that the fine be amended to a fine not exceeding 10% of the annual turnover and exports of the

608. Paragraph 2.
609. Paragraphs 41–42.
610. *Treasure Karoo Action Group and Another v Department of Mineral Resources and Others* (95261/15) [2018] ZAGPPHC 334 (16 May 2018).
611. *Minister of Mineral Resources v Stern and Others; Treasure the Karoo Action Group and Another v Department of Mineral Resources and Others* [2019] 3 All SA 684 (SCA) (4 Jul. 2019).
612. Regulation 26 General Notice 1032.
613. General Notice 863 in *Government Gazette* 36730 of 23 Aug. 2013 – in terms of s. 38(3) of the NWA 36 of 1998. This implies that the activity may not at all be undertaken or commence unless authorized in terms of the Act – s. 37(2). Also *see* Government Notice 999 in *Government Gazette* 39299 of 16 Oct. 2015 that deals with the Declaration of the exploration and/or production of onshore naturally occurring hydrocarbons that require stimulation, including but not limited to hydraulic fracturing and/or underground gasification, to extract, and any activity incidental thereto that may impact detrimentally on the water resource as a controlled activity in terms of s. 38(1) and schedule of all controlled activities in terms of s. 38(4).

right's holder's preceding financial year as reflected in its annual financial statements or imprisonment of a period not exceeding four years or both. The formulation of the sections dealing with other fines is also amended to read 5% of the annual turnover and exports or imprisonment of ten years.[614]

148. A unique appeal process is created in terms of the MPRDA and the NEMA. If a decision is taken by an official of the Department of Mineral Resources and Energy, an aggrieved person may appeal to the Minister of Mineral Resources and Energy. If the decision relates to environmental matters and issues incidental thereto and the decision is taken by the Minister of Mineral Resources and Energy, an aggrieved person may appeal to the Minister of Environmental Affairs, Forestry and Fisheries.[615] The appeal is facilitated by the NEMA.[616]

614. Clause 77. The Bill also prescribes a procedure how to determine the annual turnover of any offender if it is not possible to establish what the turnover of the preceding year was – to be inserted s. 99(1A).

615. Section 96 MPRDA and s. 48 NEMA. According to the Mineral and Petroleum Resources Development Bill [(15-2013), the section will be amended again to clearly indicate that the Minister of Environmental Affairs will be the appeal authority – Clause 68. Also *see* T. Humby and R. Krause, *Unravelling the mare's nest? The Constitutional Court interprets the duty to exhaust internal remedies in the mining setting: case notes, SA Public Law* 302–316 (2015).

616. The appeal procedure has been published – Government Notice 993 in *Government Gazette* 38303 8 Dec. 2014, as amended by Government Notice R205 in *Government Gazette* 38559 of 12 Mar. 2015.

Chapter 4. Exploitation

149. The exploitation of gas initially has been an experiment in South Africa. South Africa has limited natural gas resources in the ocean, but is also importing gas from its neighbouring country, Mozambique, and is contemplating to do so in future from Namibia and Botswana. Exploration for gas is also undertaken in the coastal regions.[617]

The exploration of shale gas by way of hydraulic fracturing also became an option as government granted exploration rights to various oil companies in South Africa.[618] The first onshore production right for gas was granted to 'Molopo South Africa Exploration ('Molopo SA') over an area of approximately 200,000 ha in the Free State province.' It will also have operations near Evander, Mpumalanga.[619] Several other Black Empower Companies received exploration rights for gas all over the country.[620] This necessitated amendments to existing mining and gas legislation and the formulation of new regulations. The exploration of coal-bed methane is being explored. Methane is also harvested from waste and other sites.

---

617. M.E. Brownfield, et al., *Assessment of Undiscovered Oil and Gas Resources of the South Africa Coastal Province, Africa, Fact Sheet 2012–3030* (US Department of the Interior, US Geological Survey, April 2012) http://pubs.usgs.gov/fs/2012/3030/ (accessed 9 Dec. 2013).
618. *See* J Glazewski and S Esterhuyse, eds, *Hydraulic Fracturing in the Karoo* (Juta 2016).
619. Molopo Energy Limited, *Molopo Awarded First Onshore Gas Production Right in South Africa*, 21 Sep. 2012, http://finance.yahoo.com/news/molopo-awarded-first-onshore-gas-110000946.html (accessed 9 Dec. 2013). Molopo Energy is already in operation at Evander and in the Free State near Virginia and is also conducting hydraulic fracturing – http://www.molopoenergy.com/assets/other-assets/virginia-evander-south-africa (accessed 28 Dec. 2013).
620. *See*, e.g., *Badimo Gas*, http://www.badimogas.co.za/rights.html (accessed 28 Dec. 2013).

Chapter 5. Transportation and Distribution

150. Gas can be transported by road, railway or via pipelines. The Gas Act regulates transportation via pipelines. Gas is, for example, transferred by pipeline from Sasolburg, approximately 60 km away from Johannesburg. Egoli Gas in Johannesburg reticulates this gas to 7500 'domestic, central heating, commercial and industrial businesses in the Greater Johannesburg metropolitan area'. Johannesburg is the only city with a piped gas network infrastructure. The Johannesburg municipality initially produced the gas and reticulated it. In 2000, the gas works were privatized. This new company distributes methane-rich natural gas instead of hydrogen-rich coal-based gas as was previously done.[621]

151. In 2005, Government developed a Gas Infrastructure Plan as 'a strategy for the development of the natural gas industry in South Africa' in order to '(i)ncrease access to affordable energy services; improve energy governance; stimulate economic activity; manage energy-related environmental impacts; secure security of supply through diversity of supply; compete within and between energy carriers [and to] promote [the] New Partnership for African Development (NEPAD) cross-border type projects'.[622]

152. The Minister of Energy may make regulations in terms of the Gas Act with regard to, *inter alia*, the keeping of records, fair administrative action, the incorporation of health, safety and environmental legislation and subordinate legislation by referral and rehabilitation.[623] In 2007, the Minister issued gas regulations[624] dealing in a more particular manner with the criteria for distribution (regulation 2), third-party access to transmission pipelines (regulation 6), third-party access to storage facilities (regulation 7), rehabilitation of land (regulation 11), determination of gas specifications (regulation 13) and mediation, arbitration and access to information (regulations 14–17). The Gas Amendment Bill, 2013 also proposes that licensees maintain their pipeline network systems and that they effect connections. If they, however, want to add, alter or reconstruct a network, they will need additional permission from the Regulator.[625]

621. Egoli Gas, *Natural Gas*, http://www.egoligas.co.za/natural-gas.html (accessed 24 Jul. 2015).
622. Department of Minerals and Energy *Gas Infra-Structure Plan*, 19 Apr. 2005, http://www.energy.gov.za/files/media/explained/statistics_gas_infrastructure_2005.pdf (accessed 10 Dec. 2013).
623. Section 34. The Gas Amendment Bill, 2013 proposes that a licensee who terminates, abandons or relinquish his or her gas operations must rehabilitate the area by insertion of s. 32A (Clause 26). In addition to this, the Gas Amendment Bill, 2013 also proposes to insert s. 36A spelling out the powers and duties of the Minister in relation to contracts, management and development activities, applying for licences, letting, hiring, etc.
624. Government Notice R321 in *Government Gazette* 29792 of 20 Apr. 2007.
625. Section 33A to be inserted by Clause 28.

153. If gas is transported by road, the National Road Traffic Act 93 of 1996 would be applicable,[626] as well as its dangerous goods regulations.[627] The Regulations incorporate several South African National Standards (SANS), giving legal effect to them.[628] Nobody may transport dangerous goods, except if they comply with the Regulations and also indicate the nature of the dangerous goods via a placard attached to the vehicle.[629] The Regulations indicate that the driver, consignor and consignee must comply with the duties set out in the relevant SANS standard.[630] The driver must undergo specific training at an approved institution[631] and must have his or her certificate available for inspection[632] by a dangerous goods inspector.[633]

The transport of dangerous goods by railroad is controlled by the National Railway Safety Regulator that may issue a safety permit[634] for the transport of dangerous goods.[635] The safety management of the Railways and accident reporting are also regulated by way of Regulations.[636]

---

626. The National Road Traffic Act 93 of 1996 prohibits the transportation of certain hazardous good per road and also appoints a dangerous goods inspectorate to oversee the enforcement of this section – ss 54–55. The Minister may issue regulations to indicate the classification of dangerous goods in this regard – s. 75(1)(h).
627. Regulations 273-283B in Government Notice R225 in *Government Gazette* 20963 of 17 Mar. 2000, as amended.
628. Regulation 274: South African National Standards SANS 1518 'Transportation of dangerous goods – design of vehicles, tanks and accessories for the transport of dangerous goods and SANS 10228 'The identification and classification of dangerous goods for transport'; SANS 10229 'Packaging of dangerous goods for road and rail transportation in South Africa'; SANS 10231 'Transportation of dangerous goods – Operational requirements for road vehicles'; SANS 10232–1, 'Transportation of dangerous goods – Emergency information systems Part 1: Emergency information system for road transport'; SANS 10232–3 'Transportation of dangerous goods – Emergency information systems Part 3: Emergency response guides'; SANS 10232–4 'Transportation of dangerous goods – Emergency information systems Part 4: Transport emergency card' and SANS 10233 'Transportation of dangerous goods – Intermediate bulk containers for road and rail transport'.
629. Regulation 275. The Minister may exempt certain dangerous goods from the list – however, they must still comply with the relevant SANS emergency standard – regulation 276.
630. Regulation 277. If there is doubt whether a substance will be a dangerous good in terms of the Regulations, South African Bureau of Standards (SABS) 0228 'The identification and classification of dangerous substances and goods' will apply – regulation 279.
631. Regulation 280. The Minister indicates approved institutions in the *Government Gazette* – *see*, for example, Government Notice R244 in *Government Gazette* 37504 of April 2014.
632. Regulation 281.
633. Inspectors are appointed in terms of regulation 282 and their duties are set out in regulation 283A. Regulation 283B deals with prima facie evidence.
634. For the application of safety permits, *see* Government Notice R549 in *Government Gazette* 38929 of 30 Jun. 2015. For the safety management system, *see* Government Notice 502 in *Government Gazette* 41632 of 18 May 2018.
635. Sections 22–24 National Railway Safety Regulator Act 16 of 2002. The Regulator may also adopt standards for the safe transportation of goods – s. 29. For the procedures to adopt standards, *see* Government Notice 718 in *Government Gazette* 30164 of 17 Aug. 2007.
636. Government Notice R866 in *Government Gazette* 26594 of 20 Jul. 2004.

Chapter 6. Consumption

154. Some residential and industrial structures make use of gas. Sasol, a South African petroleum company that produces oil and petroleum from coal, provides gas to the Gauteng region, for example.

155. The Regulator may investigate complaints by customers or any other person about unreasonable differences in the supply of gas or excessive prices or tariffs imposed by a licensee.[637] The Regulator may also act as mediator or arbitrator in disputes with regard to the trading of gas or rendering of services.[638] Section 26 makes provision for offences.[639] Section 26 is to be replaced with a new section 26 according to the Gas Amendment Bill, 2013. The Bill makes provision that the Regulator should first issue a compliance notice to the licensee if he or she is in breach of a licence condition, does not comply with a provision of the Act or is engaged in an activity that is inconsistent with the Act. The licensee may appeal or apply for review to the to be instituted Appeal Board. The compliance notice will remain valid until either the Appeal Board comes to another decision or the Regulator issue a compliance certificate.[640]

156. In 2018, consumers disputed the determination of the price of the use of gas in the case of *PG Group & others v NERSA*.[641] Sasol has a monopoly in piping gas from Mozambique. The gas is used at its own premise in Secunda. The surplus gas is enriched and piped for use by other consumers. The maximum price was determined according to an agreement with government. Subsequent to the introduction of the Gas Act, NERSA had to determine the price. It is the determination of the maximum price for piped gas that is challenged in this case. The price determination according to the agreement involved a substantial increase (more than 45%) in the tariff consumers had to pay. The court found after a lengthy discussion of the price determination methodology that NERSA's determination of the price of piped gas was 'wholly irrational and unreasonable'. The court accordingly set the price determination aside.[642]

157. During the operational phase of a landfill gas project, a maintenance plan must be prepared. The operator must keep details of the volume and types of gases that are flared and must prevent and minimize environmental pollution. When

---

637. Section 31. The Regulator may authorize entry, inspection and the gathering of information – s. 29. S. 29 is to be amended – Clause 21 Gas Amendment Bill, 2013; *see also* the proposed s. 31(4) on how to deal with complainants. Land may also be expropriated – s. 32.
638. Section 30.
639. The Gas Amendment Bill, 2013 creates additional offences in s. 34A – to be inserted by Clause 30 of the Bill.
640. Clause 17 Gas Amendment Bill, 2013. The Appeal Board will be instituted in terms of the new s. 33B to be inserted by Clause 28 of the Bill.
641. 2018 (5) SA 150 (SCA).
642. Paragraph 56. *Also see* Gen Notice 1156 in *Government Gazette* 39416 of 16 Nov. 2015 – NERSA – Invitation for public comments on Eskom's Regulatory Clearing Account (RCA) Application for Multi Year Price Determination (MYPD3) Year 1 (2013/2014).

scheduled maintenance is to be undertaken, the wells must be sealed off – gas may only escape via the natural migration processes. The operator must also keep an emergency generator and store the generator in the prescribed manner – the generator must also be operated in such a manner as to prevent or minimize environmental pollution. No smoking or fires must be allowed in the vicinity of landfill gas extraction and the necessary signs must be erected to indicate the danger. Leachate must be treated in such a manner that the environment, as well as the stability of the landfill and gas extraction, is not compromised. Contaminated soil must be removed and disposed at licensed landfill sites.[643]

158. In case of landfill to energy plants, landfill gas must be flared off during scheduled maintenance, emergency shutdowns or process upsets to machines. The landfill gas must be shut off completely and gas may only escape through natural migration processes. All liquid and solid waste must be treated and disposed of in the correct manner or must be reused or recycled. The engine performance must be measured and monitored during the whole project to ensure that it is efficient. The gas extracted from the landfill must be used to run the electricity-generating engines and all engine exhausts must be fitted with silencers.[644]

The standard dealing with landfill gas further indicates that all personnel, temporary or permanent, must be trained.[645] All emergency situations must be dealt with in terms of section 30 of the NEMA.[646]

All facilities must register with the DEA before commencement with their activities for purposes of compliance monitoring.[647] The operator must monitor its gas extraction during the project lifetime and must also conduct air quality monitoring not only at the site but also at the perimeter of the site.[648]

Each year a qualified person must undertake an environmental performance audit, and the audit must be submitted to the relevant authority on request. The performance audit must indicate whether the facility complies with the standards and other requirements of the different spheres of government, must report on any environmental incidences that may have occurred and how they were dealt with, confirm that the facility complies with its environmental management plan and air quality plan and indicate that the project is included in the agenda of the landfill site steering committee.[649]

159. The operator must also develop a rehabilitation plan, which must be implemented during the decommissioning phase.[650] The owner of the facility as well as

643. Regulation 7(1) of Government Notice 924 in *Government Gazette* 37806 of 29 Nov. 2013 – National Standards for the Extraction, Flaring or Recovery of Landfill Gas.
644. Regulations 7(2).
645. Regulation 8.
646. Regulation 9.
647. Regulation 10. The authority will be able to access or audit any facility at any time or at any frequency. All documents and records must be made available for inspection – regulation 10(3)-(4).
648. Regulation 10(5)-(6). Records must be kept of all hazardous wastes that are to be removed from the site and the records must be available for inspection – regulation 10(7).
649. Regulation 10(10).
650. Regulation 12.

subsequent owners of the facility will remain responsible for any adverse impacts on the environment even after the operations have ceased.[651]

The operators of the landfill gas recovery project must also comply with requirements in other legislation – especially the environmental legislation.[652]

651. Regulation 12(2)(g).
652. Regulation 11(1) – *see also* para. 127ff.

Part III. Regulatory Framework Concerning Petroleum

Chapter 1. General Introduction

160. Legislation controlling petroleum products was promulgated in the 1970s as a result of economic sanctions against South Africa. The real concern was not so much control of competition, as to ensure secrecy about the import and transportation of petroleum products, as well as to allow the government to introduce saving measures. The legislation dealing with petroleum products and liquid fuels is, therefore, fragmented and does not regulate the full circle of production, exploitation, transportation, distribution and consumption of petroleum products and liquid fuels. However, the Act has been amended and new regulations have been issued to address some of these issues.[653]

161. The main purpose of the Petroleum Products Act 120 of 1977 is to provide measures for the saving of petroleum products and an economy in the cost of the distribution thereof. A petroleum product is defined as 'any petroleum fuel and any lubricant used or unused (or any other substance) that can be used as such'. Biofuels and paraffin are, therefore, also regulated in terms of the Petroleum Products Act. 'Liquefied petroleum gas' is defined as 'a petroleum product which consists mainly of propane or butane or both and which can be stored as a liquid under relatively low pressure for the use as a fuel'.[654]

162. The Minister of Mineral Resources and Energy has wide powers under the Act. He or she may, for example, serve notices for the purposes of saving in the efficient use of petroleum products, regulate the manner he or she deems fit which may include the imposition of a duty or the prohibition of use, purchase, sale, supply, acquisition, disposal, storage, transportation, recovery or refinement of petroleum products.[655] For the purpose to ensure an economy based upon the cost of the distribution of petroleum products or the rendering of service, the Minister may regulate or prohibit (a) the supply of equipment intended for dispensing of any

653. *See* Petroleum Products Amendment Act 2 of 2005; Government Notices R286, 287 and 288 in *Government Gazette* 28665 of 27 Mar. 2006.
654. Section 1. 'Paraffin' is defined as 'a liquid petroleum product that is a complex mixture of predominantly aliphatic hydrocarbons ranging from C9 to C16, used mainly for lighting, cooking and heating purposes, also known as kerosene'.
655. Section 2(1)(a).

petroleum product, (b) the establishment or creation of an outlet for the sale of petroleum products, (c) the transfer of businesses from one outlet to another, (d) the change of suppliers to any business, (e) the rendering of any service and (f) the supply of petroleum products to any business or undertaking if the service to the public is not of a proper standard.[656]

163. The Minister may furthermore prescribe the price (maximum or minimum) at which any petroleum product may be sold or bought by any person, as well as conditions under which the selling or buying may take place.[657] He or she may also regulate or prohibit any business practice, method of trading, agreement, arrangement, scheme or understanding that is to his or her mind calculated to influence or cause (directly or indirectly) an increase in the purchase or selling price of petroleum products. Conditions may also be imposed regarding the price at which a product may be sold at a specific outlet.[658] A difference can be made with regard to the different classes or kinds of petroleum products or services.[659] The Minister may also require that the price of petroleum products be displayed and may also prescribe the quantities of crude oil or petroleum products that have to be maintained by specific persons.[660]

164. The Minister may appoint a Controller of Petroleum Products as well as inspectors to enforce the working of the Act.[661] Any person who manufactures petroleum products must obtain a manufacturing licence from the Controller of Petroleum Products.[662]

165. In December 2007, the then DME published a *Biofuels Industrial Strategy of the Republic of South Africa.*[663] The introduction of biofuels is a contested area in South Africa. During the discussion on the Draft Strategy, issues were raised concerning 'water limitations, food security (availability and affordability), land prices, land restitution, environmental concerns, biofuels quality, technology, crop selection/choices, support and incentives'.[664] The final decision is to proceed with the introduction of biofuels but to prescribe the types of crops that may be used for biofuels. Bioethanol may be produced from sugar cane and sugar beet, while biodiesel is to be produced from sunflower, canola and soya beans. Maize and Jatropha may not be used for biodiesel. Biodiesel support will be fixed at 2% until 2020. It is foreseen that unproductive lands in the former so-called homelands (approximately 14%) be used to introduce crops for biofuels. In times of drought, when

656. Section 2(1)(b).
657. Section 2(1)(c). The price of petroleum, paraffin and diesel is amended on a monthly basis.
658. Section 2(1)(d)–(e).
659. Section 2(2).
660. Section 2(1)(f)–(g).
661. Section 3. A Controller of Petroleum Products will be a person in the public service.
662. Section 2B.
663. Biofuels_indus_strat.pdf available at www.gov.za (accessed 18 Dec. 2013).
664. Executive Summary.

these crops usually contribute to animal feedstocks, the contribution of biofuels to the fuel production may be lessened. It is proposed that the biofuels fuel levy exemption of 40% be increased to 50%.

According to the Regulations regarding the Mandatory Blending of Biofuels with Petrol and Diesel, 2012 biofuels may only be obtained by a licensed petroleum manufacturer from a licensed biofuel producer at the specified price.[665] The biofuels must be accompanied by a quality assurance certificate.[666] The manufacturer must blend the petroleum and biofuels at his or her blending facility in accordance with the relevant SANS standards.[667] The minimum concentration for biodiesel blending is 5% v/v and for bioethanol the range is between 2% v/v and 10% v/v.[668] A licensed manufacturer must buy all the biofuel that is offered to him or her except if it can be proven that the facility[669] does not have enough petroleum or diesel to blend the biofuels. Both the petroleum manufacturer and the biofuel producer must report certain information to the relevant authorities on a regular basis pertaining to the volumes biofuels manufactured or blended, the persons to whom it was sold or from whom it was bought.[670]

665. Regulation 3(1) and (3) Government Notice R671 in *Government Gazette* 35623 of 24 Aug. 2012 (hereinafter 'Government Notice R671'). *See also* General Notice 24 in *Government Gazette* 37232 of 15 Jan. 2014 – Draft Position Paper on the South African Biofuels Regulatory Framework.
666. Regulation 3(2) Government Notice R671.
667. Regulation 3(3) Government Notice R671. SANS 1598 Unleaded Petrol. Biodiesel must comply with SANS 342 Automotive diesel fuel.
668. Regulation 3(5) Government Notice R671.
669. Regulations 3(6) and 4 Government Notice R671.
670. Regulation 5(1) Government Notice R671. Records must be kept for a period of five years – regulation 5(2).

Chapter 2. Exploration and Production

166. The exploration and production of petroleum products were until May 2004 regulated by the Minerals Act 50 of 1991. Since then the MPRDA applies.[671] Provision is made for reconnaissance permits, technical cooperation permits, exploration rights and production rights. The reconnaissance and technical cooperation permits are non-transferable and non-renewable.[672] Before an exploration right is granted, the applicant must complete an environmental management programme and should indicate that he or she has the financial resources and technical ability to do the exploration.[673] A production right is granted if the applicant complies with the financial and technical requirements. He or she should also indicate that the production will not result in unacceptable pollution, ecological degradation or damage to the environment. Financial provision should also be made for the implementation of the applicant's social and labour plans.[674]

167. Similarly, a wholesaler of petroleum products needs a wholesale licence and a retailer a retail licence.[675] A person who holds or develops a site[676] needs a site permit.[677] The application should be in the prescribed format, and the applicant should be the owner of the properties or business entity concerned.[678] The Controller must issue licences to give effect to the objectives as set out in section 2B(2) of the Act.[679] A licence remains valid for as long as the holder of the licence complies with the conditions in the licence and the licence activity is an ongoing concern. Temporary licences may also be issued for a period of six months.[680] In issuing

671. Chapter 8.
672. Sections 75–77.
673. Section 80.
674. Section 84.
675. Section 2A(1).
676. A site is defined in s. 1 as 'premises on land zoned and approved by a competent authority for the retailing of prescribed petroleum products'.
677. In the case of *ABM Motors v Minister if Minerals and Energy and Others* 2018 (5) SA 540 (KZP), the Controller of Petroleum Products refused an application for a site permit; in that there were already fifteen petroleum stations in the area of Newcastle. The Minister refused the internal appeal. The case was decided on administrative law, and the point in dispute was that the fact that the Minister also took into account the number of fuel stations in the area. The case was dismissed as the court stated that the Controller and the Minister may consider the viability of a new petrol station in the area. *See also Cianam Trading 104 CC v Peters MP and Others* (33828/2013) [2014] ZAGPPHC 974 (12 Dec. 2014). In *Snyders NO v Louistef (Pty) Ltd and Another* 2017 (6) SA 646 (CC) the court found that the site licence is a commodity with commercial value.
678. Section 2A(4). *See also* Government Notices R286, 287 and R288 in *Government Gazette* 28665 of 27 Mar. 2006 that prescribe the application formats and procedures.
679. *See infra* para. 187. The objectives include, among others, that an efficient manufacturing, wholesaling and retailing petroleum industry must be effected, that an environment conducive to efficient and commercially justifiable investment is created, as well as employment opportunities, ensure country-wide availability of petroleum products and to promote access to affordable petroleum products to low-income households.
680. Section 2B(3)–(5). Only one retail licence may be issued per site.

licences, the Controller must advance historically disadvantaged South Africans and give effect to the Charter included in Schedule 1 inserted by the Petroleum Products Amendment Act 58 of 2003.[681]

If a person engages in an activity without a licence or in contravention to a licence, the Controller must direct him or her to cease the activity. A person may continue the activity pending an application for a licence if cessation of the activities would lead to material interruption in the supply of petroleum products. If the application is unsuccessful, the applicant must be notified in writing to cease all activities.[682]

168. The Act makes provision for offences and penalties.[683] Provision is also made for appeal to the Minister as well as for arbitration.[684] A certificate issued by the Minister or any person authorized thereto setting forth the price is regarded as prima facie proof of such price. Various other presumptions are also created in terms of the Act.[685]

The Minister may make regulations regarding licences, the provision of information to the Controller of Petroleum Products, the transfer of ownership of licences, the continuity of supply of petroleum products, the blending or mixing of different petroleum products with other substances,[686] the rehabilitation of land, the lodging of financial security for rehabilitation purposes, as well as the termination of licences. He or she may also prohibit practices which may be in conflict with the objectives of the Act. Provision is made for public participation.[687]

169. The legislation dealing with petrol and liquid fuels is fragmented. In certain municipalities, inflammable liquid fuels are controlled by by-laws. Due to a lack of national and provincial legislation in this regard, it is not regulated at all in other local authority areas. Environmental issues are not always addressed.

170. The Petroleum Products Act 120 of 1977 refers to the safe and efficient use of petroleum products and that petroleum products should meet certain prescribed specifications and standards.[688] The Minister set standards for petroleum indicated

681. Section 2C.
682. Section 2A(2)–(3).
683. Section 12. The penalty for contravention is a fine of ZAR 1 million or imprisonment not exceeding ten years. If a person, however, complies with a directive, he or she will not be held criminally liable.
684. Sections 12A and 12B.
685. Section 9.
686. Government Notice R719 in *Government Gazette* 36890 of 30 Sep. 2013 determined the commencement date of the Regulations regarding the Mandatory Blending of Biofuels with Petrol and Diesel, 2012 (Government Notice R671 in *Government Gazette* 35623 of 23 Aug. 2012) as 1 Oct. 2015. *See also* para. 60.1.
687. Section 2C.
688. Section 2B(6)(c).

that by 1 July 2017 petroleum should be lead-free and also indicated level specifications for benzene, sulphur and biodiesel, among others.[689] The Minister may make regulations regarding the rehabilitation of land used in connection with a licensed activity and that financial security must be provided for any damage that may occur.[690] The licensing regulations contain environmental specifications.[691] It clearly indicates that the Controller of Petroleum Products will not approve the manufacturing, wholesale, site and retail if certain environmental authorizations have not been obtained.[692] The transport regulations incorporated standard specifications of the SABS to ensure safe transport of liquid fuels and the control of emergency incidents.

171. The NEMA will apply to the manufacture of liquid fuels as new operators will have to apply for an environmental authorization,[693] and in the case of air emissions the NEMAQA will apply.

172. Category 2 of the Government Notice 893 of November 2013[694] lists activities that have or may have a significant detrimental effect on the environment (including health, social, economic and environmental conditions or cultural heritage) and for which a licence must be obtained in terms of the NEMAQA and that specifically deals with the petroleum industry.[695] It also prescribes standards. Category 2 refers to the production of gaseous and liquid fuels as well as petrochemicals from crude oil, coal, gas or biomass. The subcategories deal with combustion installations (2.1), catalytic cracking units (2.2), sulphur recovery units (2.3), storage and handling of petroleum products (2.4) and industrial fuel oil recyclers (2.5). Government Notice 893 lists minimum emission standards that apply to both permanently operated plants and experimental or pilot plans that have a design capacity equivalent to the listed activity. The minimum emission standard is to be determined during normal operating conditions.[696] If normal start-up, maintenance,

---

689. Government Notice R627 in *Government Gazette* 28958 of 23 Jun. 2006 as amended by Government Notice R 431 in *Government Gazette* 35410 of 1 Jun. 2012; Government Notice 684 in *Government Gazette* 40047 of 3 Jun. 2016 and Government Notice R582 in *Government Gazette* 40929 of 23 Jun. 2017.
690. Section 12C(1)(g). Provision may also be made for the lodging of financial security for the rehabilitation of such premises as well as the composition of such amount.
691. Government Notices R286, R287 and R288 in *Government Gazette* 28665 of 27 Mar. 2006.
692. For example, for site, wholesale and manufacturing licences the applications for licences must include an environmental management plan indicating how site rehabilitation will take place, an environmental impact assessment, how the environmental management plan will be monitored and how performance assessment will take place and the financial security that will be provided for rehabilitation. It should also provide proof of a land use zoning certificate, an environmental authorization and the permission that is obtained from the National Roads Authority to transport dangerous goods. The applicants must also declare that they comply with all applicable laws. Government Notices R286, R287 and R288 in *Government Gazette* 28665 of 27 Mar. 2006.
693. Section 24.
694. Government Notice 893 in *Government Gazette* 37054 of 22 Nov. 2013, as amended by Gen Notice 551 in *GG* 38863 of 12 Jun. 2015.
695. Sections 21, 22 and 37.
696. According to Part II (4) ‘minimum emission standards are expressed on a daily average basis, under normal conditions of 273 K, 101.3 kPa, specific oxygen percentage and dry gas’.

upset or shutdown conditions exceed a period of 48 hours, it will be regarded as an emergency situation in terms of section 30 of the NEMA, except if another agreement was reached with the licensing authority.[697] Government Notice 893 also prescribes the standard sampling method in Annexure A.[698] Existing plants have to comply with the minimum standards for existing plants contained in Part 3 from 1 April 2015 and with the new minimum standards by 1 April 2020. However, an application for extension may be lodged.[699] Extensive monitoring and reporting provisions are also included.[700] For the first time, fugitive emissions are to be regulated too – applicants also have to include a fugitive emissions management plan in their atmospheric emission licence application if their operations will generate such emissions.[701]

173. The then Minister of Environmental Affairs also declared certain areas in South Africa as priority areas in terms of section 18 of the NEMAQA. She did this as she reasonably believes that the ambient air quality standards may be exceeded in these areas and that specific air quality management action is necessary. Such action allows the Minister to publish a priority area air management plan following a consultative process.[702] The plan has to coordinate air quality management in the area, address issues relating to air quality management in the area and must provide for the implementation of the plan by a committee representing role players.[703] The Minister may also make regulations dealing with the implementation and enforcement of the air quality management plan.[704] The petroleum refineries fall within two of the areas that were proclaimed priority areas, namely the Highveld Priority Area and the Vaal Triangle Air-Shed Priority Area.[705]

174. In 2017 greenhouse gas emissions were declared as priority air pollutants.[706] The implication of such declaration will be that an applicant that falls under the scope of the declaration will have to prepare a pollution prevention plan[707] in

697. Part II (1)-(3).
698. Part II (5)-(7). Other sampling methods may only be used with permission of the licensing authority.
699. Part II (8)-(11). *See also* the Department of Energy *National Framework for Air Quality Management in the Republic of South Africa, 2012* – Government Notice 919 in *Government Gazette*, 37078 of 29 Nov. 2013. An extension for an additional five years may be granted (13). The air quality officer may review the postponement from time to time – (14). For the new framework, *see* DEA, *The 2017 National Framework for Air Quality Management in the Republic of South Africa* – Government Notice 1144 in *Government Gazette* 41996 of 26 Oct. 2018.
700. Part II (15)-(19).
701. Part II (20).
702. Section 19.
703. Section 19(6).
704. Section 20.
705. *See*, e.g., Government Notice 144 in *Government Gazette* 35072 of 2 Mar. 2012 (Highveld Priority Area Air Quality Management Plan), Government Notice R614 in *Government Gazette* 32254 of 29 May 2009 (Regulations for implementing and enforcing the Vaal Triangle Air-Shed Priority Area Air Quality Management Plan).
706. Government Notice 710 in *Government Gazette* 40996 of 21 Jul. 2017.
707. Compiled in terms of Government Notice 712 in *Government Gazette* 40996 of 21 Jul. 2017 – National Pollution Prevention Plans Regulations, 2017.

terms of the NEMAQA. All sectors of the economy must also report their emissions,[708] as well as their greenhouse gas emissions.[709]

175. In addition to the Act, Durban Metro promulgated the Schedule Trade and Occupation Bylaws,[710] in terms of which refineries and bulk storage of petroleum products have been declared a scheduled trade and occupation which is regulated by an authorization by Durban Metro. Only two refineries are subject to local by-laws – the refineries in Sasolburg and Cape Town are not. In the absence of technical standards in South Africa, most South African refineries and handlers of bulk petroleum products adopted the American Petroleum Industry Standards (API).[711]

176. Section 20 of the NWA and section 30 of the NEMA regulate emergency incidents. When an incident occurs, the responsible person has certain obligations relating to controlling the incident, clean-up of the terrain, remediation or rehabilitation. Petroleum industries usually prepare emergency response plans to be implemented in the case of a spill or environmental disaster. Industries have to comply with all legislation with regard to reporting – reports must be sent not only to the Department of Human Settlement, Water and Sanitation but also to the Department of Environment Affairs, Forestry and Fisheries, local government, the South African Police Services and the Department of Health (in the case of hazardous substances). The fragmentation of legislation places an unnecessary burden on industry, but however ensures that all the key departments are informed.

---

708. Government Notice R283 in *Government Gazette* 38633 of 2 Apr. 2015 – National Atmospheric Emission Reporting Regulations, 2015.
709. General Notice 275 in *Government Gazette* 40762 of 3 Apr. 2017 – National GHG Emissions Reporting Regulations, 2016.
710. Municipal Notice 134 of 22 Mar. 1979 in terms of s. 27 of the Local Authorities Ordinance 25 of 1974.
711. The National Environmental Management: Air Quality Act 39 of 2004 provides for the setting of standards. *See also* J. Glazewski & L. du Toit, eds, *Environmental Law*, 22–1–22–21 (2nd edn, LexisNexis 2014 Service Issue 2).

Chapter 3. Transportation and Distribution

177. In 2003, the Petroleum Pipelines Act 60 of 2003 was promulgated to establish a national regulatory framework for petroleum pipelines.[712] The National Energy Regulator is responsible for the issuing of licences, obtaining information, undertaking investigations, setting and approving tariffs and charges, monitoring and taking appropriate action to ensure access to facilities.[713]

Licences are issued for '(i) the construction and conversion of petroleum pipelines, loading facilities[714] and storage facilities[715] and (ii) the operation of petroleum pipelines, loading facilities and storage facilities'. Applications for licences must be made by the owner of the pipeline or facility in the prescribed format and must among others include a description of the proposed pipeline, loading facility or storage facility to be constructed or operated, including maps and diagrams; a description of tariff policies to be applied; the plans and ability of the applicant to comply with applicable labour, health, safety, security and environmental legislation; and the identification of the individual who will be responsible for the control, management and operation of the pipeline or facility.[716] The applicant must publish a notice of the application in at least two newspapers in any two of the official languages. It must also be stated that objections may be lodged to the Regulator.[717] Conditions may be added to the licence as described in section 20, for example health, safety and environmental standards as well as standards for the operation or

712. As of May 2005, the Act had not been put into operation but it will come into force on 1 Nov. 2005.
713. Established in terms of the National Energy Regulator Act 40 of 2004. The Regulator will undertake the functions described in s. 4 of the Petroleum Pipelines Act and for which a Petroleum Pipelines Regulatory Authority was foreseen – s. 4(1)(b). The Regulator is authorized to enter and inspect premises to obtain information or conduct an investigation (ss 29 and 30). It may expropriate land in certain circumstances (s. 32).
714. A 'loading facility' is defined in s. 1 as 'any marine facility that is or can be used to load or off-load petroleum and includes any auxiliary pipelines connected thereto but excludes bunkering facilities'.
715. 'Storage facility' is defined in s. 1 as 'any bulk storage facility and its auxiliary equipment that is or is intended to be used for the storage of petroleum and excludes storage facilities (a) on premises at which petroleum products are manufactured and where such storage facilities are integral to the process of manufacture; (b) for own final use; (c) used for the retailing of petroleum products to the public; (d) used by an agricultural cooperative exclusively for its members; and (e) used to transport petroleum by road, rail, sea and air'.
716. Section 16. Provision is made for a transitional period in which persons owning petroleum pipelines, loading facilities or storage facilities prior to commencement of the Act may within six months apply for a licence – s. 35. For a discussion on tariffs and levies *see* Part VI.
717. Section 17.

construction of a pipeline or facility.[718] A licence is issued for a period of twenty-five years after which it may be renewed. A licence may at any time be amended or revoked under certain conditions.[719]

It may be required from the licensee to submit financial security to ensure compliance with licence conditions dealing with health, safety, security or the environment, prior to or during the validity of the licence.[720]

Petroleum is also transported and distributed by road. The same legislation as discussed in the case of gas will be applicable. In the case of *Transnet Soc Ltd v Total South Africa (Pty) Ltd and Another*,[721] the tariff for the transportation of crude oil via the petroleum pipeline was in dispute. The court found that Transnet may allow discount and that differentiation between customers based on contract was not discrimination.

718. Section 20. If a licensee contravenes or fails to comply with a condition in the licence or a provision of the Act, the Regulator may serve a notice to direct the licensee to comply with the condition. If a person fails to comply, the Regulator may act as a tribunal and impose a penalty or fine not exceeding ZAR 2,000,000 per day for each day on which the contravention or failure continues – s. 25.

719. Sections 23–24. The licence may also be revoked by the High Court on application of the Regulator – s. 26. Provision is also made for the use of arbitration if all parties agreed (s. 30).

720. Section 27.

721. [2016] ZASCA 116.

Chapter 4. Consumption

178. The Minister may in terms of the Petroleum Pipelines Act make regulations regarding *inter alia* the rehabilitation of land used for the licensed activity, the provision of financial security for rehabilitation purposes and the composition of such an amount. The Regulations must be published for public comment.[722]

179. The Hazardous Substances Act provides for the control of substances that may cause injury to or death of human beings by reason of their toxic, corrosive, irritant, strongly sensitizing or flammable nature.[723] Four groups of hazardous substances are identified.[724] Once a substance is declared as a Group I or III substance, its sale is regulated.[725] A licence[726] must be obtained, and the Director General of the Department of Health may impose any conditions he or she deems fit.[727] The sale, letting, use, operation, application and installation of Group III substances are similarly regulated.[728]

180. The director general may appoint inspectors to ensure the implementation of the Act. The inspectors have wide-ranging powers, for example entry, embargo, taking of samples and seizure.[729] The Act also makes provision for secrecy. Disclosure of information by an official must be authorized by the director general or be disclosed for the purposes of legal proceedings.[730]

181. The Minister may make regulations with regard to various matters dealing with hazardous substances.[731] In some instances, the control of hazardous substances may be assigned to local authorities. In terms of section 24, however, local

722. Section 33.
723. Preamble to the Act. *See*, for example, the construction regulations issued in terms of the Act – Government Notice 1010 in *Government Gazette* 25207 of 18 Jul. 2003 – regulation 23 which provides that a contractor must comply with the general safety regulations dealing with inflammable liquids – the inflammable liquids must, for example, be stored in a safe manner and in a properly ventilated place. Fire resistant containers should be used and access to the premises should be controlled.
724. Groups I and II – to be declared by Minister of Health – any substance or group of substances which, in the course of customary or reasonable handling or use, including ingestion, might, by reason of its toxic, corrosive, strongly sensitizing or flammable nature or because it generates pressure through decomposition, heat or other means, cause injury, ill health or death to human beings. Group III hazardous substances deal with electronic products and Group IV with radioactive material found outside nuclear installations.
725. Section 2. The Minister may also exempt certain persons or categories of persons from the working of the Act – s. 3(1A).
726. Government Notice R453 in *Government Gazette* 5467 of 25 Mar. 1977. The Regulations make provision for, *inter alia*, the conditions and supply of Group I hazardous substances (regulation 4); record-keeping (regulation 5); labelling (regulation 8) and disposal of empty containers (regulation 10).
727. Section 3(1)(a) read with s. 4. The licence can be cancelled or suspended at any time – s. 7.
728. Section 3(1)(b) read with s. 4.
729. Sections 8–12.
730. Section 17. For offences, proof and presumptions, liability of principals, right to prosecute, restriction of liability, *see* ss 18–28.
731. Section 29.

authorities must apply for authorization to enforce the Regulations.[732] These regulations deal with the transportation of hazardous waste by road tankers.[733]

182. The Department of Health prescribes ionizing radiation dose limits and annual limits on the intake of radioactive material.[734] Similarly, protective measures to be taken in the event of an accident involving radioactivity are described.[735] Other matters regulated by the Department are standards for the safe use of industrial gauges containing radioactive sources,[736] requirements for leak testing facilities,[737] code of practice for the safe use of soil moisture and density gauges,[738] guidelines for the safe transportation of radioactive material,[739] requirements for the safe use of unsealed radioactive nuclides[740] and code of practice for the management and disposal of non-nuclear radioactive waste.[741]

183. The National Health Act 61 of 2003 provides a framework for a structured uniform health system within South Africa. The Director General of Health is responsible for issuing norms and standards with regard to environmental conditions which may constitute health hazards. He or she must also facilitate the provision of indoor and outdoor environmental pollution control services which is important as many people in South Africa still make use of paraffin as their source of energy in their houses.[742] Similar functions are given to provincial and local authorities.[743]

184. In terms of regulations dealing with fires and explosions issued in terms of the Mine Health and Safety Act 29 of 1996, a duty of care regarding the transport, store, deposit, use and disposal of inflammable liquids, gases and materials is placed on mines to prevent fires and health risks.[744] The Occupational Health and Safety

---

732. *See*, for example, Upington – Government Notice R566 in *Government Gazette* 17921 of 18 Apr. 1997.
733. Government Notice R73 in *Government Gazette* 9556 of 11 Jan. 1985. These regulations must be read with the road transport regulations – *see infra* Ch. 3.
734. Department of Health – Directorate: Health Technology, *Ionising Radiation Dose Limits and Annual Limits on the Intake of Radioactive Material*, DLUG91-1 (Feb.), 1997.
735. Department of Health – Directorate: Health Technology, *Protective Measures to be Taken in the Event of an Accident Involving Radioactivity*, FIRE (Feb.), 1997.
736. Department of Health – Directorate: Health Technology, *Standards for the Safe Use of Industrial Gauges Containing Radioactive Sources*, GAUGE (August), 1996.
737. Department of Health, Radiation Control Directorate, *Requirements for Leak Testing Facilities* (October), 1999.
738. Department of Health – Directorate: Health Technology, *Code of Practice for the Safe Use of Soil Moisture and Density Gauges Containing Radioactive Sources*, SOIL (August), 1997.
739. Department of Health – Directorate: Radiation Control, *Guidelines for the Safe Transport of Radioactive Material*, TRUG91-1 (Apr.), 1997.
740. Department of Health – Directorate: Health Technology, *Requirements for the Safe Use of Unsealed Radioactive Nuclides*, UNSEAL (Feb.), 1997.
741. Department of Health – Directorate: Health Technology, *Code of Practice for the Management and Disposal of Non-nuclear Radioactive Waste*, WSCP91-1 (Feb.), 1997.
742. Section 21. The same will be true for the indoor use of coal stoves for heat and cooking.
743. Sections 25 read with section 1 – definition of 'municipal services'.
744. General Notice R1237 in *Government Gazette* 25404 of 29 Aug. 2003.

Act was promulgated to provide for the health and safety of persons at work or hazards arising out of or in connection with their working activities. The Act itself applies to the petroleum and liquid fuel industry as to any other workplace, but it is the Regulations that are of importance to the petroleum and liquid fuel industry. Asbestos and lead are still used, and, therefore, the industries have to comply with regulations in this regard.[745] The industry must also comply with the major hazardous installation regulations.[746]

185. In terms of the Fire Brigade Services Act, the Minister may after consultation with the Fire Brigade Board[747] make regulations with regard to the use, manufacture, storage or transportation of *inter alia* petroleum or any other flammable or combustible substance, gas or dangerous substance. The Minister issued draft regulations in this regard, but they were never put into operation. However, municipalities used the draft regulations to issue their own by-laws in this regard.[748]

186. If a municipality, government Department or any other person fails to comply with a requirement, standard or specification in the Act, the competent official may serve a written notice to comply. If such a person or authority fails to give effect to the notice, the official may take steps against them and recover the costs from such a person or authority.[749]

187. Various municipal by-laws control inflammable liquids and substances and gases. These by-laws deal, *inter alia*, with the storage and supply of these liquids and substances, as well as with applications for registration.[750]

---

745. Government Notices 773 and 745 in *Government Gazette* 10700 and 10693 (respectively) of 10 Apr. 1987; Government Notice 745; Government Notice R586 in *Government Gazette* 13082 of 22 Mar. 1991. Regulations pertaining to lead and asbestos were published in 1999 – Government Notice R236 in *Government Gazette* 23175 of 28 Feb. 2002 and Government Notice R959 in *Government Gazette* 20359 of 16 Aug. 1999.
746. Government Notice R60 in *Government Gazette* 18608 of 16 Jan. 1998. Other specifications include Standards Specifications for Symbolic Safety Signs (SABS 1186); Government Notice R1179 in *Government Gazette* 16596 of 25 Aug. 1995 – regulations for hazardous chemical substances; *Government Notice* R1449 in Government Gazette 17403 of 6 Sep. 1996 – reporting of incidents, handling of hazardous chemical substances, recording and investigation of incidents and material safety data sheet (MSDS) specifications.
747. Instituted in terms of s. 2.
748. In terms of s. 16.
749. Section 17. A Chief Fire Officer may at any reasonable time enter premises to determine whether the provisions of the Act are complied with – s. 18.
750. *See*, for example, AN 567 of 18 Jul. 1956 – Municipality of Springs: Inflammable Liquids and Substances Bylaws; PN 264 of 20 May 1983: Vredenburg Saldanha Municipality: Bylaw relating to Flammable Liquids and Gases; City of Johannesburg Metropolitan Municipality: Emergency Services Bylaws (Notice 826 Provincial Gazette Extraordinary 179 of 21 May 2004).

Part IV. Regulatory Framework Concerning Coal

Chapter 1. General Introduction

188. Coal is one of the major energy sources in South Africa. The production, exploitation, transportation, distribution and consumption of coal as such are not regulated in a single Act. They are regulated in terms of general mining and environmental legislation.[751] The MPRDA changed the concept of mineral rights to recognize the internationally accepted right of the state to exercise sovereignty over all the mineral and petroleum resources in South Africa and to give effect to the state's custodianship of the nation's mineral and petroleum resources.[752]

Recently mining companies embarked on the gasification of coal seams that are too deep to exploit properly or where coal of a lesser quality is found. It is also considered as a source of alternative energy.[753]

189. The MPRDA is the principal Act on mining and activities connected thereto. The Act was enacted to achieve the following aims: *inter alia* to (a) promote equitable access to all South Africa's mineral resources, to promote economic growth and mineral and petroleum resources development; (b) give effect to section 24 of the Constitution by ensuring that the nation's mineral and petroleum resources are developed in an ecologically sustainable manner while promoting justifiable

751. *See* M. Mabiletsa & W. Du Plessis, *Impact of Environmental Legislation on Mining in South Africa*, 8 SAJELP 185–213 (2001) for a discussion of the pre-2004 position.
752. Sections 2(a)–(b) and 3. The legal nature of the mineral rights of previous owners changed – it is still regarded as a limited real right, but the right is subject to approval by government and is only allocated for a specific period of time – *see* s. 5. On the public trust doctrine, *see* E. van der Schyff, *Unpacking the Public Trust Doctrine: A Journey into Foreign Territory*, 13 PELJ 122–159 (2010); E. van der Schyff, *Who Owns the Country's Mineral Resources? The Possible Incorporation of the Public Trust Doctrine through Section 3(1) of the Mineral and Petroleum Resources Development Act 28 of 2002*, Journal of South African Law 757–768 (2008).
753. *See* M. Green, *Underground Coal Gasification – A Clean Indigenous Energy Option*, http://www.ucgengineering.com/publishedarticleonucg.html (accessed 19 Dec. 2013); Eskom, *Underground Coal Gasification*, COP17 Fact Sheet, 2011 http://www.eskom.co.za/AboutElectricity/FactsFigures/Documents/Underground_Coal_Gasification_UCG.pdf (accessed 19 Dec. 2013); for an explanation of the technology.

social and economic development; and (c) ensure that holders of mining and production rights contribute towards the socio-economic development of the areas in which they are in operation.[754] The Act was put into operation on 1 May 2004.[755]

754. Section 2(e), (h)–(i).
755. Proclamation R25 in *Government Gazette* 26264 of 23 Apr. 2004. On the Mineral and Petroleum Resources Act 28 of 2002 – *see* E. van der Schyff, *Property in Minerals and Petroleum*, Juta, 2016.

Chapter 2. Licensing and Authorization Regime

190. Where the Minerals Act 50 of 1991 only referred to prospecting and mineral rights, the 2002 Act makes provision for (a) reconnaissance permissions, (b) prospecting rights, (c) mining permits, (d) mining rights, (e) retention permits, (f) reconnaissance permits, (g) technical cooperation permits, (h) exploration rights, and (i) production rights (in the case of petroleum and gas).[756]

When an application for the mining of coal is made, the applicant must apply to the regional manager in the prescribed manner for a mining right of the area where the mine is to be situated.[757] If the regional manager accepts the application, the applicant has to apply for an environmental authorization and submit the necessary environmental reports as prescribed in terms of section 24 of the NEMA.[758] The mining right will not be granted if the applicant had not obtained an environmental authorization.[759] The applicant must consult with all interested and affected parties as well as the landowner and lawful occupiers of the land. The result of the consultation must form part of the environmental reports that are to be submitted.[760] The applicant must provide proof that the mineral can be mined optimally in accordance with the mining work programme and that the applicant has the technical and financial resources to conduct the proposed mining operation optimally. The regional manager must further be certain that the mining will not result in unacceptable pollution, ecological degradation or damage to the environment. The applicant must also prove that financial provision is made to comply with the mine's social and labour plan.[761] A mining right is granted for thirty years and may be renewed.[762]

756. Chapters 4 and 5.
757. Section 22. A mining right is granted for a period of thirty years and may be extended only once. Preference may be given to communities if they can prove that the right shall be used to contribute to the development and social upliftment of the community, they submit a development plan and they have access to technical and financial assistance – s. 104. *See also* regulations 2–3, 12–14, Government Notice R527 in *Government Gazette* 26275 of 23 Apr. 2004 – hereinafter 'GN R527'.
758. Section 22(4). The application for an environmental authorization is to be done in terms of s. 24 of NEMA. An environmental management programme will have to be compiled in terms of s. 24N of NEMA. Section 24N was put into operation on 8 Dec. 2014. A mine may be required to submit its environmental management programme with its application for an environmental authorization – s. 24N(1) as amended by the National Environmental Management Laws Amendment Act 25 of 2014. *See also* regulations 48–52 of General Notice R527. Since December 2014, the mine will also have to conduct an environmental impact assessment in terms of the environmental impact assessment regulations – Government Notice R982 in *Government Gazette* 38282 of 4 Dec. 2014 and item 21 Government Notice R983 in *Government Gazette* 38282 of 4 Dec. 2014. Item 33 of Government Notice R983 refers to the underground gasification of coal and item 58 to the expansion of such operations. These requirements will be amended again with the introduction of the Mineral and Petroleum Resources Development Amendment Bill [B15B-2013]. The Act specifies that the mine will have to consult community and their relevant structures with regard to the implementation of the social and labour plan (previously this was not necessary) and that the mine will have to apply for a water use licence (to be inserted s. 22(4)(c) and (d)).
759. Section 23(1)(d) MPRDA.
760. Section 24(2)(b) MPRDA.
761. Section 23. *See also* regulations 40–56 of General Notice R527.
762. Sections 23(6) and 24.

A mining permit is granted if a mineral can be mined optimally within a period of two years and the mining area does not exceed 1.5 ha in extent.[763]

191. Mines are bound to the sustainable development principles as set out in section 2 of NEMA.[764] Mines are also obliged to give effect to the general objectives of integrated environmental management as set out in Chapter 5 of NEMA. Before 2014 all environmental impacts had to be managed in accordance with an environmental management plan or approved environmental management programme.[765] Environmental management plans could have been amended from time to time.[766] Since 8 December 2014, new mines will have to submit an environmental management programme indicating the management, mitigation and remedial measures that will be undertaken.[767] The mine must specifically indicate how it will deal with pollution and environmental degradation, comply with environmental management standards or practices and the responsibilities to pump and treat extraneous water.[768] Provision is also made for monitoring and performance assessments of the environmental management programmes and plans.[769]

192. All mines, including coal mines, must, as far as it is reasonably practicable, rehabilitate the environment affected by prospecting or mining to its predetermined state or to a land use which conforms to the generally accepted principle of sustainable development.[770] All buildings and structures (including mining equipment) must be demolished or removed, except if they are to be preserved under the National Heritage Resources Act 25 of 1999 or if they are to be retained in terms of an agreement between the holder of the right and the owner or occupier of the land.[771]

A mine must provide the prescribed financial provision before an environmental authorization will be issued. Financial provision includes insurance, bank guarantee, trust fund or cash.[772] If the holder of a right or permit fails to rehabilitate or manage negative impacts on the environment, the Minister may after given written

763. Section 27. The same procedures are followed except that the applicant has to hand in an environmental management plan only.
764. The Mineral and Petroleum Resources Development Amendment Bill (B15B-2013) amends this position and states that government departments must take these principles into account in their decision-making – once the Bill is signed into an Act and comes into operation the principles will only have indirect application on mines.
765. Section 38 MPRDA.
766. Section 39(6) MPRDA.
767. Section 24N NEMA.
768. Sections 24N(2)(g) and 3(b) NEMA.
769. Regulation 55 of General Notice R527 read with s. 24N(7)(d) NEMA.
770. Before 8 Dec. 2014 – s. 38(1)(d) MPRDA; after this date s. 24N(2)(f) NEMA.
771. Section 44.
772. Defined in s. 1 NEMA, previously in MPRDA. *See* Government Notice R1147 in Government Gazette 39425 of 20 Nov. 2015 for financial regulations. *See also* in this regard A.A. Smithen, *Environmental Considerations in the Preparation of Bankable Feasibility Documents*, 99 The Journal of the South African Institute of Mining and Metallurgy 317–320 (1999); G.D. Coppin, *Should Mines take Account*, Mar., Mining World 26–27 (2000); G. Charles, *Providing for Mine Rehabilitation – Making your Environmental Trust Work for You*, Mar., Mining World 28 (2000); Anon., *Facing Early Closure Funding Shortfalls*, May, Mining World 32 (2000).

notice use the funds for rehabilitation.[773] Several mines are threatened with lawsuits dealing with pollution. Other communities resist the opening of new mines.[774]

193. Holders of rights or permits remain liable for environmental damage or pollution until a closure certificate has been issued by the Minister.[775] Applications for closure certificates must be made upon lapsing, abandonment or cancellation of the right, the cessation of the prospecting or mining operations or the relinquishment of land to which a right or permit relates or on completion of the prescribed closing plan.[776] The application must be made within 180 days after the occurrence of activities mentioned above.[777] The application should, among others, include an environmental risk report and the risks should be qualitatively marked as potential, uncertain and insignificant risks. The amended sections do not refer to environmental risk reports but to 'information, programmes, plans and reports' in terms of the NEMA only.[778]

194. Closure certificates may only be issued once the Chief Inspector of Mines and each government department (charged with the administration of laws affecting the environment) confirmed in writing that the provisions pertaining to health and safety and management of potential pollution to water resources have been addressed.[779] It is sometimes difficult to obtain a closure certificate, as the Department of Mineral Resources and Energy and the Department of Human Settlement, Water and Sanitation are not always convinced that all potential environmental risks have been eliminated. However, a mine might receive a closure certificate but its liabilities in terms of, for example, section 28 of the NEMA (polluter pays principle) continue.[780] The new amendments in terms of the Mineral and Petroleum Resources Development Amendment Bill (B15B-2013) propose that the holder of a

773. Section 41(2).

774. *See*, for example, *Coal of Africa Limited and Another v. Akkerland Boerdery (Pty) Ltd* (38528/2012) [2014] ZAGPPHC 195 (5 Mar. 2014); Anon., *Coal Rail Plan Faces Farmers' Resistance*, 23 Apr., Business Report (2012), http://www.iol.co.za/business/companies/coal-rail-plan-faces-farmers-resistance-1.1281325#.VKvOzbTNzaE (accessed 5 Jan. 2015), G. Ashton, *Adding Insult to Injury: The Impacts of Coal Extraction*, The South African Civil Social Information Service, 16 Jan. 2012, http://sacsis.org.za/site/article/810.1 (accessed 5 Jan. 2015).

775. Section 43(1) MPRDA read with s. 24R NEMA.

776. Section 43(3).

777. Section 43(4).

778. Regulation 60 of General Notice R527. *See also* the other regulations dealing with the closure certificate – regulations 56–62. This regulation should be read with the amended s. 43(4) MPRDA and s. 24N(2)(v) and (2)(f) NEMA. *See also* the inserted s. 24(5)(bA) NEMA with regard to the possible documents that may be required – environmental risk assessments are included in the list – National Environmental Management Laws Amendment Act 25 of 2014.

779. Section 43(5). When a closure certificate is issued, the Minister must return a portion of the financial contribution. He or she may, however, retain an amount for latent or residual environmental damage which may only be known in future – s. 43(6). These sections are to be amended again by the Mineral and Petroleum Resources Development Amendment Bill [B15B-2013]. The Chief Inspector of Mines will in future only have to consult with the Department of Water and Sanitation.

780. *See also* T. Molete, *Environmental Risk Exposures – A Thorny Issue for Mine Closures*, January/February, The Journal of the South African Institute of Mining and Metallurgy, 55 (1999); *see also* F. Cessford, *Mine Water Monitoring – Past, Present and Future*, February, Mining World 26 (2000).

closure certificate would remain liable for any 'latent or residual environmental liability, pollution, ecological degradation, the pumping and treatment of extraneous water which may become known in the future'.[781]

195. Due to the Merriespruit disaster,[782] a new code of practice (SANS 0286) was published to deal with the disposal of mine residue deposits. The code is based on ISO 14001 to ensure continual improvement: 'the primary focus of the new code is to ensure that the appropriate safety and environmental objectives are set and achieved'. It is recommended in the code that residue disposal should be integrated into the main activities of the mine, taking into consideration the variety of residue types, disposal methods and climatic conditions.[783] The MPRDA initially dealt with the management of residue stockpiles and deposits. Only sites that were indicated in the environmental management programme could be used for this purpose.[784] However, in 2013 the position was amended, and the NEMWA now regulates residue stockpiles and residue deposits. The Minister of Mineral Resources and Energy is the responsible organ of the state. However, the Minister of Environmental Affairs, Forestry and Fisheries may make regulations on standards and specifications for these stockpiles and deposits. Residue stockpiles and residue deposits are regarded as hazardous waste in terms of NEMWA.[785]

196. Extensive provision is made for consultation with interested and affected parties. Within fourteen days after receipt of the application, the regional director must inform interested and affected parties of the application as well as inform them to their right to comment on the application within thirty days of the application. If a person objects to the application, the regional director must refer the objection to the Regional Mining Development and Environmental Committee to consider the objections and to advise the Minister thereon.[786] In terms of the Minerals Act 50 of 1991, the then Director of Mineral Development granted an initial approval for mining, without addressing the concerns of interested groups. In terms of the legislation, he was not obliged to do so but the SCA ordered him to adhere to the principle

781. The proposed insertion of s. 43(1A) by the Bill.
782. A sludge dam of a mine burst, resulting in the death of several people and the destruction of a part of Virginia, a town in the Free State Province.
783. Anon., *SABS Mine Residue Code Published*, April, Mining World 6 (2000).
784. Section 42. *See also* regulation 73 in General Notice R527.
785. Schedule 3 Category A NEMWA. The Minister issues regulations in terms of s. 24(5)(b)(vi) NEMWA. The Minister issued regulations on the planning and management of these deposits and stockpiles – Government Notice R632 in *Government Gazette* 39020 of 24 Jul. 2015.
786. Section 10.

of *audi alteram partem.*[787] In 2011, the Constitutional Court in *Bengwenyama Minerals (Pty) Ltd v. Genorah Resources (Pty) Ltd*[788] confirmed the importance of consultation with at least the landowner – even where the MPRDA did not explicitly prescribe it (in the case of prospecting rights). In terms of section 6 of the MPRDA, all administrative processes must be conducted in accordance with the Promotion of Administrative Justice Act 3 of 2000. It must also be conducted within a reasonable time and in accordance with the principles of lawfulness, reasonableness and procedural fairness.[789] In 2018, the Gauteng High Court in the case of *Baleni and Others v Minister of Mineral Resources and Others*[790] a community challenged the mining authorization on the basis that they had not given prior and informed consent. Neither the MPRDA nor the NEMA provides for such consent. However, the court applied the Interim Protection of Informal Land Rights Act 31 of 1996 to construe this consent in the case where the holders of the land have informal land rights, for example in the case of traditional communities.

Applications for reconnaissance permissions are also lodged at the regional manager. The regional manager must be certain that the applicant has access to financial resources and has the technical ability to conduct the operations.[791] A holder of a reconnaissance permission may not prospect or mine, and the permission does not give the holder an entitlement to be allocated the prospecting or mining right.[792] The permission is granted for a period of two years and is not renewable.[793]

197. An application for a prospecting right is lodged similar to the lodging of a mining right.[794] The regional manager must request the applicant to lodge all environmental reports in terms of NEMA and must consult with interested and affected parties and must include the results of the consultation in his or her environmental reports.[795] If the regional manager is satisfied that the applicant has the financial and technical ability to conduct the prospecting and that the prospecting would not result

787. *The Director: Mineral Development, Gauteng and Sasol Mining (Pty) Ltd v. Save the Vaal and Others* 1999 2 SA 709 (A). *See also* K. Farina, *Public Participation and Mining*, Conference: Developments in the Contemporary Constitutional State, 2–3 Nov. 2000, Potchefstroom, South Africa; M. Kidd, *Vaal Environment Saved? The Director: Mineral Development, Gauteng and Sasol Mining (Pty) Ltd v. Save and Others*, 6 SAJELP 149–160 (1999); G. Ferreira, W. Du Plessis & K. van der Walt, *A License to Mine, audi alteram partem and NEMA*, 6 SAJELP 245–256 (1999).

788. 2011 4 SA 113 (CC) [62]-[68].

789. *Bengwenyama Minerals (Pty) Ltd v. Genorah Resources (Pty) Ltd supra* [69]-[74]. *See also* para. 84.

790. [2019] 1 All SA 358 (GP); 2019 (2) SA 453 (GP).

791. Sections 13–14.

792. Section 15.

793. Section 14.

794. Section 16(1).

795. Section 16(4). *See also* the *Bengwenyama Minerals* case *supra* para. 82. Before 8 Dec. 2014 s. 16(4) referred to notification only. The Mineral and Petroleum Resources Development Amendment Act 49 of 2008 amended the position as from 8 Dec. 2014. In *Global Environmental Trust and Others v Tendele Coal Mining (Pty) Ltd and Others* [2019] 1 All SA 176 (KZP), the applicants averted that the respondents did not have the necessary environmental and planning authorizations. The court found that the respondents received approval of their mining right applications and environmental management programme, long before the MPRDA and NEMA's amendments came into operation. The waste legislation as well as the planning laws were also not in operation at the time.

in unacceptable pollution or damage to the environment, he or she may grant the right. A prospecting right is valid for five years and may be renewed once for a period not exceeding three years.[796] As stated above, the land must be rehabilitated.

198. The Minister may facilitate assistance to persons from historically disadvantaged groups to conduct prospecting or mining operations.[797] The assistance may be given subject to certain conditions. The Minister must take certain factors into account, namely the need to promote equitable access to the nation's mineral resources, the financial position of the applicant, the need to transform the ownership structure of the mining industry and the extent to which the proposed mining or prospecting meets the objects as set out in section 2 of the Act.[798] Several individuals and communities received royalties from mines. Due to the new dispensation, these people and communities can no longer automatically rely on these royalties. According to item 11 in Schedule II to the Act (transitional arrangements), any existing consideration (royalty or contractual consideration) that accrued to a community will continue to accrue to a community. The community, however, must annually furnish certain particulars to the Minister regarding the usage and disbursement of the consideration. The Minister may place certain conditions on communities which may include the manner in which the royalty will be used for purposes of promoting rural, regional and local economic development, proper financial control, the compilation of a development plan, the use of the royalty for the benefit of the community, the right of the Minister to intervene if the royalties are not being utilized according to the conditions and the establishment of a trust or company to administer the funds.[799] A Mining Charter was also agreed upon by government and the mining industry that set out the rules of the game with regard to empowerment of formally disadvantaged persons and communities.[800] If the consideration accrues to a natural person, the royalties may still be paid out if the discontinuation thereof will cause undue hardship or if the person uses the consideration or royalty for social upliftment.[801]

199. Various rural communities have mineral deposits such as coal on their land. The mineral rights of these communities were taken away in terms of apartheid legislation.[802] Some communities received their land back in terms of the Restitution of Land Rights Act 22 of 1994.[803] Rural communities or persons from disadvantaged groups who want to mine will have to comply with the requirements of the

796. Sections 17–18.
797. Section 12.
798. Section 12(3).
799. Item 12(3) Sch. II. Such communities or persons must keep records that should be available to inspection by the director general and must have annual audited financial statements.
800. Now referred to as the *Amended Broad Based Socio-Economic Empowerment Charter for the South African Mining and Minerals Industry* of 2010 drafted in terms of s. 100(2) MPRDA – Government Notice 838 in *Government Gazette* 33573 of 20 Sep. 2010.
801. Item 11(7) Sch. II.
802. Development Trust and Land Act 18 of 1936.
803. In *Alexkor Ltd v. Richtersveld Community and Others* 2004 5 SA 460 (CC), a community received their land back in terms of the 1994 Act – the land is subject to diamond mining. The community was also involved in another claim for their mineral rights. In terms of the new mineral legislation

Act. The implementation of environmental management programmes is not only costly, but these communities or groups also need technical assistance in this regard. In order for this Act to operate efficiently, provision should be made for training in this regard. Communities or holders of mining rights should also know their responsibilities regarding the environment.

200. If a person can prove that his or her land has been expropriated in terms of the Act, he or she may claim compensation from the state. The following must, however, be indicated if compensation is claimed, namely the extent and nature of actual loss or damage suffered, the current use of the property, proof of ownership, history of acquisition of the property and the price paid for it, detail of the nature of the property, the market value and the extent of state assistance and benefits received in respect of the property. Other factors that will be taken into account in order to calculate the compensation are the state's obligation to redress past discrimination and the state's commitment to promote equitable access to all South Africa's natural resources in terms of section 25(8) of the Constitution.[804] However, South African mining legislation does not regulate small-scale mining effectively, and illegal mining occurs in abandoned mines or sometimes on traditional land.[805]

201. The 2004 regulations issued in terms of the Act extensively provide for pollution control and waste management regulation.[806] These measures deal, *inter alia*, with air quality, fire prevention, noise management, blasting, vibration and shock management and control, water and pollution control, disposal of waste material, soil pollution and erosion, sanitation of surface and the management of residue stockpiles and deposits.

202. In regulation 63 of GN R527, the principles of pollution control and waste management are set out. The holder of a mining right, prospecting right or mining permit must avoid the generation and production of pollution, waste and mine residue at source or where it cannot be avoided, it should be minimized and recycled or disposed in a responsible and sustainable manner.

203. Regulation 64 of GN R527 stipulates that a holder of a right or permit should comply with all legislation dealing with air quality management and control. The assessment of impacts relating to air quality should form part of the EIA and

---

all minerals belong to the state and the legal question before the court was whether the group had an entitlement to the right or not. *See also Ga-Magashula Community Trust v. Marsfontein and Others* (LCC105/00) [2000] ZALCC 50 (19 Dec. 2000).

804. Item 12 Sch. II. *See* in this regard E. van der Schyff, *Who Owns the Country's Mineral Resources? The Possible Incorporation of the Public Trust Doctrine through section 3(1) of the Mineral and Petroleum Resources Development Act 28 of 2002*, Journal of South African Law 757–768 (2008).

805. *See* in this regard W. Du Plessis and J.M. Pienaar, *Illegal Mining: The Continued Struggle for Mineral Resources, Communities and the Environment*, t. In In the shadow of an African Boabab, (C. Rautenbach (ed), Juta 2018).

806. Part IV of GN R527. These regulations were amended by Government Notice R1288 in *Government Gazette* 26942 of 29 Oct. 2004 and Government Notice R1203 in *Government Gazette* 29431 of 30 Nov. 2006 and have to be read in conjunction with the NEMWA, NEMAQA and NEMA.

environmental management programme or plan.[807] All coal debris and bituminous rock must be deposited in terms of the Mine Health and Safety Act 29 of 1996 at an identified and specified site. The holder of a mining right dealing with coal will be responsible for all damages resulting from the combustion of coal residue stockpiles or deposits.[808]

204. The provisions of the Mine Health and Safety Act 29 of 1996 regarding noise management and control must be complied with as well as other legislation dealing with noise pollution. Noise pollution should also be addressed in the environmental impact assessment or environmental management programme.[809] Many coal mines in South Africa are opencast coal mines and some of them are in the vicinity of towns or settlements. In the case of blasting, the provisions of the Mine Health and Safety Act must be complied with and the matter should also be dealt with in the environmental impact assessment and environmental management programme.[810]

205. The Regulations refer to the provisions in the NWA regarding water management and pollution control at all proposed or existing mining operations. As set out above, water pollution should be taken into account in the compilation of the EIA and the environmental management programme.[811] Mines also have to comply with the specific regulations issued for the control of water pollution at mines.[812]

206. Waste must be disposed of as specified in the environmental management programme and by the NEMWA. The impact of waste should be assessed in the applications for rights or permits. It is stated that waste material from reduction works, beneficiation plants, coal preparation plants, screening and washing installations and generating stations at a mine shall be disposed of in accordance with the environmental management programme and on an approved site. Rubble, litter, garbage, rubbish and any other discards must only be dumped at a demarcated site. Slimes dams and sand dumps may not be established on the bank of any stream, water, river, dam, pan, wetland or lake without the Minister's permission and in consultation with the Department of Human Settlement, Water and Sanitation. Coal debris may not accumulate on any ground where there are surface fissures or cavities as a result of underground operations. This will also be the case if there is a possibility that such fissures or cavities may result.[813]

207. Provision should also made for soil pollution and erosion control. Again, the holder of a right or permit is obliged to manage and control soil pollution and erosion in terms of existing legislation. The impacts of soil erosion and pollution should also be assessed. The spillage of hazardous chemicals into the ground or its

807. Regulation 64(2) GN R527.
808. Regulation 65 GN R527.
809. Regulation 66.
810. Regulation 67.
811. Regulation 68.
812. Government Notice 704 in *Government Gazette* 20119 of 4 Jun. 1999.
813. Regulation 69 GN R527.

migration into surrounding soils must be prevented. Oil, grease and hydraulic fluids must be disposed of in the correct manner at an acceptable waste disposal site. The acidification, salination and mineralization of soils through seepage of polluted water and the irrigation of land must take place within the prescribed limits or as set out in the environmental management programme or plan. The chemical and physical properties of topsoil used for rehabilitation should not be changed by the introduction of foreign material, gravel, rock, rubble or mine residue.[814]

Provision is also made for proper toilet facilities for workers to prevent pollution of groundwater.[815]

814. Regulation 70 GN R527.
815. Regulation 71 GN R527.

Chapter 3. Exploitation

208. Mining is one of the activities that has a severe impact on the environment.[816] The impacts range from those impacting on soil, water, human health, the built-up environment, to air, plants and animal life, and differ from one mining activity to another. The aim of mining companies is to maximize the extraction of ore in South Africa to ensure wealth creation. Their first priority is not necessarily the environment.

209. For many years, mining companies and the former DME have made decisions regarding mining and environmental issues. The Department was the decision-maker not only with regard to licences but also in approving the environmental management programmes of the mines. In the 1990s, a conflict arose, as it was felt that all decision-making with regard to environmental matters should rest with the then DEAT.

As is apparent from the MPRDA and subsequent amendments and proposals for amendments, the Department of Mineral Resources and Energy retains all decision-making powers regarding mining matters, whether on environmental issues or not. Since September 2014, the Minister of Mineral Resources and Energy has the authority to appoint his or her own mineral resource inspectors to investigate any environmental transgressions on mines.[817] However, the Constitution[818] and the NEMA[819] encourage cooperative governance.[820] The Department of Mineral Resources and Energy, Department of Environmental Affairs, Forestry and Fisheries and Department of Human Settlement, Water and Sanitation are aligning their application processes to ensure better integration and coordination of the authorization system. The NEMA also allows for the issuing of an integrated environmental authorization.[821]

210. In many instances, mines in the previous dispensation provided their own water. Since the introduction of the NWA, new priorities have been identified and the mining sector has 'to compete on equal footing with other interests which may

816. *White Paper on a Mineral Policy for South Africa* of 1998 – Government Notice R2359 in *Government Gazette* 19344 of 10 Oct. 1998.
817. Section 31BB NEMA. The Minister of Environmental Affairs, Forestry and Fisheries appoints all other environmental inspectors in the Environmental Management Inspectorate who are responsible for the investigation of all other environmental transgressions. This Inspectorate is under the control of the Department of Environmental Affairs, Forestry and Fisheries.
818. Sections 40 and 41.
819. Chapter 2.
820. For a discussion of the conflict, *see also* J. Nel & W. Du Plessis, *Unpacking Integrated Environmental Management – a Step Closer to Effective Cooperative Governance?* 19 SA Public Law 181–190 (2004); W. Du Plessis, *Legal Mechanisms for Cooperative Governance in South Africa: Successes and Failures*, 23 SA Public Law 87–110 (2008); L.J. Kotzé and A. Du Plessis, *A Gold Rush to Nowhere? The Rights-based Approach to Environmental Governance in South Africa's Mining Sector in Question*, 47 Verfässung und Recht Übersee 447–481 (2014).
821. Sections 24(2C) and 24L(1) NEMA.

be of greater or lesser importance when it comes to demands placed on the use of the country's resources. The playing fields have been levelled'.[822]

In terms of the Water Services Act 108 of 1997, industrial use of water is regulated. In terms of section 7(1), no person may obtain water for industrial use from any source other than the distribution systems of a water service provider nominated by the relevant water services authority. In the same manner, no person may dispose of industrial effluent other than in the approved manner.[823] A person who obtained water from a source or disposed of industrial effluent into that source before the commencement of the Act has to apply for a new authorization.[824] Mines could in terms of the Water Services Act also be service providers if they provide water to communities or individuals outside the mining area.

The NWA has given the Minister of Human Settlements, Water and Sanitation the responsibility of regulating water use. In order to ensure equitable allocation and beneficial use of water in the public interest, water use is defined among other things as including activities which reduce stream flow, waste discharges and disposals altering a watercourse or removing underground water for certain purposes.[825]

Previous mining legislation gave certain persons the right to use water (water rights) as a right ancillary to or attached to existing mineral rights or mining rights. These water rights were, however, not uniform in character and were granted on different terms and conditions, depending on the legislation authorizing such issue.[826] Section 4(2) of the NWA recognizes these rights as constituting a lawful water use, which use has to be registered in terms of section 26(1)(c) of the Act. Since most of these water rights are linked to mineral rights or mining rights, it means any enforcement of the mineral rights or mining rights in a form of a prospecting or mining right will have a direct impact on the water quality and the availability of such water as a resource. The existing lawful use of mines, therefore, continues (subject to the conditions in section 34 of NWA) until reviewed by the Department of Human Settlements, Water and Sanitation. This Department drafted regulations with limitations, restrictions and prohibitions relating specifically to mining activities aimed at the protection of water resources.[827]

In terms of the Regulations, a person intending to mine has to notify the Department of Human Settlement, Water and Sanitation at least fourteen days before the commencement of the mining activity.[828] An existing activity or mine must submit a copy of its environmental management programme and amendments to the

---

822. C. Dixon, *The Puzzle of Media and Sector Legislation: Putting the Pieces Together to Create the Legal Picture for the Mining Industry*, 99 The Journal of the South African Institute of Mining and Metallurgy 149 (1999).
823. Section 7(2).
824. Section 7(3).
825. Section 21. *See*, e.g., Government Notice 406 in *Government Gazette* 40229 of 26 Aug. 2016 providing for a general authorization in relation to impeding or diverting the flow of water in a watercourse (s. 21(c)) and altering the bed, banks, course or characteristics of a watercourse (s. 21(i)).
826. For example, there were rights granted in terms of the Precious Stones Act 73 of 1964 and the Mining Rights Act 20 of 1967.
827. Government Notice R104 in *Government Gazette* 20119 of 4 Jun. 1999, the Regulations have been made in terms of s. 26(1)(b), (g) and (i) of the NWA.
828. Regulation 2(1).

Department.[829] The Department must be notified if the activity is suspended and when it resumes. In cases of emergency incidents or potential emergency incidents involving a water resource, the Department must also be notified. Detailed information must be furnished about the incident and measures the applicant intends to take to correct or prevent the reoccurrence of the incident.[830]

No person may use material that is likely to cause pollution to a water resource for the construction of a dam or other impoundment or for any other purpose that is likely to cause pollution of a water resource.[831] Every person in control of a mine must have the capacity to determine, construct, maintain, operate and confine a clean water system at the mine to avoid spillage into a dirty water system for more than once in fifty years. A person in control of a mine must collect dirty water into a dirty water system and be able to design, construct, maintain and operate a dirty water system at a mine so that it is not likely to spill into any clean water system for more than once in fifty years.[832]

Every person in control of a mine must take reasonable measures to prevent water containing waste from entering any water resource, to construct and maintain all water systems, have effective measures to minimize the flow of surface water or floodwater into *inter alia* mine workings and opencast workings through cracks or openings.[833] Access to areas that contain any poisonous, toxic or injurious substances must be restricted by fencing-off those areas. Such an area may not be used for any purpose if such use might cause or is likely to cause pollution of a water resource.[834]

Any cessation of mining activities, whether permanent or temporary, must have all pollution control measures in place.[835] There are additional regulations dealing with the rehabilitation of coal residue deposits, technical investigation, monitoring and offences and penalties.[836]

211. In cases where a mining activity is being carried out, the owner or person in control has the responsibility of avoiding pollution of the water resource.[837] The mining companies also have to control emergency incidents according to section 20. Any spills must *inter alia* be reported and cleaned up. The question still remains what the relationship between the NWA, NEMA and the MPRDA would be in the case of the control of pollution and emergency incidents. In 2005, for example, the Department of Human Settlement, Water and Sanitation applied for an interdict against three mining companies that did not comply with conditions regarding the

829. Regulation 2(2)(a).
830. Regulation 2(2)(b) and (c). *See also* s. 19 NWA.
831. Regulation 5.
832. Regulation 6.
833. Regulation 7.
834. Regulation 8.
835. Regulation 9.
836. On the rehabilitation of mines, *see* S. Hartzer and W. Du Plessis, *The liability of historical mine authorization holders for rehabilitation of old order mine dumps*, Southern African Public Law 469–493 (2014).
837. Section 19.

pumping of water in the area, resulting in flooding and posing a danger to the community and surrounding mines.[838] The court ordered the mine to comply with its obligations.

In terms of sections 45 and 46 of the MPRDA, the Minister may recover costs incurred in the case of ecological degradation, pollution or environmental damage. The Minister may direct the holder of a permit or right to assess the impact and to take certain measures. If the holder fails to comply, the Minister may take such measures as is necessary to protect the health and well-being of affected persons, to remedy ecological degradation or to prevent further pollution. The Minister may, based on a High Court order, seize and sell the property of the holder to cover the expenses of the implementation of the measures. If the holder of the right or permit is deceased or cannot be traced, the Minister may instruct the regional manager to take the necessary steps. The financial provision made by the holder must be used, or if not available, funds allocated by Parliament. If the land is remedied it should be noted against the title deed of the land in the deeds registry.

212. Mines have to take notice of the sections in the NWA dealing with the safety of dams.[839] The definition of 'dams' refers to 'any existing or proposed structure, which is capable of containing, storing or impounding water (including temporary impoundment or storage) whether that water contains any substance or not'.[840] Sludge dams can also be interpreted as a 'dam with a safety risk'[841] – these dams have to be registered.[842]

213. Dust is controlled by the Minister of Environmental Affairs, Forestry and Fisheries or the MEC responsible for environment in a province.[843] Dust control in mining areas is also the obligation of the Department of Mineral Resources and Energy,[844] resulting again in having more than one department responsible for mining matters. If the mine will cease its activities within five years, the owner of the mine must inform the Minister of Environmental Affairs, Forestry and Fisheries in

838. *Minister of Water Affairs and Forestry v. Stilfontein Gold Mining Company Ltd and Others* 2006 JOL 17516 (W); *Harmony Gold Mining Co Ltd v. Regional Director: Free State, DWAF* 2006 SCA 65; *Kebble v. Minister of Water Affairs* 2007 SCA 111; *Harmony Gold Mining Company Ltd v. Regional Director: Free State Department of Water Affairs* 2014 3 SA 149 (SCA).

839. Sections 117–123.

840. Section 117(b).

841. Section 117(c) read with s. 121 (factors to be considered in declaring a dam or category of dams with safety risk). *See also* Government Notice R1560 in *Government Gazette* 10366 of 25 Jul. 1986.

842. Section 120. NWA prescribes the control measures that an owner of a dam must introduce to avoid the risk – s. 118.

843. Dust is regulated in s. 32 of the NEMAQA. The definition of 'pollution' in s. 1 also defines 'air pollution' as 'any change in the composition of the air caused by smoke, soot, dust (including fly ash), cinders, solid particles of any kind, gases, fumes, aerosols and odorous substances'. National Dust Control Regulations were published in 2013 in terms of NEMAQA – Government Notice R827 in *Government Gazette* 36974 of 1 Nov. 2013.

844. Section 6(2)(a)–(b) – *see also* dust control regulations under the repealed Mines and Works Act 27 of 1956 and Government Notice R992 in *Government Gazette* 2741 of 26 Jun. 1970 – Ch. 10. These regulations were not repealed.

writing about the fact. The owner must also convince the Minister that the necessary plans are in place to rehabilitate the area and to ensure dust control.[845]

214. Coal mines cannot hide behind the fact that the Department of Mineral Resources and Energy is the only responsible authority that they have to deal with. They can no longer ignore the legislation that is applicable to them. They must adhere to all legislation they have not explicitly been exempted from. They have to adhere not only to the legislation but also to the various international conventions and treaties that are applicable to them.

In order to solve the problems, it is suggested that the rights and obligations of mining concerns, government officials and all interested and affected parties in terms of legislation and other measures must be spelled out clearly, especially when it gets to decision-making. This should also be done with regard to the various government departments in the national, provincial and local sphere. The NEMA can be used as the tool to ensure cooperative governance as indicated above.

215. However, the importance of mining cannot be ignored. A large section of the economy in South Africa is dependent on mining – the coal industry is the main source of energy in this country. Coal mining also provides jobs to a great number of people. In a country like South Africa, where development is urgently needed, mines cannot be ignored – they also cannot be closed down just because they cause damage to the environment. A solution must be found, where mines take the responsibility for their actions and where proper plans and systems are introduced to ensure legal compliance and to give effect to section 24 of the 1996 Constitution.[846]

845. Section 33 NEMAQA.

846. *See Director: Mineral Development, Gauteng Region and Another v. Save the Vaal Environment and Others* [1999] 2 All SA 381 (A); *Harmony Gold Mining Company Ltd v. Regional Director: Free State Department of Water Affairs* 2014 3 SA 149 (SCA).

Chapter 4. Transportation

216. Coal is transferred by rail rather than by road. If the coal is transferred by road, the National Road Traffic Act 93 of 1996 and in the case of road and rail the Road Transportation Act 74 of 1977 will apply. If non-hazardous goods are transferred, a permit has to be obtained.[847] The National Road Traffic Act deals mainly with driver licences, the fitness of vehicles, operator fitness, road safety and dangerous goods. There are no specific regulations dealing with coal only.

847. Sections 12–29 of the Road Transportation Act 74 of 1977. If hazardous, the Hazardous Substances Act may apply.

Chapter 5. Consumption

217. Coal is mostly used for electricity generation and exportation – *see* Part I. On the health issues associated with the use of coal in households for cooking and heating, *see* the General Introduction, Chapter 1, § 5 III.

Part V. Interaction Between Energy Law and Environmental Law

Chapter 1. General

218. The generation of electricity as the main source of energy in South Africa has for many years been coal-based. Other forms of energy were also used, but not on the same scale. As the generation of energy was state-controlled, not much attention was given to the environment and the legislation protecting the environment.

Petroleum, however, was a scarce commodity in the apartheid era, and, therefore, the industries providing petroleum were also not strictly regulated.

The matters regarding nuclear energy were regarded as confidential information and, therefore, controlled only by the state.

219. The new democratic dispensation in South Africa also brought about new thinking about the environment. The Constitution includes an environmental clause, and since 1994 numerous new environmental acts have been introduced. Suddenly South Africa could participate in the international market again. With this came the realization that in order to import and export goods, South African industries will have to comply not only with their own country's standards but also with international standards. Eskom, Sasol and various other energy-generating industries embarked on a process to voluntarily obtain ISO 14001 certification. In some instances in the absence of South African standards, these companies strive to comply with either international or American standards.

220. Since the introduction of the interim Constitution in 1993[848] and the final Constitution in 1996, the courts also make use of the environmental clause in the Constitution to interpret legislation. In the case of *The Director: Mineral Development, Gauteng Region and Sasol Mining (Pty) Ltd v. Save the Vaal Environment,*[849] the court made use of the environmental clause in the Constitution to force the Director: Mineral Development to heed the objections of landowners in the region

848. 1993 Constitution.
849. [1999] All SA 381 (A). *See* in this regard also M. Kidd, *Vaal Environment Saved? The Director: Mineral Development, Gauteng and Sasol Mining (Pty) Ltd v. Save and Others*, 6 SAJELP 149–160 (1999); G. Ferreira, W. Du Plessis & K. van der Walt, *A License to Mine, Audi Alteram Partem and NEMA*, 6 SAJELP 245–256 (1999); P.J. Badenhorst & M. Carnelley, *Application for a Mining License and the Audi Alteram Partem Rule*, 63 Tydskrif vir Hedendaags Romeins-Hollandse Reg 689–698 (2000).

before he could issue a temporary mining permit. In terms of the Mineral Act 50 of 1991, he was not obliged to do so. The fact that the courts are prepared to take environmental considerations into account is an important factor that brought about change in the energy industry's thinking.[850] This case was followed by several others, and in the *Bengwenyama Minerals (Pty) Ltd v. Genorah Resources (Pty) Ltd*,[851] the court again confirmed the importance of consultation.

850. *See also*, among others, *Minister of Health and Welfare v. Woodcarb (Pty) Ltd* 1996 3 SA 155 (N); *Wildlife Society of Southern Africa v. Minister of Environmental Affairs and Tourism of the Republic of South Africa* 1996 3 SA 1095 (Tk); *Van Huyssteen NO v. Minister of Environmental Affairs and Tourism* 1995 9 BCLR 1191 (C); *Bareki NO and Another v. Gencor Ltd and Others* 2006 8 BCLR 920 (T); *Fuel Retailers Association of Southern Africa v. Director-General Environmental Management, Department of Agriculture, Conservation and Environment, Mpumalanga Province and Others* 2007 10 BCLR 1059 (CC); *Joseph and Others v. City of Johannesburg* 2010 4 SA 55 (CC); *HTF Developers v. Minister of Environmental Affairs and Tourism and Others* [2007] 4 All SA 1108 (SCA); *Maccsand (Pty) Ltd v. City of Cape Town and Others* 2012 4 SA 181 (CC). *See also* E. Couzens & M. Lewis, *South Africa*. In International Encyclopaedia of Laws: Environmental Law, paras 72–79 (K. Deketelaere, ed., Kluwer Law International 2013).

851. 2011 4 SA 113 (CC) [62]-[68].

Chapter 2. Constitution of the Republic of South Africa, 1996

221. The energy industry is obliged to take notice of the Constitution of the Republic of South Africa, 1996, as section 8 states that Chapter 2 of the Constitution (Bill of Rights) binds both natural and juristic persons.[852] Section 24 of the Constitution of the Republic of South Africa, 1996, states as follows:

> Everyone has the right –
> (a) to an environment that is not harmful to their health or well-being; and
> (b) to have the environment protected, for the benefit of present and future generations, through reasonable legislative and other measures that –
> (i) prevent pollution and ecological degradation;
> (ii) promote conservation; and
> (iii) secure ecologically sustainable development and use of natural resources while promoting justifiable economic and social development.

222. Everyone has a right and a duty to ensure that the environment is not detrimental to another's health and well-being.[853] The duty is placed on the state, however, to enforce section 24.[854] The state does not always have the capacity to do so, and it results in either having the legislation ignored or the implementation of self-regulation (ISO 14001) by industry, including the energy industry.[855]

---

852. *See also* J. Glazewski & L. du Toit, *Environmental Law*, 5-1-5-54 (2nd edn, LexisNexis 2014 Service Issue 2).
853. *See also* A.A. Du Plessis, *The promise of 'wellbeing' in Section 24 of the Constitution of South Africa*, South African Journal on Human Rights (2018) https://doi.org/10.1080/02587203.2018.1475116.
854. *See also* A.A. Du Plessis, *Perceptive Approaches to the Interpretation and Realization of South Africa's Constitutional Environmental Right*, 6 SAJELP 129–156 (2009); A.A Du Plessis, *A Government in Deep Water? Some Thoughts on the State's Duties in Relation to Water Arising from South Africa's Bill of Rights*, 19 Review of European Community and International Environmental Law (RECIEL) 316–327 (2010); A.A. Du Plessis, *South Africa's Constitutional Environmental Right Generously Interpreted: What is in it for Poverty?* 27 South African Journal on Human Rights 299–307 (2011); A. Du Plessis and A. van der Berg, *RA Le Sueur v Ethekwini Municipality 2013 JDR 0178 (KZP): An Environmental Law Reading*, Stellenbosch Law Review 25(3) 580–594 (2014); L. Chamberlain, *Beyond Litigation: The Need for Creativity in Working to Realise Environmental Rights* 13(1) *LEAD Journal* (2017) http://lead-journal.org/2017.htm (accessed 16 May 2019).
855. If a mine is, for example, in possession of a certified internationally recognized environmental management system (ISO 14001), it may in some instances be exempted from an Environmental Management Programme Performance Assessment in terms of Government Notice R801 in *Government Gazette* 20219 of 25 Jun. 1999 – regulation 15(18)(2). *See also* J. Nel & W. Du Plessis, *ISO14001 and Environmental Law*, 9 SAJELP 51–60 (2002); J. Nel & L.J. Kotzé, *Environmental Management: An Introduction*, 10. In Fuggle and Rabie's Environmental Management in South Africa (H.A. Strydom & N.D. King, eds, Juta 2009); Nel, J & R. Alberts. *Environmental Management and Environmental Law in South Africa: An Introduction*, 1–55. In Fuggle and Rabie's Environmental Management in South Africa (King, N.D, Strydom, H.A. & F.P. Retief, eds, 3rd edn, Juta 2018).

223. Another question that arises is whether section 24 has horizontal application or only vertical application. Writers argue that section 24(a) has horizontal application due to the nature of the right and the duty imposed by the right.[856] From the wording of section 24(b), it is clear that the right can only be vertically enforced, although reference to 'other measures' may perhaps include instruments such as ISO 14001, which changes the argument.[857]

224. Section 24 is not an absolute right but is limited in the sense that on the one hand the environment must be protected, while on the other hand justifiable economic and social development must be promoted. In a country such as South Africa, development is urgently needed and a too strict interpretation of the right could eventually lead to no development taking place at all. In the case of development, the emphasis is shifted towards environmental and social sustainable development rather than development for the sake of development itself.[858]

225. The energy industry has to take notice of certain other rights in the Constitution. In terms of section 25(2), property may be expropriated in terms of a law of general application for a public purpose or in the public interest. The public interest includes the nation's commitment to land reform, and to bring about equitable access to South Africa's natural resources.[859] Section 25, therefore, allows the state to become the custodian of all South Africa's natural resources. The NWA and the MPRDA are examples of legislation that aim to achieve equitable access to natural resources.

226. Section 25 deals with property. In the 1993 Constitution rights in land were protected. Section 25 of the 1996 Constitution only states that no one may be deprived of property except in terms of law of general application and no law may permit arbitrary deprivation of property. Property may be expropriated in the public interest. The public interest includes the nation's commitment to land reform and to bring about equitable access to all South Africa's natural resources. Property is not

856. Section 8 of the Constitution. *See* in this regard G.M. Ferreira, *Grondwetlike waardes en sosio-ekonomiese regte met verwysing na die reg op 'n skoon en gesonde omgewing*, Tydskrif vir Suid-Afrikaanse Reg 285–303 (1999); G.M. Ferreira, *Volhoubare ontwikkeling, regverdigbare ontwikkeling en die fundamentele reg op 'n skoon en gesonde omgewing*, Tydskrif vir Suid-Afrikaanse Reg 434–453 (1999); J. Glazewski, *Environmental Law*, 74–75 (2nd edn, Butterworths 2005).

857. *See also* W. Du Plessis, *Hichange – A New Direction in Environmental Matters? – Hichange Investments (Pty) Ltd v. Cape Produce Co (Pty) Ltd T/A Pelts Products and Others*, 11 SAJELP 135–151 (2004); J. Nel & W. Du Plessis, *ISO 14001 and Environmental Law*, 9 SAJELP 51–59 (2002).

858. *See* T. Scheepers, *A Practical Guide to Law and Development*, 33–105 (Juta 2000). *See also Fuel Retailers Association of Southern Africa v. Director-General Environmental Management, Department of Agriculture, Conservation and Environment, Mpumalanga Province and Others* 2007 10 BCLR 1059 (CC) where the court emphasized the economic dimension of sustainable development. This case was discussed in detail in the SAJELP 15:1 (2008).

859. Section 4(a). Property may be deprived in terms of a law of general application (s. 25(1)), and it is important to note that s. 4(b) states that property is not limited to land. *See also* W. Freedman, *The Constitutional Protection of Property, the Conservation of the Environment, and the Doctrine of Constructive Expropriation*, 9 SAJELP 61–71 (2002); W. Freedman, *Environmental Conservation and the Concept of Ownership as an Absolute and Unrestricted Right*, 8 SAJELP 128 (2001).

limited to land. Persons with insecure tenure are entitled to tenure, which is legally secure, or to comparable redress. The implications of section 25 are that natural resources must be accessible to all and that it can be expropriated to ensure land restitution. This has implications for national parks and other nature reserve areas.[860]

227. Section 8 of the Constitution states that the Bill of Rights applies to all law and binds all the different levels of the state, natural and juristic persons. Juristic persons are also entitled to the rights in the Constitution. Section 9 (equality clause) also promotes the achievement of equality, legislative and other measures designed to protect or advance persons that were disadvantaged by unfair discrimination (section 9(2)). This could allow the state, for example, to reduce the environmental laws applicable to implement a housing or development project.[861]

228. In terms of section 22, every citizen has the right to choose a trade, occupation or profession freely. The practice of a trade may be regulated by law, which includes environmental law. This right does not give a carte blanche to the energy industry to ignore all laws in order to pursue its trade.

Every person has a right to adequate housing, and the state must within its available resources achieve this right in terms of section 26. This may also have implications for the environment as stated above.[862]

In terms of section 27, everyone has the right to have access to, *inter alia*, sufficient food and water, which again the state must provide within its available resources. Read with sections 25 and 26, the implications become even clearer that the environment may suffer as a result of this.[863]

---

860. *See also* E. van der Schyff, *Who Owns the Country's Mineral Resources? The Possible Incorporation of the Public Trust Doctrine through Section 3(1) of the Mineral and Petroleum Resources Development Act 28 of 2002*, Journal of South African Law 757–768 (2008); E. van der Schyff & G. Viljoen, *Water and the Public Trust Doctrine – the South African Perspective*, The Journal for Transdisciplinary Research in Southern Africa 339–353 (2008); E. van der Schyff, *Unpacking the Public Trust Doctrine: A Journey into Foreign Territory*, 13 PELJ 122–189 (2010).

861. *See*, for example, the *Minister of Public Works v. Kyalami Ridge Ratepayer's Association* 2001 3 SA 1151 (CC) case where the applicants argued that the interim resettlement of a community in a pristine area should comply with environmental and planning legislation. The case involved the removal of informal settlers on the bank of the Juskei River – the river was flooding and there was a possible health, safety and environmental risk to the people. Various government departments were granted an interdict to remove these people to the Leeukop Prison Area in order to provide shelter. The court shied away from the environmental issues and relied on s. 26 of the Constitution the right to shelter. Another argument that the court could have used was the s. 9 argument. *See also* W. Freedman, *Environmental Conservation and the Concept of Ownership as an Absolute and Unrestricted Right: Minister of Public Works and Others v. Kyalami Ridge Environmental Association and Another*, 8 SAJELP 128–134 (2001); M. Kidd, *The Constitutional Court's dilution of NEMA: Minister of Public Works and Others v. Kyalami Ridge Environmental Association and Another*, 8 SAJELP 117–127 (2001).

862. *See*, e.g., *Residents of Joe Slovo Community, Western Cape v. Thubelisha Homes and Others* 2010 3 SA 454 (CC); *Government of the Republic of South Africa and Others v. Grootboom and Others* 2001 1 SA 46 (CC); *Mbatha and Others v. City of Johannesburg Metropolitan Municipality and Others* (40067/2014) [2014] ZAGPJHC 370 (5 Dec. 2014).

863. *See also Mazibuko and Others v. City of Johannesburg and Others* 2010 4 SA 1 (CC); E. Couzens, *Avoiding Mazibuko: Water Security and Constitutional Rights in Southern African Case Law*, 18(4)

Section 32 provides that everyone has the right of access to (a) any information held by the state and (b) any information held by another person that is required for the exercising and protection of any rights. To give effect to this right, national legislation must be enacted. The Promotion of Access to Information Act 2 of 2000 was enacted to give effect to this constitutional provision. Several court decisions deal with the right so access to information and a number of them with the right of access to environmental information.[864]

Section 33 provides for just administrative action. In environmental matters, one mostly deals with administrative actions of state, provincial and local authority organs. The section states that everyone has the right to administrative action that is lawful, reasonable and procedurally fair. Written reasons have to be given for decisions that adversely affect persons (e.g., permits, licences, etc. that were not granted). National legislation had to be enacted to give effect to this section. The Promotion of Administrative Justice Act 3 of 2000 serves this purpose.[865] The rights in the 1996 Constitution may be limited in terms of laws of general application to the extent that the limitation is reasonable and justifiable in an open and democratic society based on human dignity, equality and freedom, taking into account all relevant factors mentioned in the section.[866]

229. Chapter 3 of the Constitution makes provision for cooperative government. The principles of cooperative government promote effective, transparent, accountable government and not assuming any power or function except those conferred on the different spheres of government by the Constitution. The different spheres of government must cooperate with each other by support and assistance, informing

---

Potchefstroom Electronic Law Journal 1161–1186 (2016); P. King and C. Reddell, *Public participation and water use rights*, 18(4) Potchefstroom Electronic Law Journal 943–968. Also *see* A. Belinsjkij, L.J. Kotzé and O. Fuo, *Domestic manifestations of international law's right to water: A comparative analysis of emerging rights obligations in Finland and South Africa*,' 25 African Journal of International and Comparative Law 261–292 (2017).

864. *See*, e.g., *Company Secretary of Arcelormittal South Africa and Another v. Vaal Environmental Justice Alliance* (69/2014) [2014] ZASCA 184 (26 Nov. 2014); *Centre for Environmental Rights v. Director-General: Department of Mineral Resources*: Deemed refusal of access to information about financial provision for rehabilitation under the Mineral and Petroleum Resources Development Act, 2002 (MPRDA); Centre for Environmental Rights, Barricading the doors, February 2013, http://cer.org.za/wp-content/uploads/2013/03/Barricading-The-Doors-Feb-20131.pdf (accessed 9 Jan. 2014); W. Du Plessis, *Access to Information* 197–221. In Environmental Compliance and Enforcement in South Africa: Legal Perspectives (A.R. Paterson & L.J. Kotzé, eds, Juta 2009); W. Du Plessis & S. de la Harpe, *The Duty to Disclose and the Right to Refuse: Undefined Dilemma of Environmental Practitioners: South Africa and other Jurisdictions*, 14 SAJELP 83–103 (2007).

865. *See also* C. Hoexter, *Administrative Law in South Africa* (2nd edn, Juta 2012); M. Murcott, *The Role of Administrative Law in Enforcing Socio-Economic Rights: Revisiting Joseph*, 29 South African Journal of Human Rights 481–495 (2013); E. Bray, *Administrative Justice* in *Environmental Compliance and Enforcement in South Africa: Legal Perspective*, 152–196 (A. Paterson & L.J. Kotzé, eds, Juta 2009).

866. Section 36.

each other of matters of common interest, coordinate their actions and legislation with one another and adhere to agreed procedures.[867] These principles are included in the NEMA.[868]

The objects of local government include promoting a safe and healthy environment as well as social and economic development.[869] Municipalities can no longer hide behind the fact that they do not have capacity. There is a Constitutional obligation on them to ensure a clean and healthy environment within the framework of social and economic development.

867. Section 41. Municipalities have to comply with s. 154.

868. *See also* P.G.W. Henderson, *Some thoughts on Distinctive Principles of South African Environmental Law*, 8 SAJELP 139–184 (2001).

869. Section 152.

Chapter 3. Environmental Framework Legislation

230. In 1998, South Africa adopted legislation which can be regarded as environmental framework legislation.[870] The NEMA partially repealed the ECA. The two acts should be read together as the overarching environmental framework legislation in South Africa. NEMA read with the ECA has some of the characteristics of environmental framework legislation, but is still lacking in some other respects.[871]

231. The purpose of the ECA was to coordinate all environmental matters. The Act did not serve its purpose. One of the reasons was that the institutions created in terms of the Act did not manage to ensure collaboration between different line ministries.

In terms of section 2 of the Act, an environmental policy was issued.[872] The policy was drafted by the then DEAT. The policy was published for comment in the *Government Gazette*. There was, however, no general consultation process in the drafting of the policy. During 1996–1997, a wide consultative process (known as Consultative Process (CONNEP)) was followed to draft a new policy. The *White Paper on Environmental Management* was published in 1997,[873] which eventually led to the implementation of NEMA.

232. Part IV of the ECA dealt with pollution but was not a general codification of pollution measures; it placed a prohibition on littering only and made provision for a permit system for waste sites (mostly municipal waste sites).[874]

---

870. J. Nel & W. Du Plessis, *An Evaluation of NEMA Based on a Generic Framework for Environmental Framework Legislation*, 8 SAJELP 1–37 (2001). Environmental framework legislation aims to define overarching and generic principles in which sector-specific legislation is embedded as well as to enhance cooperative environmental governance among fragmented line ministries. Also *see*, Oosthuizen, M., Van der Linde, M. & E. Basson, *National Environmental Management Act 107 of 1994 (NEMA)*, 125–207. In Fuggle and Rabie's Environmental Management in South Africa (King, N.D, Strydom, H.A. & F.P. Retief, eds, 3rd edn, Juta 2018).
871. Some of the aspects include a lack of definition of the roles and responsibilities of the different role players; there is no indication of the relationship between NEMA and other environmental legislation and certain command and control instruments (such as compliance auditing, a single authorization system, reporting by the private sector). Economical instruments are to a lesser extent included. *See also* J. Nel, *Unsustainable EIA Partnerships: Poorly-Defined Rights, Roles, Responsibilities and Duties of EIA Stakeholders*, 8 SAJELP, 103–118 (2001).
872. Government Notice 51 in *Government Gazette* 15428 of 21 Jan. 1994. Since s. 2 has been repealed, it is questionable whether the policy is still enforceable. J. Glazewski, *Environmental Law*, 159 (2nd edn, Butterworths 2005), argues that the policy can still be regarded as law in terms of the saving clause in s. 51 in NEMA. In *Corium (Pty) Ltd v. Myburgh Park Langebaan* 1995 3 SA 51 (C), the court disallowed a development next to a national park based on the enabling provision namely s. 2, and not on the policy itself – *see also* Glazewski 159.
873. Government Notice 1096 in *Government Gazette* 18164 of 28 Jul. 1997.
874. Section 19 read with s. 19A (removal of litter) and s. 20 dealt with waste permits.

233. Government embarked on a process to integrate all legislation dealing with waste by publishing the *White Paper on Integrated Pollution and Waste Management*.[875] The White Paper culminated in the NEMWA and the NEMAQA. NEMWA replaced the ECA's provisions dealing with waste.

In 2002, the then Minister of Environmental Affairs and Tourism published regulations dealing with the banning of thin plastic bags.[876] Plastic bags are a by-product of the petroleum industry. The petroleum industry indicated that the creation and use of plastic bags are less environmentally sensitive than the production of paper bags. As a result of these discussions, specifications regarding the thickness of plastic bags were promulgated.[877]

234. The ECA was the first act to introduce environmental impact assessments (EIA) in South Africa. The first EIA regulations were issued in 1997 and subsequent lists amended and replaced the initial lists.[878] Once an application was approved, a record of decision was issued. This process was replaced by section 24 of NEMA, whereby applicants have to apply for an environmental authorization.

235. The NEMA follows a different approach than the ECA.[879] The Act relies on principles which apply to all organs of state that may significantly affect the environment.[880] The principles apply alongside other considerations, such as the state's responsibility to fulfil the social and economic rights in Chapter 2 of the Constitution, serve as a general framework within which environmental management and implementation plans must be formulated and as guidelines for decision-making by government departments. The principles must also guide the interpretation, implementation and administration of the Act.

Various principles are listed in section 2(2) stating that 'environmental management must place people and their needs at the forefront of its concern, and serve their physical, developmental, cultural and social interests equitably. Development must be socially, environmentally and economically sustainable'.[881]

---

875. Government Notice 227 in *Government Gazette* 20978 of 17 Mar. 2000.

876. General Notice R543 in *Government Gazette* 23393 of 9 May 2002; Government Notice R651 in *Government Gazette* 36808 of 6 Sep. 2013. *See also* E. Witbooi, *Plastic Bag Regulation in South Africa: Just a Load of Rubbish?* 10 SAJELP 67–91 (2003).

877. General Notice R522 in *Government Gazette* 243734 of 17 Apr. 2003 – proposed compulsory specification for plastic carrier bags in terms of the Standards Act 29 of 1993; General Notice R625 in *Government Gazette* 24839 of 9 May 2003 specifications of plastic carrier bags and plastic flat bags.

878. Sections 21, 22 and 26. Government Notices 1183 and 1184 in *Government Gazette* 18261 of 5 Sep. 1997.

879. *See* W. Bray, *Cooperative Governance in the Context of the National Environmental Management Act 107 of 1998*, 6 SAJELP 1–8 (1999); E. Couzens, *NEMA – A Step Closer to Coherence?* 6 SAJELP 13–20 (1999); F. Soltau, *The National Environmental Management Act and Liability for Environmental Damage*, 6 SAJELP 21–32 (1999); R. Lawrence, *How Manageable is South Africa's New Framework of Environmental Management?* 6 SAJELP 61–66 (1999); J. Glazewski, *Environmental Law*, 133–166 (2nd edn, Butterworths 2005).

880. Section 2.

881. Section 2(3).

In section 2(4), various factors are listed when one deals with the term sustainable development. These include that the disturbance of ecosystems and loss of biological diversity are avoided, or where they cannot be avoided, minimized and remedied; that waste is to be avoided or minimized, reused or recycled; that environmental justice must be pursued; that all interested and affected parties' participation in environmental governance must be promoted; and that decisions must be taken in an open and transparent manner.

Although these principles are not directly applicable to the private sector, one can argue that they are indirectly applicable. It would be in the private sector's interest to ensure that they comply with these principles as they form the basis of decision-making by government.

236. The Act initially made provision for the National Environmental Advisory Forum[882] that had to advise the then Minister of Environmental Affairs and Tourism on the application and monitoring of the principles of the Act, as well as on environmental management and governance. The first forum was established in 2005, including among others people from industry, academia and environmental activists.

The Act also provided for a Committee for Environmental Co-ordination[883] consisting of the Directors General of various government departments. The functions of the committee were *inter alia* to promote integration and coordination of environmental functions by organs of state and to make recommendations on the harmonization of environmental functions in all national departments and spheres of government. The section dealing with these committees was repealed in 2009. The Minister of Environmental Affairs, Forestry and Fisheries may now establish any forum or committee she or he may wish and may determine the functions and composition of such committees.[884]

237. The point of departure of the Act is cooperative governance. Cooperative governance is one of the principles set out in the Constitution.[885] Cooperative governance is to be effected by the environmental implementation and management plans.[886] The Departments of Environmental Affairs, Forestry and Fisheries, Rural

882. Sections 3–6.
883. Sections 7–10.
884. Section 3A.
885. For other forms of cooperative governance and problems experienced, *see* W. Du Plessis, *Legal Mechanisms for Cooperative Governance in South Africa: Successes and Failures*, 23 SA Public Law 87–110 (2008); J. Nel & W. Du Plessis, *Unpacking Integrated Environmental Management – a Step Closer to Effective Co-operative Governance?* 19 SA Public Law 181–190 (2004); W. Du Plessis & J. Nel, *Environmental Framework Law: A Strategy towards Integrating Pluralist Legislation*, 90 Archiv für Rechts und Sozialphilosophie 197–208 (2004); A. Du Plessis and R. Alberts, *Cooperative environmental governance: At the coalface of sustainable infrastructure development in South Africa*, 29(2) Southern African Public Law 441–468 (2014).
886. Sections 11–16.

Development and Land Reform, Agriculture, Forestry and Fisheries, Human Settlements, Water and Sanitation, Transport and Defence, Trade and Industry, and Military Veterans, as well as every province must compile an environmental implementation plan.[887] These departments exercise functions which may affect the environment.

Departments whose functions are described as involving the management of the environment (Departments of Environmental Affairs, Forestry and Fishers, Human Settlements, Water and Sanitation, Mineral Resources and Energy, Rural Development and Land Reform, Health and Labour) must also compile an environmental management plan, which may be combined with the implementation plan, where applicable. These plans must be compiled or revised every five years. The purpose and objects of these plans are *inter alia* to coordinate and harmonize environmental policies, plans, programmes and decisions of national departments, to minimize duplication of procedures and functions, promote consistency in the exercise of functions that may affect the environment, secure the protection of the environment across the country and prevent unreasonable actions by provinces in respect of the environment.[888]

The Minister would also be able to make use of the Intergovernmental Relations Framework Act 13 of 2005 to establish committees between government departments and the different spheres of government to reach the goals of NEMA.

238. In the Act, the general objectives of integrated environmental management are set out.[889] These objectives include the promotion of the section 2 principles in all decision-making processes, the identification, prediction and evaluation of the actual and potential impact on the environment, socio-economic conditions and cultural heritage, risks and consequences as well as alternatives to minimize negative impacts on the environment and to ensure that all impacts received due consideration. There should also be adequate and appropriate opportunity for public participation.[890]

Since 2004 section 24 of the Act has been extensively amended to provide for environmental authorizations which apply to the whole life cycle of a project and not only certain upgrading or construction activities or the change of land use for which a record of decision was to be issued.[891] Section 24 now also applies to mining activities. The Minister or an MEC of a province may (a) identify activities for which an environmental authorization is necessary; (b) identify geographical areas

887. Listed in Sch. 1.

888. Sections 11–12. *See*, for example, the Department of Environmental Affairs' Consolidated Environmental Management Plan – Government Notice 530 in *Government Gazette* 39998 of 19 May 2016 and its 2015–2020 3rd edition Environmental Management Plan – Government Notice 255 in *Government Gazette* 39816 of 16 Mar. 2016; Department of Energy, Government Notice 255 in *Government Gazette* 39816 of 16 Mar. 2016 – Department of Energy: 2015–2020, 3rd edition Environmental Management Plan.

889. Section 23.

890. *See also* A.A. Du Plessis, *Public Participation, Good Environmental Governance and Fulfilment of Environmental Rights*, 11 PELJ 1–29 (2008).

891. Section 24E – 'Every environmental authorization must as a minimum ensure that – (a) adequate provision is made for the ongoing management and monitoring of the impacts of the activity on the environment throughout the life cycle of the activity'.

based on environmental attributes, and as specified in spatial development tools, in which specified activities may not commence without an authorization; (c) identify geographical areas in which specific activities may be excluded; and (d) identify individual or generic activities which may have a detrimental effect on the environment.[892] The listed activities must be published for comment in the *Government Gazette* and persons must be invited to submit written comments.[893] In the past, it was not always clear which competent authority had to approve an EIA. In terms of section 24C, a procedure is laid down to identify the competent authority during the listing process. The Minister of Environmental Affairs, Forestry and Fisheries is identified as the competent authority for all activities that give effect to the Integrated Resource Plan.[894]

The procedure for an application for an authorization is described in section 24(4) read with the Regulations.[895] It is an offence to commence a listed activity without proper authorization.[896] It is possible to rectify an unlawful commencement of a listed activity or waste management activity. The Minister of Environmental Affairs, Forestry and Fisheries or Minister of Mineral Resources and Energy or responsible MEC may direct the applicant, among others, to cease his or her operations, to remedy the adverse effects, to rehabilitate the area, to conduct an EIA or to compile a report indicating, for example, the need and desirability of the project.[897] The applicant has to pay an administrative fee and may still be prosecuted for failure to obtain an environmental authorization.[898] The Act provides for the registration of environmental assessment practitioners in terms of section 24H.[899]

If the Department does not have the expertise or technical knowledge to consider an application, it may appoint expert consultants and may recover the costs from the applicant.[900] Provision is made for appeal in section 43 of the Act.

---

892. Section 24(1). *See* Government Notice R983–985 in *Government Gazette* 38282 of 4 Dec. 2014. These Regulations were amended – *see* Government Notice Government Notice 324–327 in *Government Gazette* 40772 of 7 Apr. 2017. In 2019, the Minister issued Regulations for the adoption of spatial tools and other environmental instruments – Government Notice 542 in *Government Gazette* 42380 of 5 Apr. 2019. *See* in this regard also, Kidd, M, Retief, F and R. Alberts. *Integrated Environmental Assessment and Management*, 1213–1277. In Fuggle and Rabie's Environmental Management in South Africa (King, N.D, Strydom, H.A. & Retief F.P., eds, 3rd edn, Juta 2018).
893. Section 24A. The same procedure is followed to delist an activity – s. 24B.
894. Government Notice 779 in *Government Gazette* 40110 of 1 Jul. 2016.
895. Government Notice R982 in *Government Gazette* 38282 of 4 Dec. 2014.
896. Section 24F read with s. 34.
897. Section 24G. *See also* Department of Environmental Affairs and Tourism, *NEMA Section 24G*, Integrated Environmental Management Guideline Series 2 (2005); L Kohn, *The Anomaly that is Section 24G of NEMA: An Impediment to Sustainable Development*, 19 SAJELP 1–24 (2012).
898. *See also York Timbers Proprietary Limited v. National Director of Public Prosecutions* 2015 (1) SACR 384 (GP); 2015 (3) SA 122 (GP); *Magaliesberg Protection Association v. MEC: Department of Agriculture, Conservation, Environment and Rural Development, North West Provincial Government and Others* [2013] 3 All SA 416 (SCA); *The Body Corporate of Dolphin Cove v. Kwadukuza Municipality and Another* (8513/10) [2012] ZAKZDHC 13 (20 Feb. 2012).
899. *See* Government Notice 849 in *Government Gazette* 40154 of 22 Jul. 2016 with regard to the authority.
900. *See EarthLife Africa (Cape Town) v. Director-General: DEAT* (Case No. 7653/03 (CCT) 26 Jan. 2005). *See also supra* paras 17 and 120.

Section 23A of the NEMA allows for the adoption of environmental management instruments proposed by a specific industry. The procedure for identifying spatial or environmental management tools has been described in 2019.[901]

239. Section 28 of NEMA deals with the duty of care and remediation of environmental damage. The polluter pays principle is also included in this section.[902] The courts had to pronounce on the retroactive application of section 28 in the case of *Chief Pule Shadrack VII Bareki NO and Another v. Gencor Limited and Others.*[903] The court found that section 28 cannot apply retroactively and only applies to pollution generated from the commencement of NEMA. Section 28 was subsequently amended in 2009 to ensure that polluters could be held liable for historical pollution in the sense that they have to rehabilitate the area, for example. They cannot be held criminally liable for their actions. The 2009 amendment made pollution or degradation of the environment an offence. The control of emergency incidents is regulated in terms of section 30. Sections 28 and 30 overlap with similar provisions in the NWA (sections 19 and 20). This may create confusion as to which authority should be informed first of a spill or an emergency incident.

240. The Act contains various measures to ensure conflict resolution in environmental matters.[904] The courts or tribunals may refer disputes regarding the protection of the environment to conciliators. The records of the conciliation must be made available to the public. Disputes may also be referred to arbitration in terms of the Arbitration Act 42 of 1965. The Minister of Environmental Affairs, Forestry and Fisheries may at any time appoint a commission of enquiry in terms of the Commissions Act 8 of 1947 to assist him or her in the evaluation of a matter relating to the protection of the environment. All records pertaining to environmental conflict management must be kept and made available for inspection to the public.

241. In Chapter 6 of the Act, considerations are set out that should be taken into account before an international environmental instrument is signed. The considerations include the available resources to ensure implementation, the views of interested and affected parties, benefits and disadvantages to the Republic and the responsibilities of the national departments involved.[905] An international obligation must be ratified in terms of the Constitution.[906]

---

901. Government Notice R542 in *Government Gazette* 42380 of 5 Apr. 2019.
902. *See supra* para. 132 and *Hichange Investments (Pty) Ltd v. Cape Produce Co (Pty) Ltd T/A Pelts Products and Other* 2004 2 SA 393 (E) where the court ordered the provincial environmental department to address the issue in terms of s. 28.
903. (19895/03) [2005] ZAGPHC 109 (19 Oct. 2005); *see also* L.J. Kotzé & W. Du Plessis, *Absolving Historical Polluters from Liability through Restrictive Judicial Interpretation: A Matter of (Misguided) Principle*, 18 Stellenbosch Law Review 161–193 (2007).
904. Sections 17–22. *See also* General Notice 638 in *Government Gazette* 36585 of 21 Jun. 2013 – Accreditation standard for a panel of environmental mediators.
905. Section 25(1).
906. Sections 231–233.

242. The Minister must also report once a year to Parliament regarding international environmental instruments for which he or she is responsible. An Annual Performance Report on Sustainable Development must also be published to meet the government's Agenda 21 commitment.[907] The introduction of international obligations regarding energy will have to follow the same route. South Africa is signatory to various conventions and treaties[908] dealing with energy – a yearly report must, therefore, also be given on this topic.

243. The Act contains various other provisions that may impact on the energy industry. Workers who refuse to do environmentally hazardous work are protected in terms of section 29. Provision is also made for the protection of whistle-blowers.[909] A whistle-blower on environmental issues can rely on NEMA or the Protected Disclosures Act 26 of 2000.[910]

244. NEMA contains a legal standing clause similar to that of the Constitution. The legal standing clause is, however, extended to provide that a person may act in the interest of protecting the environment.[911] Provision is further made for the possibility of private as well as criminal proceedings with the possibility of cost allocation outside the normal rules of cost allocation.[912]

245. The Act provides for the enforcement of specific environmental management acts (including the NEMA)[913] and the legislation listed in Schedule 3 to the Act. The supervision of sections 31A–31L is undertaken by both national and provincial governments. The functions of supervision may be delegated to other authorities, such as municipalities.

In terms of the Act, environmental management inspectors are appointed, commonly referred to as 'Green Scorpions'.[914] The functions of the inspectors include

907. Section 26.

908. For example, the *Treaty on the Non-Proliferation of Nuclear Weapons* of 1961; *Vienna Convention for the Protection of the Ozone Layer* of 1985; *Montreal Protocol on Substances that Deplete the Ozone Layer* of 1987; *UN Framework Convention of Climate Change* of 1992; *Paris Agreement* of 30 Nov. to 11 Dec. 2015.

909. Section 31(4)–(8). *See also* the Protected Disclosures Act 26 of 2000.

910. Also *see* M. Toxopeüs and L.J. Kotzé. *Promoting Environmental Justice through Civil-Based Instruments in South Africa*, 13/1 Law, Environment and Development Journal 47 (2017), http://www.lead-journal.org/content/17047.pdf.

911. Section 32(1)(e). The court may decide not to award costs against a person or group of persons who fails to secure relief. The court must be of the opinion that these persons acted out of concern for the public interest or in the interest of protecting the environment – s. 32(2)–(3). *See also Petro Props (Pty) Limited v. Barlow and Another* (29663/05, 29663/05) [2006] ZAGPHC 46 (12 May 2006).

912. Sections 33–34. *See also Biowatch Trust v. Registrar Genetic Resources and Others* 2009 6 SA 232 (CC).

913. ECA; the NWA; the National Environmental Management Biodiversity Act 10 of 2004; NEMAQA; NEMICMA; NEMWA; World Heritage Convention Act 49 of 1999 – s. 1 NEMA.

914. Also *see* Government Notice R480 in *Government Gazette* 40879 of 31 May 2017 – Regulations relating to qualification criteria, training and identification of, and forms to be used by environmental management inspectors and environmental mineral resource inspectors.

among others the questioning of a person on an act or omission, the issuing of written notice to persons who refuse to answer questions requiring a person to answer questions, inspection or copying of documents, books, written or electronic information. They may also take samples, remove waste or any other matter, dig or bore into soil, seize items, stop and search vehicles/vessels and hold routine inspections after obtaining a warrant to do so. They may issue compliance notices in terms of section 31L.[915]

The so-called Green Scorpions take their work seriously and they already successfully prosecuted numerous environmental transgressions.[916] To provide for the enforcement of specific environmental management acts, the Minister may issue regulations on a wide range of matters pertaining to the environment.[917]

246. An interesting provision in the Act is the possibility of environmental management cooperation agreements.[918] Such a contract may be concluded with any person/community after agreement of all organs of state which have jurisdiction over the activity. The agreement may only be entered into if every organ of state that has jurisdiction on any activity to which the agreement relates agrees to it and the procedures for public participation have been complied with. These agreements may contain an undertaking by a person or the community to improve on standards laid down by law for the protection of the environment, a set of measurable targets for fulfilling the previous undertaking as well as provision for periodic monitoring and reporting, independent verification of reports, regular independent monitoring and inspection and verifiable indicators of compliance with any targets, norms and standards agreed upon. An example of such an agreement is one concluded by the then DEAT with a community in Midrand, Gauteng, the local government and a company called Vesuvius South Africa (Pty) Ltd. The community complained for many years about excessive dust fall out and emissions from the plant. The DEAT tried to address their complaints by placing further restrictions on emissions. In 2002, the Department ordered the company either to clean up or close down. The community realized that if the company closed down, it will result in job losses and petitioned government not to do so. In 2004, an environmental management cooperation agreement was concluded that the company will improve its emissions by

915. In the case of *Mineral Sands Resources (Pty) Ltd v Magistrate for the District of Vredendal, Kroutz NO and Others* [2017] 2 All SA 599 (WCC) (20 Mar. 2017), the environmental inspectors of the DEA acted against a mine as a result of a collapse of cliff and the fact that they are mining within 10 metres from a protected area, among others. The court found that only the inspectors appointed by the then Minister of Mineral Resources could act on mining land and not the DEA inspectors.

916. DEA *National Environmental Compliance & Enforcement Report 2012/2013*, https://www.environment.gov.za/sites/default/files/docs/necer_report2012_13.pdf (accessed 9 Jan. 2015).

917. *See*, for example, regulations pertaining to the control of vehicle use in the coastal zone – Government Notice R1426 in *Government Gazette* 27066 of 7 Dec. 2004; Regulations pertaining to the identification of environmental management inspectors – Government Notice R619 in *Government Gazette* 27713 of 1 Jul. 2005.

918. Section 35 read with s. 45. *See also* DEAT, *Guideline Series 1: Environmental management co-operation agreements*' (2005), J. Hanks, *Achieving Industrial Sustainable Development in South Africa: What Role for 'Self-Regulatory' and 'Co-Regulatory' Instruments*, 5 SAJELP 298–354 (1998); W. Scholtz, *Milieuconvenanten, oftewel omgewingbestuursamewerkingsooreenkomste, as self-regulerende instrument in the omgewingsreg: 'n regsvergelykende ondersoek* (LLD Thesis, Leiden University 2001).

March 2004.[919] A similar agreement, although not a formal agreement in terms of NEMA, was reached between mining companies, the then Department of Water Affairs and Forestry (DWAF), the then Department of Mining and Energy, the local municipality of Potchefstroom and mining companies on pollution of the Mooi River which is the source of drinking water for the City of Potchefstroom.[920]

In *Earthlife Africa Johannesburg v Minister of Environmental Affairs and Others*,[921] the granting of an environmental authorization was challenged in that the environmental impact assessment did not include a climate change impact study. Although the NEMA does not directly provide for such a study, the court agreed that some of the provisions of NEMA indirectly allow such a study.

919. Anon, *Deputy Minister applauds win-win air pollution agreement*, www.environment.gov.za/news/newsmedia/medstat/ (accessed 27 Jan. 2004).

920. *See* in this regard C. Bosman, L. Kotzé & W. Du Plessis, *The Failure of the Constitution to Ensure Integrated Environmental Management from a Cooperative Governance Perspective*, 19 SA Public Law 411–421 (2004).

921. [2017] 2 All SA 519 (GP). *See* in this regard J-C. N. Ashukem, *Setting the Scene for Climate Change Litigation in South Africa: Earthlife Africa Johannesburg v Minister of Environmental Affairs and Others [2017] ZAGPPHC 58 (2017) 65662/16*, 13/1 Law, Environment and Development Journal 35 (2017), http://www.lead-journal.org/content/17035.pdf.

Chapter 4. Other Environmental Legislation

247. The energy industry must comply with nearly every other piece of environmental legislation.[922] The specific environmental issues pertaining to electricity, gas, petrol and liquid fuels, coal, nuclear energy and renewable energy have been discussed above. In this section, the applicable environmental legislation will only be referred to briefly.

§1. Climate Change

248. In 2018 the Climate Change Bill, 2018 was published for comment.[923] The purpose of the Bill is to:[924]

(a) provide for the coordinated and integrated response to climate change and its impacts by all spheres of government in accordance with the principles of cooperative governance;
(b) provide for the effective management of inevitable climate change impacts through enhancing adaptive capacity, strengthening resilience and reducing vulnerability to climate change, with a view to building social, economic, and environmental resilience and an adequate national adaptation response in the context of the global climate change response;
(c) make a fair contribution to the global effort to stabilise greenhouse gas concentrations in the atmosphere at a level that avoids dangerous anthropogenic interference with the climate system within a timeframe and in a manner that enables economic, employment, social and environmental development to proceed in a sustainable manner.

The interpretation of the Bill will be guided by the section 2 principles of NEMA as well as additional principles set out in the Bill. These principles relate to the protection of climate systems for the benefit of current and future generation and the international principles of equity and common but differentiated responsibilities. The need for 'a just transition towards an environmentally sustainable economy and society in the light of national circumstances and developmental goals' is also indicated.[925] All government departments must revise their legislation to ensure that climate change risks and vulnerabilities are addressed in light of the adaptation and mitigation measures set out in the Bill.[926] The Bill further set out how provinces and municipalities should develop a climate change response.[927] A national adaptation

922. The most important legislation in this regard will be discussed thematically.
923. Government Notice 580 in *Government Gazette* 41689 of 8 Jun. 2018. Also *see* A. Gilder and E. Swanepoel, *Climate Change*, 745–803. In Fuggle and Rabie's Environmental Management in South Africa (King, N.D, Strydom, H.A. & F.P. Retief, eds, 3rd edn, Juta 2018).
924. Clause 2 read with Clause 8 that provides for institutional cooperative governance.
925. Clause 3.
926. Clause 7.
927. Chapter 3.

strategy will be developed.[928] Chapter 5 of the Bill addresses the greenhouse gas emissions and mitigation strategies. Clause 13 of the Bill provides for the introduction of a carbon budget. All regulations will be subject to consultation and public participation.[929] The Bill also criminalize the non-submission of greenhouse gas emission reports as well as the exceedance of greenhouse case emissions, as set out in the specific person or industry's carbon budget.[930] In 2019, a Climate Change Adaptation Strategy was also published for comment.[931]

§2. WATER

249. The NWA and the Water Services Act 108 of 1997 regulate water use in South Africa.[932] This became necessary as the realization dawned that water is a scarce commodity in South Africa. The NWA repealed the Water Act 54 of 1956. The 1956 Act was first introduced to regulate agricultural use of water but was later extended to regulate industrial use of water. Environmental concerns played a lesser role. Only in the 1980s the polluter pays principle was introduced into this Act. The NWA has saving clauses to validate anything done under a repealed law to the extent that it is not inconsistent with the 1998 Act or until it is repealed.[933] The saving clauses give an afterlife to the 1956 Act. Section 34, for example, gives authority to continue with existing lawful water uses.[934] Some of these water uses had to be reregistered within two years from the commencement of the 1998 Act,[935] and others are still in existence.

250. In terms of the Water Services Act 108 of 1997, no person may make use of water services other than those nominated by the water services authority.[936] The industrial use of water is regulated by section 7. Both the acquisition and disposal of water must be approved by the water services authority. This authorization does not relieve the industry of compliance with other laws relating to the use and conservation of water or the disposal of effluent.

---

928. Chapter 4.
929. Clauses 16 and 17.
930. Clause 19. Also *see* General Notice 497 in *Government Gazette* 40949 of 30 Jun. 2019 – the Draft Third National Communication Report for the Republic of South Africa to the United Nations Framework Convention on Climate Change that was published for comment.
931. Government Notice 644 in *Government Gazette* 42446 of 6 May 2019.
932. Also *see* C. Bosman, M. Kidd & R. Alberts. *Water Quality Management,* 995–1054. In Fuggle and Rabie's Environmental Management in South Africa (King, N.D, Strydom, H.A. & F.P. Retief, eds, 3rd edn, Juta 2018).
933. Section 163(3).
934. *See also* s. 4.
935. Section 32 deals with the definition of existing lawful water uses and s. 33 with the declaration of water use as existing lawful water use.
936. A municipality, district or rural council. Persons who used water from another source could continue for a period of sixty days, after which they had to apply for approval – s. 6(2). *See also Mazibuko and Others v. City of Johannesburg and Others* 2010 (3) BCLR 239 (CC); *Anglogold Ashanti Ltd v. Merafong City Local Municipality and Others* (23558/2011) [2014] ZAGPPHC 85 (26 Feb. 2014).

251. The Minister of Human Settlement, Water and Sanitation may among other things prescribe compulsory national standards relating to the provision of water services, the quality of water taken from or discharged into any water services or water resource system, the effective and sustainable use of water, the nature, operation, sustainability, efficiency and economic viability of water services.[937] In subscribing norms and standards in respect of tariffs for water services, the Minister may differentiate on an equitable basis between different users and type of water services.[938] He or she may also take into account different geographical areas as well as the socio-economic and physical attributes of each area. Limitation can be placed on surplus or profit as well as on the use of income generated by the recovery of charges. This may impact on the energy industry, as the Minister may decide to levy higher charges on industry as they have the potential to pollute the environment. Poorer communities are then to benefit as a result of these charges. Government provides a certain amount of water free of charge to all users. A surplus charge is added on users, depending on the amount of water used. This has resulted already in one of the petroleum companies, Sasol, designing closed water systems. The company's industries are in catchment areas,[939] and they have to compete with, for example, informal settlements and the Gauteng Province for water. The company as far as possible reuses water rather than acquires and disposes water from a service provider.

252. In the 1956 Water Act, a distinction was drawn between private and public water. Virtually no restrictions existed with regard to private water. In terms of the 1998 NWA, however, it is stated that all water, including underground aquifers, belongs to the government as public trustee of the nation's water resources.[940] The purpose of the Act is *inter alia* to ensure that the nation's water resources are protected, used, developed, conserved and managed to meet the basic human needs of present and future generations, to promote equitable access to water, to redress the results of past discrimination and to facilitate social and economic development.[941]

253. Water may only be used in terms of a general authorization or licence under this Act.[942] Water use includes the taking of water from a water resource, storing water, impeding or diverting the flow of water in a watercourse, engaging in stream

937. Section 9(2).

938. *See*, for example, Government Notice R1353 in *Government Gazette* 20615 of 12 Nov. 1999 – pricing strategy for water use charge.

939. South Africa is divided into catchment areas. Each catchment management agency must develop a catchment management strategy for the water in its region. The cooperation and agreement of stakeholders and interested persons are necessary in the development of this strategy. The agency may set principles for allocating water to existing and prospective users taking into account various factors such as protection, use, development and conservation – *see* ss 8–11.

940. Section 3. This is made possible as s. 25(8) of the Constitution states that 'no provision of this section may impede the state from taking legislative and other measures to achieve land, water and related reform, in order to redress the result of past racial discrimination'. Section 25(1) provides that 'no one may be deprived of property except in terms of law of general application, and no law may permit arbitrary deprivation of property'.

941. Section 2.

942. *See also* ss 40–42 with regard to the licence application.

flow reduction activities, discharging waste or water containing waste into a water resource through a pipe, canal, sewer, sea outfall or any other conduit, disposing of waste which may have a detrimental impact on a water resource and removing, discharging or disposing water found underground.[943] Most of the activities of the energy industry involve water and will fall under the definition of water use. The electricity industry in particular makes use of huge amounts of water.

An industry that uses water must comply with the conditions of the general water authorization[944] and is further subject to all limitations, restrictions and prohibitions imposed upon it by this Act or any other law.[945] Where waste is disposed of, the industry must comply with applicable waste standards[946] and must return any seepage, runoff or water containing waste to the water resource unless directed otherwise.[947] If an application for a water use or renewal of a licence[948] has been refused or a licence for a lesser use has been granted, resulting in severe prejudice to the economic viability of the undertaking in respect of which the water was beneficially used, the applicant may claim compensation for the financial loss suffered.[949]

254. Section 19 of the Act deals with the prevention and remedying of the effects of pollution. An owner of land or the person in control of land must take all reasonable measures to prevent pollution from occurring, continuing or recurring.[950] It also contains the polluter pays principle.[951] Persons who negligently failed to prevent the activity or process being performed or undertaken or the situation from coming about will also be held liable. A catchment management agency may direct an industry that fails to take the necessary measures to commence, complete or continue with the remedying of the pollution.[952] If such an industry fails, the catchment agency may take the steps necessary to remedy the situation and recover the costs from the industry.[953]

943. Section 21.
944. *See also* Government Notice 1191 in *Government Gazette* 20526 of 8 Oct. 1999.
945. The Minister may make special arrangements with regard to geographic areas under water stress – *see* ss 43–48.
946. Prescribed in terms of s. 26(1)(h) and (i).
947. Section 22.
948. Sections 49–52. *See also* Government Notice 2834 in *Government Gazette* 20606 of 12 Nov. 1999.
949. Section 22(6). The amount of compensation is to be determined in accordance with s. 25 of the Constitution. The claim must be lodged within six months to the water tribunal – s. 22(7)–(10). For an example of a case before the water tribunal, *see Escarpment Environment Protection Group and Another v. Department of Water Affairs and Others, In Re; Escarpment Environment Protection Group and Another v. Department of Water Affairs and Others, In Re; Escarpment Environment Protection Group and Another v. Department of Water Affairs and Others* (A666/11, 4333/12, 4334/12) [2013] ZAGPPHC 505 (20 Nov. 2013).
950. Section 19(1).
951. Section 19(5).
952. If a person fails to comply with a directive, he or she may also be held criminal liable in terms of ss 152–155 of the Act. *See also* ss 53–55; *Minister of Water Affairs and Forestry v. Stilfontein Gold Mining Company Ltd and Others* 2006 JOL 17516 (W); *Harmony Gold Mining Co Ltd v. Regional Director: Free State, DWAF* 2006 SCA 65; *Kebble v. Minister of Water Affairs* 2007 SCA 111; *Harmony Gold Mining Company Ltd v. Regional Director: Free State Department of Water Affairs* 2014 3 SA 149 (SCA).
953. Section 19(2)–(5).

255. Emergency incidents are controlled by section 20. As has been stated before, this control is in addition to the regulation of emergency incidents in the NEMA. The energy industries must identify their activities, risks and substances in order to draft an emergency plan. A procedure must also be developed in order to facilitate the reporting of such incidents to the officials mentioned in the Act.

Section 20 of the NWA and section 30 of the NEMA should be read with the Disaster Management Act 57 of 2002.[954] The purpose of the Act is to provide for 'an integrated and coordinated disaster management policy, that focuses on preventing or reducing the risk of disasters, mitigating the severity of disasters, emergency preparedness, rapid and effective response to disasters and post-disaster-recovery'. A 'disaster' is defined as 'a progressive or sudden, widespread or localized, natural or human-caused occurrence which – (a) causes or threatens to cause – (i) death, injury or disease, (ii) damage to property, infrastructure or the environment; or (iii) disruption of the life of a community and (b) is of a magnitude that exceeds the ability of those affected by the disaster to cope with its effects using only their own resources'.[955] The Act does not apply if the occurrence can be dealt with effectively in terms of other legislation.[956]

256. The safety of dams is an important factor. The safety of dams is regulated by sections 117–123 of the NWA. Dams which can contain, store or dam more than 50,000 cubic metres of water or any other substance such as sludge (whether it is empty or not) and which have a wall of a vertical height of more than 5 metres are regarded as dams with a safety risk.[957] Such dams have to be registered and are subject to inspections.[958] The Minister may also direct that the dam be repaired or altered to limit the safety risk.[959] The energy industry makes use of dams to store water or to dispose of water and must, therefore, register the dams on their premises.

257. A section of the Act is devoted to servitudes.[960] It allows a person who is authorized to use water to claim a servitude over another person's land if it is necessary to make his or her use effective. The servitudes are acquired by agreement between the water user and the landowner and must be registered with the Registrar of Deeds. An industry within the energy sector will, therefore, be allowed to register servitudes if necessary to produce energy effectively.

---

954. Certain chapters of the Act came into operation on 1 Apr. 2004 and the remaining chapters on 1 Jul. 2004 – Proclamation R23 in *Government Gazette* 26228 of 31 Mar. 2004. The Minister of Cooperative Governance and Traditional Affairs is designated as the member of cabinet responsible for the administration of the Act – General Notice 563 in *Government Gazette* 26228 of 31 Mar. 2004. *See also* the proposed national disaster framework that was published for comment – General Notice 974 in *Government Gazette* 26390 of 28 May 2004.
955. Section 1.
956. Section 2.
957. Section 117(c). A dam can also be declared as one with a safety risk in terms of s. 118(3).
958. *See also* ss 124–125 dealing with inspections and entry upon land.
959. Section 118(3)(c).
960. Sections 126–134.

258. Water quality standards are prescribed in terms of Government Notice R991 of 1984.[961] The Regulations provide for a general and special standard as well as a general phosphate standard.[962] These standards can be included as conditions in a water licence.

§3. Soil and Biota

259. The Conservation of Agricultural Resources Act 43 of 1983 controls soil erosion, weeds, the protection of wetlands and other matters on land which fall under the jurisdiction of the energy industry.[963] These industries have to comply with the measures in the Act. The Act also deals with the protection of wetlands.[964] Some mines are situated in areas with internationally declared wetlands and, therefore, have to comply with the Ramsar Convention to which South Africa is a signatory. Weeds[965] are controlled by Chapter 5 of the Act. The person in control of a piece of land is directly liable to control invaders on that land. The energy industry will, therefore, be responsible for the control of these species. This Act has to be read with the NEMBA that also provides measures for the control of alien and invasive species.[966]

260. Forestry is an aspect of the environment. Sustainable forest management and use benefit the environment and contribute to economic development as well. The mining industry, for example, has an effect on forestry conservation. The National Forest Act 84 of 1998[967] recognizes that and regulates such.[968] In terms of section 23(e), any use of land in a state forest for commercial purposes has to be licensed. In terms of the Forestry Regulations,[969] the mining industry (and, therefore, the coal industry) is such an activity. A licence can only be issued for a period

961. *Government Gazette* 9225 of 18 May 1984. These regulations continue to exist in terms of s. 163. *See also* www.dwaf.gov.za/Documents/ (accessed 28 May 2005).
962. These standards should be read with SANS0257 – water standards issued by Standards South Africa.
963. *See* in this regard, T.C. Meyer, et al., *Soil, Land and Agriculture,* 283–350. In Fuggle and Rabie's Environmental Management in South Africa (King, N.D, Strydom, H.A. & F.P. Retief, eds, 3rd edn, Juta 2018).
964. 'Water course' in s. 1 read with ss 3 and 6 and regulation 7 in Government Notice R1048 in *Government Gazette* 9238 of 25 May 1984. Some wetlands are also declared as Ramsar sites. *See also* the *Ramsar Convention* and M. Kidd, *Environmental Law*, 96–98 (Juta 1997). By May 2005, the Act was being revised to be replaced by a new Act. A Sustainable Use of Agricultural Resources Draft Bill is currently under discussion.
965. *See* Government Notice R1048 in *Government Gazette* 9238 of 25 May 1984 for a list of weeds. It also deals with soil loss, *vleis* and the salination of land, etc.
966. *See* in this regard R. Alberts & J. Moolman, *Protecting Ecosystems by Way of Biological Control: Cursory Reflections on the Main Regulatory Instruments for Biological Control Agents, Present and Future*, 16 PELJ 184–212; A. Paterson, *Clearing a Path Towards Effective Alien Invasive Control: the Legal Conundrum*, 9 PELJ 1–56 (2006).
967. *See also* J. Glazewski, *Environmental Law*, 179–184 (2nd edn, LexisNexis 2005).
968. The Minister may declare certain tree species to be protected trees. Once it is so declared, it may not be cut, damaged, disturbed or removed without a licence from the Minister – ss 12 and 15. *See* Government Notice 650 in *Government Gazette* 37941 of 29 Aug. 2014 for a list of protected trees.
969. Regulation 14 – Government Notice R466 in *Government Gazette* 32185 of 29 Apr. 2009.

of not more than ten years.[970] This licence can only be issued together with a prospecting or mining authorization under the MPRDA.[971]

261. The energy industry also has to take notice of the National Veld and Forest Fire Act 101 of 1998.[972] The purpose of this Act is to prevent and combat veld, forest and mountain fires throughout the Republic.[973] Owners may form fire protection associations for the purpose of predicting, preventing, managing and distinguishing veld fires. The association may apply for registration to Department of Environmental Affairs, Forestry and Fisheries.[974] The energy industry also has to comply with the Regulations regarding firebreaks.[975]

262. In terms of the Fertilizers, Farm Feeds and Stock Remedies Act 36 of 1947, the energy industries may only use qualified and registered pest control operators[976] to apply registered pesticides and herbicides on their land.[977]

263. Mines and the energy industry are also subject to the various nature conservation ordinances and must protect plant and animal species on their land.[978]

§4. AIR QUALITY

264. Before the introduction of the NEMAQA, the Atmospheric Pollution Prevention Act 45 of 1965 regulated air quality. If an activity was listed in Schedule 2 of the Act, permission was needed from the chief atmospheric pollution control officer.[979] Various processes used in the energy industry were listed.[980] The chief atmospheric pollution control officer could have granted a provisional or final registration certificate.[981]

970. Section 24 National Forest Act.
971. Regulation 14 of GN R466. J. Glazewski & L. du Toit, eds, *Environmental Law*, 4.31–4.54 (2nd edn, LexisNexis 2014 Service Issue 2).
972. *Ibid.* at 4-42–4-44.
973. Section 1.
974. Section 3.
975. Sections 12–17.
976. The registered pest control operator must before administering the pesticide or herbicide notify the land owner of the purpose of the administration, the registered name and number of the substance used, the registration certificate and precautions taken during and after the administration – s. 10.
977. Section 3.
978. *See also* J. Glazewski, *Environmental Law*, eds, 379–380 (2nd edn, Butterworths 2013).
979. Section 8.
980. For example, item 39 – waste incineration processes; item 29 – power generation processes; item 33 – producer gas processes; item 34 – gas, coke and charcoal processes; item 59 – the bulk storage and handling of ore and coal; item 69 – animal matter reduction processes. Item 29(c) deals with 'processes in which … (c) any fuel burning appliance is used that is not controlled in terms of Part III of this Act, excluding appliances in private dwellings'. This item is sometimes overlooked by the energy industry that has fuel-burning appliances other than the generation of electricity for public purposes or boilers capable of burning fuel at a rate of 10 tons per hour to raise steam for the supply of energy (item 29(a)–(b)).
981. Sections 10–11.

265. In 2005 the NEMAQA was promulgated.[982] The aim of the Act is to protect the environment by providing reasonable measures for '(i) the protection and enhancement of the quality of air in the Republic; (ii) the prevention of air pollution and ecological degradation and (iii) securing ecologically sustainable development while promoting justifiable economic and social development'. The Act also has to give effect to section 24 of the Constitution.[983] The Act is to be read with the NEMA.[984] Air quality is monitored by the national, provincial and local spheres of government.[985]

The NEMAQA provides for the establishment of a National Air Quality Advisory Committee who has to advise the Minister.[986] All spheres of government should appoint air quality officers to coordinate matters pertaining to air quality management,[987] and national and provincial government should include an air quality management plan into their environmental management and environmental implementation plans.[988]

266. The Act provides various tools to manage air quality in the country, namely the declaration of priority areas by the Minister or two or more MECs,[989] the listing of activities that may result in atmospheric emissions and measures dealing with controlled emitters.[990] Listed activities require a licence.[991] The Minister issued a list of activities and associated minimum air quality standards in 2013.[992]

267. The Minister or an MEC may also declare substances or mixtures of substances which result in emissions that may harm the health and well-being of people or the environment as controlled substances. He or she may also declare substances as priority air pollutants. If a pollutant is declared as such, the person in control of the pollutant must prepare a pollution prevention plan and submit the plan to the Minister. The Minister declared her intention to declare certain greenhouse gases as

982. Also *see* Rumble, O., et al., *Air Quality*, 401–457. In Fuggle and Rabie's Environmental Management in South Africa (King, N.D, Strydom, H.A. & F.P. Retief, eds. 3rd edn, Juta 2018).
983. Section 2. For a discussion of s. 24 of the Constitution, *see supra* paras 130–133.
984. Section 4. For a discussion of NEMA, *see supra* paras 136, 140–148.
985. Sections 8–11.
986. Section 13.
987. Section 14.
988. Section 15 – the plans are compiled in terms of NEMA.
989. Sections 18–20. The Vaal Triangle, Waterberg-Bojanalo and Highveld areas were declared priority areas in terms in the Act – *see* Government Notice 365 in *Government Gazette* 28732 of 21 Apr. 2006; Government Notice 1123 in *Government Gazette* 30518 of 23 Nov. 2007; Government Notice 495 in *Government Gazette* 35435 of 15 Jun. 2012. For an example of an air quality management plan for these areas, *see* the Highveld Priority Area Air Management Plan – Government Notice 144 in *Government Gazette* 35072 of 2 Mar. 2012.
990. Sections 21–25.
991. Sections 36–49. The procedure for application of licences is set out in ss 37 and 38. The Act makes provision for both provisional atmospheric emission licences and atmospheric emission licence once the facility complies with the conditions set out in the provisional permit – s. 42. The contents of the licence are described in s. 43. Provision is made for transfer of these licences – s. 44. Licences may be reviewed, amended or renewed – ss 45–47. Offences and penalties are dealt with in Ch. 7 of the Act. The Act includes some transitional arrangements regarding registration certificates that were issued in terms of the Atmospheric Pollution Prevention Act 45 of 1965 – ss 61–63.
992. Government Notice 893 in *Government Gazette* 37054 of 22 Nov. 2013.

priority air pollutants.[993] A controlled substance must comply with prescribed standards.[994] Other measures include atmospheric impact reports, recognition programmes, the control of dust, rehabilitation when mining operations cease,[995] control of noise and offensive odours.[996]

268. In terms of section 30, the licensing authorities must in consideration of a licence application consider the standards set for emissions and air quality, the possible pollution and its effect on health, social conditions, economic conditions, cultural heritage and ambient air quality as well as the best practicable options available to prevent, control, abate or mitigate the pollution. Tradable emission schemes should also be taken into account. Certain persons or companies may make an application to be exempted from certain provisions of the Act in terms of section 59.

269. The Minister must address transboundary pollution and its effect on South Africa's neighbouring countries.[997] Both the Minister and MEC may make regulations regarding a broad range of manners, including environmental management cooperation agreements, open fires and incinerators, trading schemes, labelling and ozone-depleting substances.[998] The Act also makes explicit provision for consultation and public participation.[999] The Minister issued regulations with regard to the phasing out and management of ozone-depleting substances and air dispersion models.[1000]

270. Initially in the absence of prescribed air quality standards, the chemical industry, government and the general public negotiated an agreement for the reduction of VOCs. The NEMAQA, however, provides for a national framework that includes mechanisms, systems and procedures to attain compliance with ambient air quality standards as well as national norms and standards for the control of emissions from point and non-point sources, for air quality monitoring and air quality management planning to which all industries have to comply with.[1001]

---

993. Section 29. General Notice 172 in *Government Gazette* 37421 of 14 Mar. 2014.

994. Sections 23–28. *See*, for example, General Notice 1138 in *Government Notice* 37062 of 29 Nov. 2013 that proposed to declare temporary asphalt plants as control emitters; Government Notice 831 in *Government Gazette* 36973 of 1 Nov. 2013 declared small boilers as controlled emitters.

995. Also *see* Centre for Environmental Rights, *Full disclosure: The truth about mining rehabilitation in South Africa* (June 2018) https://fulldisclosure.cer.org.za/ (accessed 12 May 2019).

996. Sections 30–35. *See*, e.g., Government Notice 747 in Government Gazette 36904 of 11 Oct. 2013, as amended by Government Notice R284 in Government Gazette 38633 of 2 Apr. 2015, for regulations dealing with the format of the atmospheric impact report; Government Notice 827 in Government Gazette 36974 of 31 Oct. 2013 for national dust control regulations.

997. Section 50.

998. Sections 53–54.

999. Sections 56–57.

1000. *See* Government Notice R351 in *Government Gazette* 37621 of 8 May 2014; Government Notice R533 in *Government Gazette* 37804 of 11 Jul. 2014.

1001. Section 7(1). The national norms and standards must ensure that public participation takes place, that the public has access to air quality information and to reduce the discharges that may impair air quality. It must also promote the efficient and effective management of air quality – s. 7(2). The national standards may differentiate between geographical areas and may provide for phasing

271. In terms of the 2004 Act, local authorities play a crucial role in the implementation of licensing procedures and the monitoring of air quality. Not all local authorities have the capacity to do so, and until such time either national government or a provincial government will deal with licensing in the jurisdiction of those municipalities lacking capacity. Local authorities may issue their own air quality by-laws and draft air quality by-laws were published in this regard.[1002]

272. Dust control in mining areas (also coal mining areas) is transferred to the Department of Mineral Resources and Energy.[1003] In terms of the NEMAQA, a mine that foresees closure within five years must notify the Minister of the likely cessation of the mining operations and the rehabilitation of the area in order to control dust.[1004]

§5. Nuclear Energy

273. In terms of the Nuclear Energy Act 131 of 1993,[1005] mines were regarded as a nuclear plant if they complied with certain requirements dealing with radioactive waste on their mines. These mines had to obtain a registration certificate from the then relevant council. In terms of the National Nuclear Regulator Act 47 of 1999,[1006] mines are no longer regarded as nuclear plants and the control over them was reduced.[1007]

§6. Waste

274. One of the main challenges of the energy industry is the generation of waste. In many instances, even in the case of renewable energy, hazardous waste is generated. Waste can take different forms.

For purposes of this discussion, a distinction can be drawn between hazardous waste and other waste. For example, in the case of hazardous waste, energy industries with clinics that use isotopes or where closed isotopes are used to measure products must obtain licences from the Department of Health.[1008] Radioactive waste is regulated by nuclear legislation. The NWA regulates waste that contaminates water resources. Mining waste is regulated by the MPRDA and the NEMWA.

---

in of its provisions – s. 7(4). *See* Government Notice 909 in *Government Gazette* 37078 of 29 Nov. 2013 for the National Framework for Air Quality Management in the Republic of South Africa. This framework amends the 2007 Framework.

1002. Government Notice 579 in *Government Gazette* 33342 of 2 Jul. 2010.

1003. Section 6(2)(a)–(b) – *see also* dust control regulations under the repealed Mines and Works Act 27 of 1956 and Government Notice R992 in *Government Gazette* 2741 of 26 Jun. 1970 – Ch. 10.

1004. Section 33.

1005. *See* discussion on nuclear energy Part I *supra*.

1006. Section 47 of 1999.

1007. Section 1 – 'definition of nuclear installations'. *See* s. 1 of the Nuclear Energy Act 131 of 1993 – definition of 'nuclear installations' where mines with certain processes were regarded as nuclear installations.

1008. Schedule 4 Hazardous Substances Act 15 of 1973.

The NEMWA also regulates domestic and industrial waste.[1009] Waste is defined in section 1 as 'any substance, whether or not that substance can be reduced, re-used, recycled or recovered – (a) that is surplus, unwanted, rejected, discarded, abandoned or disposed of; (b) which the generator has no further use of for the purposes of production; (c) that must be treated or disposed of; or (d) that is identified as waste by the Minister by notice in the *Government Gazette*'. A general duty is placed on the holders of waste to avoid the generation of waste and where it cannot be avoided to at least minimize its toxicity and the amount of waste generated, to reduce, reuse and recycle and to manage the waste in such a manner as not to endanger the health, well-being of person as well as the environment through noise, odour and visual impacts. Waste may also not be used for unauthorized purposes. If someone sells a product that may result in the generation of hazardous waste, such a person must be informed about the impact of such waste on his or her health or the environment.[1010]

The Minister may by notice in the *Government Gazette* identify activities which may have a detrimental effect on the environment. Once an activity is listed, an applicant must apply for a waste management licence in terms of the Act and comply with the standards set out in the Regulations.[1011] The licence procedure must be coordinated and consolidated with the environmental authorization procedure in terms of section 24 of the NEMA or any other authorizations that need to be obtained. The licensing authority may issue an integrated licence.[1012] The licence may be reviewed and amended at any time.[1013]

The Minister must set national norms and standards for the classification of waste as well as for the storage, treatment and disposal of waste. The norms and standards may differentiate between geographical areas, classes or categories of waste as well as between users of waste management services.[1014]

The authority may require the licence holder to appoint a waste management control officer depending on the size and nature of the waste generated. The waste management control officer must, among other functions, work towards the introduction of clean production technologies to minimize waste, take reasonable steps to ensure that the holder of the licence comply with the conditions in the licence and report

---

1009. Also *see* C. Bosman, R. Alberts & C. Roos. *Integrated Waste Management,* 1055–1097. In Fuggle and Rabie's Environmental Management in South Africa (King, N.D, Strydom, H.A. & F.P. Retief, eds, 3rd edn, Juta 2018).

1010. Section 16.

1011. Sections 19–20. The activities and standards are to be found in Government Notice 921 in *Government Gazette* 37083 of 29 Nov. 2013 (as amended by Government Notice 322 in *Government Gazette* 37604 of 2 May 2014, Government Notice R633 in *Government Gazette* 39020 of 24 Jul. 2015 and Government Notice 1094 in *Government Gazette* 41175 of 11 Oct. 2017). The application procedure is set out in ss 44, 47–51. The licence may be renewed – s. 55.

1012. Section 44.

1013. Sections 53–54.

1014. Section 7. An MEC may also set provincial norms and standards – s. 8. A municipality must deliver waste management services in accordance with the norms and standards set in terms of ss 7 and 8 – s. 9. Government Notice 634 in *Government Gazette* 36784 of 23 Aug. 2013 (waste classification and management); Government Notice 635 in *Government Gazette* 36784 of 23 Aug. 2013 (standards for the assessment of waste water landfill disposal); Government Notice 926 in *Government Gazette* 37088 of 29 Nov. 2013 (standards for the storage of waste).

any non-compliance to the licence conditions to the authorities.[1015] The environmental management inspectors appointed in terms of section 31A of the NEMA may also investigate compliance to the Act and the licence conditions. In addition to their powers set out in NEMA, the inspectors may require the holder of the licence to submit a waste impact report if the inspector has reasonable grounds to suspect contravention of the law or the licence conditions.[1016]

It is an offence to dispose waste on land or in a water body without any authorization or to litter.[1017]

The Minister may also declare certain waste as a priority waste if he or she is of the opinion that such waste poses a threat to health, well-being or the environment. The Minister must further specify which specific management measures need to be undertaken, for example the preparation of a waste management plan, the prohibition on the generation of such waste, measures pertaining to the storage and monitoring of the waste.[1018] The Minister has to follow a consultative process before he or she can introduce such a process.[1019] The effect of the declaration is that the waste may not be imported, exported, manufactured or sold without compliance with the prescribed plan and measures.[1020]

If waste is reduced, recycled, reused or recovered, the person undertaking the activity must ensure that the process will 'use less natural resources than the disposal of the waste and to the extent that it is possible, is less harmful to the environment than the disposal of such waste'.[1021] The Minister may also provide by way of regulation for extended producer responsibility for a specific product or a class of products. Again, the Minister has to follow a consultative process before publishing such a notice in the *Government Gazette*.[1022]

275. A specific industry, for example the shale gas industry or the electricity industry, may be obliged to prepare an industry waste management plan if the activity is conducted in more than one province. This plan will have to address the impact or potential impact of the waste on health and the environment, the environmentally sensitive nature of the natural resource or the amount of the natural resources that is to be consumed in the manufacturing or production processes that result in waste. The plan will have to indicate how these impacts will be minimized, reduced or avoided and how natural resources will be conserved.[1023]

1015. Section 58.
1016. Section 66. Waste management licences may also be revoked or suspended – s. 56.
1017. Sections 26 and 27.
1018. Section 14.
1019. Sections 72 and 73 describe the procedure for consultation.
1020. Section 15. The Minister of Environmental Affairs, Forestry and Fisheries is the licensing authority if hazardous waste is involved, if the licensing follows an international obligation, if the activity is undertaken by a government department of a statutory body or if the activity traverses the boundaries of two or more provinces. A province or a statutory body may also in certain other circumstance be the licensing authority – *see* s. 43.
1021. Section 17.
1022. Section 18.
1023. Section 28 read with s. 30. The Minister may also require a province to prepare such a plan – s. 29.

The Minister must determine a national waste management strategy to determine, among others, the objectives, plans, guidelines, systems and procedures relating to the protection of the environment and generation and management of waste, the raising of awareness on waste matters, cooperative governance and approaches to ensure compliance with the requirements of the Act.[1024]

The Act has extensive provisions for contaminated land and extended liability for contaminated land. If energy is generated on specific land and the land is contaminated, the owner or the person undertaking the high-risk activity may be hold responsible for remedial measures. Such persons may be directed to prepare a site assessment report of the contamination of the land as well as its impact on health or the environment, the substances present in or on the land, the exposure to pathways, the use or proposed use of the land and the possible migration of the substances from the land. The Minister must keep a contaminated land register, and the Registrar of Deeds must note on its register that the land has been a remediation site.[1025]

The Act also provides for the establishment of a national waste information register that will keep information on all waste generated, locations of waste sites and licences issued. The idea is to use the information for education and awareness raising, research, planning, safety and to determine the impact of waste on health and the environment.[1026] The Minister may require any person to provide certain information on waste to the system on a regular or once off basis. The Promotion of Access to Information Act 2 of 2000 regulates access to this information and will protect commercial confidential information, where applicable.[1027]

276. Some of the petrol refineries and the Koeberg Nuclear Station are near the seaside. These industries also have to comply with legislation dealing with the sea, such as the Sea-Shore Act 31 of 1935 (as assigned to the provinces), the NEMICMA,[1028] the Dumping at Sea Control Act 73 of 1980 and the Marine Pollution Act 6 of 1981. Where waste is transported by sea, the various conventions dealing with transportation of hazardous waste at sea and pollution at sea should also be taken into account.[1029]

1024. Section 6. Government Notice 625 in *Government Gazette* 35583 of 13 Aug. 2012 (regulations national waste information system).

1025. Sections 35–41. *See also* National Norms and Standards for Remediation of Contaminated Land and Soil Quality – Government Notice 331 in *Government Gazette* 37603 of 2 May 2014.

1026. Sections 60–61. An MEC may also establish a provincial register – s. 62. *See also* Government Notice R625 in *Government Gazette* 35583 of 13 Aug. 2012 – National Waste Information Regulations.

1027. Sections 62–63.

1028. *See also* Government Notice 711 in *Government Gazette* 40996 of 21 Jul. 2017 – Dumping at Sea Regulations – issued in terms of this Act.

1029. The *Law of the Sea Convention* (in South Africa Maritime Zones Act 15 of 1994), *International Convention for the Prevention of Pollution from Ships* of 1974 (in South Africa incorporated into International Convention for the Prevention of Pollution from Ships Act 2 of 1986), *International Maritime Goods Code* (incorporated into regulations issued under the Merchant Shipping Act 57 of 1951), *International Convention on Civil Liability for Oil Pollution Damage* of 1969 (incorporated into Marine Pollution (Control and Civil Liability) Act 6 of 1981), *International Convention on Liability and Compensation for Damage in connection with the Carriage of Hazardous and Noxious Substances at Sea* of 1996 (South Africa has acceded to the Convention but has not

§7. Hazardous Substances

277. The Hazardous Substances Act 73 of 1973 deals with the control of substances which may cause injury or ill health to or death of human beings by reason of their toxic, corrosive, irritant, strongly sensitizing or flammable nature.[1030] The Act distinguishes between four groups of hazardous substances. Group IV is classified as radioactive material that is outside a nuclear installation as defined in the Nuclear Energy Act 46 of 1999 and does not form part of or is used in the nuclear fuel cycle. To be classified as a Group IV hazardous substance, the radioactive material should have an activity concentration of more than 100 becquerels per gram and a total activity of not more than 4,000 becquerels, or have an activity concentration of 100 becquerels or less per gram or a total activity of 4,000 becquerels or less, and which the Minister of Health has declared a Group IV substance.[1031] The material is to be used for medical, scientific, agricultural, commercial or industrial purposes. Radioactive waste arising from radioactive material is also regarded as a Group IV substance. To acquire, use, dispose of, import or export a Group IV hazardous substance, written authority from the Director General of Health is necessary.[1032]

278. The nuclear industry is the only energy-producing technology that has to take full responsibility for all its wastes and fully costs it into the product. According to the *Nuclear Issues Briefing Paper 9*,[1033] the amount of waste is relatively small compared to fossil-fuel electricity generation. Three types of radioactive waste can be distinguished, namely low-level waste generated by hospitals, industry and the nuclear fuel cycle. It mostly contains articles of clothing, paper, filters, etc., which have short-lived radioactivity. Intermediate-level waste has higher amounts of radioactivity, and some require shielding, such as resins, chemical sludge and metal fuel cladding and material from reactor decommissioning. It is solidified in concrete or bitumen for disposal. This waste is buried in shallow repositories, while long-lived waste is to be buried deep underground. High-level waste is generated by the use of uranium fuel in a nuclear reactor. This waste is highly radioactive and hot to the touch. This type of waste accounts for the radioactivity produced in the process of nuclear electricity generation.

279. An unfortunate outcome of nuclear energy is the radioactive waste that is generated and must be disposed of in a specific manner. In 2008, a National Radioactive Waste Disposal Institute Act 53 of 2008 was published to establish the National Radioactive Waste Disposal Institute[1034] and to regulate radioactive waste

---

yet incorporated it into domestic law) – *see* in this regard J. Glazewski & L. du Toit, *Environmental Law*, 25–29–25–30 (2nd edn, LexisNexis 2013 Service Issue 2). *See also* the Dumping at Sea Control Act 73 of 1980 and the Wreck and Salvage Act 94 of 1996.

1030. Preamble.

1031. Section 1. *See also* Government Notice 246 in *Government Gazette* 14596 of 26 Feb. 1993.

1032. Section 3A.

1033. Anon, *Waste Management in the Nuclear Fuel Cycle*, August 2000, www.uic.com.au/ nip09.htm (accessed 7 May 2001).

1034. Established in terms of ss 3–33.

disposal. The functions of the Institute are, among others, to issue certificates for radioactive waste disposal, as well as to manage, operate and monitor radioactive waste disposal facilities or close them.[1035] If the Institute operates a waste disposal site, it must comply with the provisions of the Act with regard to security, safety, record-keeping and access.[1036]

A generator of radioactive waste who wants to dispose of radioactive waste must apply to the Chief Executive Officer of the Institute for a waste disposal certificate.[1037] The certificate may be granted subject to conditions and the conditions may be amended from time to time.[1038] While the radioactive material is stored on site, the generator must manage the waste in accordance with a site-specific radioactive waste management plan and must act in accordance with other national laws. They remain liable for any damage caused by the waste until it is disposed of in a proper manner.[1039]

§8. Protection of Cultural Resources

280. Mines (and, therefore, coal and uranium mines) were exempted from section 12(2A) of the National Monuments Act 28 of 1969.[1040] They need not protect *inter alia* meteorites, fossils, drawings, paintings or objects of anthropological or archaeological interest in the normal course of mining. The finder of the item had, however, to report the find to the relevant institution. The National Heritage Resources Act 25 of 1999[1041] does not contain a similar provision.

Exemption is only allowed where an environmental impact assessment or an environmental management programme is submitted in terms of NEMA, the MPRDA or any other legislation.[1042]

The heritage resource consenting authority must, however, ensure that the requirements set out in section 38(3) are met.[1043] Otherwise, a separate heritage

1035. Section 5.
1036. Sections 26–27.
1037. Section 23.
1038. Section 24.
1039. Section 25.
1040. Section 12(3).
1041. The Act commenced on 1 Apr. 2000.
1042. Section 38(8).
1043. Section 38(3) determines that the following must be completed: '(a) The identification and mapping of all heritage resources in the area affected; (b) an assessment of the significance of such resources in terms of the heritage assessment criteria set out in Section 4(2) or prescribed under Section 7; (c) an assessment of the impact of the development on such heritage resources; (d) an evaluation of the impact of the development on heritage resources relative to the sustainable social and economic benefits to be derived from the development; (e) the results of consultation with communities affected by the proposed development and other interested parties regarding the impact of the development on heritage resources; (f) if heritage resources will be adversely affected by the proposed development, the consideration of alternatives; and (g) plans for mitigation of any adverse effects during and after the completion of the proposed development.'.

impact assessment will have to be undertaken.[1044] The comments and recommendations of the relevant heritage resource authority must be taken into account prior to the granting of the consent.

281. In terms of the National Monuments Act, a historical site was defined as any identifiable building older than fifty years[1045] that cannot be demolished without the permission of the relevant authority.[1046] In terms of the Minerals Act 50 of 1991, however, buildings had to be demolished as soon as a prospecting permit or mining authorization was suspended, cancelled, terminated or lapsed.[1047] Many mines demolished buildings older than fifty years and were not aware of this provision in the National Monuments Act. In terms of the National Heritage Resources Act, the period is extended to sixty years. In the case of demolition, the permission of the relevant provincial heritage resources authority is needed.[1048] The MPRDA also includes a clause that buildings, structures and objects have to be removed after a prospecting or mining right is cancelled, relinquished or abandoned.[1049] However, this cannot be done if another law (such as the National Heritage Resources Act) prohibits it.[1050]

282. In terms of section 28(1), South African Heritage Resources Agency (SAHRA)[1051] may designate land covered by a mine dump as a protected area. They must issue regulations for the protection of such areas if they are seen to be of national importance.[1052] The designation must be done in consultation with the owner, the Minister of Mineral Resources and interested and affected parties within the mining community. This Act places a burden on mines on the one hand, but on the other hand may ensure a mind change by the mining authorities towards conserving the environment. Interested and affected parties also have to be consulted, which was not done in the past.

§9. Land Use Planning

283. All energy-related projects must comply with the relevant planning legislation. Land has to be rezoned to the relevant category (e.g., industrial) before any

1044. Section 38(2)-(3).
1045. Section 1.
1046. Section 2A(f). *See also* J. Glazewski, *Environmental Law*, 518–525 (2nd edn, LexisNexis 2005).
1047. Section 40. *See also* General Notice 500 in *Government Gazette* 27424 of 30 Mar. 2005 – Draft Policy on the Protection, Management and Conservation of Heritage Objects.
1048. Section 34(1). It seems that grade 3 structures will be dealt with by the local authorities – J. Glazewski & L. du Toit, eds, *Environmental Law*, 19.11–19.21 (2nd edn, LexisNexis 2013 Service Issue 2).
1049. Section 44.
1050. The Director: Mineral Development may also grant an exemption. The structures also need not to be demolished if the owner of the land wishes to retain the structures – S. 44(1)(a)–(c). Bona fide mining equipment may be removed – s. 44(2).
1051. SAHRA established in terms of s. 11.
1052. Section 28(4).

development can take place.[1053] Land use planning differs from one province to another. This led to the question when one has to apply for a planning authorization and when not. In the case of *Maccsand (Pty) Ltd v. City of Cape Town and Others*,[1054] the dispute was whether a mining company had to apply for rezoning if it had already obtained a mining right. It was argued on behalf of the applicant that such authorization would not be necessary. The Court found, however, that the applicant had to apply for both a mining right and rezoning before the mining could commence. The mining took place in the Western Cape where the Land Use Planning Ordinance of the Cape lists mining as one of the categories for which zoning was necessary. In KwaZulu-Natal, the court found that an application for rezoning was not necessary in the case of sand mining as the provincial ordinance did not specify mining as an activity for which permission was necessary.[1055] However, the KwaZulu-Natal Planning and Development Act 6 of 2008 now provides that mines will have to apply for rezoning before they could mine. In the Western Cape High Court, it was also found in the *Maccsand* case that the mine has to apply for an environmental authorization before it could proceed. As hydraulic fracturing is to be undertaken in the Western Cape, gas exploration companies shall also have to submit rezoning applications before they would be able to proceed. Similarly, any other project involving energy will have to apply for all environmental and planning authorizations before it would be able to commence with construction.[1056]

In the case of any housing development, the developer must in addition indicate that electricity can be provided to the development in accordance with the municipality's energy plan.

§10. Spatial Planning and Land Use

284. Spatial planning and land use management takes place in terms of a myriad of legislative rules in the national and provincial sphere, with legacies from the apartheid era.[1057] In 2013, the Spatial Planning and Land Use Management Act 16 of 2013 was promulgated. The Act introduces a new spatial planning and land use management system for South Africa and states as its aims to introduce a uniform

1053. *See*, for example, General Notice 106 in *Government Gazette* 37337 of 21 Feb. 2014 – Notice of amendment of Land Use Management Scheme in terms of Town Planning Ordinance 15 of 1986. Eskom applies for rezoning of land on which a power station is situated from agricultural to industrial. On Land Use and Planning *see* E. Couzens & M. Lewis, *South Africa*. In International Encyclopaedia of Laws: Environmental Law (K. Deketelaere, ed., Kluwer Law International 2013), Part IV.

1054. 2012 4 SA 181 (CC).

1055. *Mtunzini Conservancy v. Tronox KZN Sands (Pty) Ltd and Another* 2013 4 BCLR 467 (KZD).

1056. *See also* J. van Wyk, *Planning in All Its (dis)guises: Spheres of Government, Functional Areas and Authority*, PELJ 288–318 (2012).

1057. The main national legislation dealing with land use planning and management includes, for example, the Development Facilitation Act 67 of 1995; Physical Planning Act 88 of 1967; Less Formal Township Establishment Act 113 of 1991; Physical Planning Act 125 of 1991 and the Removal of Restrictions Act 84 of 1967. There is also provincial land use planning ordinances and acts and some former homeland legislation that is still in place. *See* J. van Wyk, *Planning law in South Africa* (2nd edn, Juta 2012).

and effective system, to ensure social and economic inclusion, to ensure sustainable and effective use of land and to provide for cooperative governance between the different spheres of government.[1058] A national spatial development framework will indicate the desired land use patterns in the country, while a provincial spatial development framework will do the same for a specific province. Similarly regional spatial development frameworks may be developed.[1059] The implication of these frameworks is that they may indicate where energy development may occur or where not. These frameworks will inform planning decisions. All planning must be done in accordance with a municipal spatial development framework and executed in terms of land use schemes; however,[1060] The Municipal Planning Tribunal may on application change a permitted land use.[1061] The Minister may in the public interest exempt a piece of land or an area from the application of the Act.[1062] An Infrastructure Development Act 23 of 2014 commenced in July 2014. The purpose of the Act is, among others, to identify and implement strategic projects that are of significant economic and social importance to South Africa and to expedite the approval procedures of authorizations that apply to these projects.[1063] The projects include energy and energy-related projects mentioned in the schedules, such as electricity transmission and distribution, mines, oil and gas pipelines, refineries and other installations, power stations and other installations used to harness energy. Although the Act specifically states that the procedures for applications for authorizations in terms of other legislation (e.g., in relation to environmental impact assessments[1064]) must be adhered to, Schedule 2 of the Act sets an expedited time frame for submission, amendments, consultation and decision-making.[1065] It is doubtful whether environmental impacts would get the attention they deserve.

1058. Section 3. Also *see* J. van Wyk, *Can legislative intervention achieve spatial justice*, 48 Comparative and International Law Journal of Southern Africa 381–400 (2015); J. Van Wyk and P. Steyn, *Planning law Casebook* (Juta 2015); Van Wyk, J. *The Law on Planning and the Environment*, 1131–1176. In Fuggle and Rabie's Environmental Management in South Africa (King, N.D, Strydom, H.A. & Retief F.P., eds, 3rd edn, Juta 2018).
1059. Sections 13–19.
1060. Sections 22 and 24.
1061. Section 26(4) read with ss 35–46.
1062. Section 55.
1063. Section 2.
1064. Sections 17–18. Existing projects listed in Sch. 3 are also regarded as strategic projects that fall under the scope of the Act.
1065. Also *see* Government Notice 1124 in *Government Gazette* 39412 of 13 Nov. 2015 – Commencement of Spatial Planning and Land Use Management Regulations: Land Use Management and General Matters, 2015.

Chapter 5. Other Applicable Legislation

285. The demarcation of the whole of South Africa into local government areas in terms of the Local Government: Municipal Demarcation Act 27 of 1998 also had an influence on the energy industry. These industries fall under either municipal areas or district municipalities. In terms of the Constitution, the developmental duties of municipalities are set out as follows:[1066]

> A municipality must –
>
> (a) structure and manage its administration, budgeting, and planning processes, to give priority to the basic needs of the community, and to promote the social and economic development of the community; and
> (b) participate in national and provincial development programmes.

This implies that energy industries falling under the jurisdiction of local authorities will also be responsible for contributing to the development of the community around them. This places a new responsibility on these industries whose responsibilities have always been elsewhere.

Municipalities must, among other things, promote a safe and healthy environment,[1067] which places an obligation on municipalities to ensure that in the exercise of their discretion with regard to energy-related development projects not only economic development is furthered but also that health, environmental and safety issues are considered. In *Le Sueur v. Ethekwini Municipality*,[1068] the High Court decided that the Constitution authorizes municipalities to 'legislate in respect of environmental matters to protect the environment at the local level', although it is not directly stated as such.

286. The energy industry is subject to the Explosives Act 26 of 1956.[1069] Only authorized explosives may be used.[1070] The industry has to obtain several licences, authorizations and permits in this regard.[1071] In 2003, a new Explosives Act 15 of 2003 was promulgated but it has not been put into operation yet.

1066. Section 153. *See also* s. 19 of the Local Government: Municipal Systems Act 119 of 1998. Municipalities also have to compile integrated development plans – the energy industry will have to form part of the process in which these plans are formulated – *see*, *inter alia*, ss 1, 44(2), 56(2) and 83(3).
1067. Section 152(1)(d) of the Constitution.
1068. (9714/11) [2013] ZAKZPHC 6 (30 Jan. 2013) para. 40. *See* in this regard, A. Du Plessis and A. van der Berg, *RA Le Sueur v Ethekwini Municipality 2013 JDR 0178 (KZP): An Environmental Law Reading*, 25(3) Stellenbosch Law Review 580–594 (2014); A. Muir, *The Le Sueur case and a local government's constitutional right to govern: case notes*, *SA Public Law* 556–579 (2015).
1069. *See also* Government Notice R991 in *Government Gazette* 2741 of 26 Jun. 1970 – regulations 8 and 9 (arrangements for safe use of explosives).
1070. Section 5.
1071. *See*, for example, s. 6 – prohibition of storage of authorized explosives except in licensed premises; prohibition of blasting of explosives without a permit – s. 9; s. 22 – magazines for storage; s. 8 – importation of explosives must be done with a permit. *See also* Government Notice R1412 in *Government Gazette* 7648 of 3 Jun. 1981 for authorized explosives and Ch. 6 of Government

287. The energy industry must comply with the National Building Regulations and Building Standards Act 103 of 1977. Mines are, however, exempted from this Act, which is an indication of how mines were not properly controlled by the previous government.[1072] This led, for example, to poor housing for mine workers resulting in *inter alia* ill health and poor living conditions.[1073]

288. In terms of the Promotion of Access to Information Act 2 of 2000, the energy industry will have to divulge information to individuals protecting a right or to the state acting in the public interest.[1074] Information can only be refused if it falls under one of the grounds for refusal.[1075] On request, the industry has to disclose information in the public interest if there was a substantial contravention or failure to comply with a law or if an imminent and serious public safety or environmental risk exists.[1076]

Information may also be obtained from the state[1077] if it does not fall under one of the grounds for refusal of records.[1078] The state has a similar obligation as private bodies to reveal information with regard to the contravention or failure to comply with a law or an imminent and serious public safety or environmental risk. The public interest must clearly outweigh the harm contemplated.[1079] There are concerns that the right of access to information is not always adhered to.[1080]

Notice R1604 in *Government Gazette* 3648 of 8 Sep. 1972 (transportation of explosives); Ch. 7 (licensing of storage magazines); Ch. 8 (storage of blasting materials); Ch. 15 (destruction and disposal of explosives).

1072. Section 2(6).
1073. *See also Magidiwana and Another v. President of the Republic of South Africa and Others* [2014] 1 All SA 76 (GNP), where one of the issues, the living conditions of the workers on the mine, led to a long, violent and drawn out mine worker strike. Section 100(3) of the MPRDA is to be inserted to ensure that the Department of Mineral Resources and Energy may also consider the housing conditions of workers as one of the factors before issuing an authorization – Mineral and Petroleum Resources Development Bill (B15B-2013).
1074. Section 50.
1075. Sections 62–69. Grounds for refusal include the mandatory protection of privacy of a third party who is a natural person, of commercial information of a third party, of certain confidential information of a third party, of the protection of safety of individuals and the protection of property, records privileged in court proceedings, research information. The protection of commercial information of the private body itself is discretionary. A record may not be refused if it contains information about the results of any product or environmental testing carried out by or on behalf of the private body and its disclosure would reveal a serious public safety or environmental risk – s. 68(2). *See also* W. Du Plessis, *Access to Information* in Environmental Compliance and Enforcement . In South Africa: Legal Perspectives, 197–221 (A.R. Paterson & L.J. Kotzé, eds, Juta 2009); W. Du Plessis & S. de la Harpe, *The Duty to Disclose and the Right to Refuse: Undefined Dilemma of Environmental Practitioners: South Africa and other Jurisdictions*, 14 SAJELP 83–103 (2007).
1076. Section 70. This Act should be read with the Protected Disclosures Act 26 of 2000, which protects whistle-blowers.
1077. Section 11.
1078. Sections 33–45.
1079. Section 46.
1080. *See* Centre for Environmental Rights, *Turn on the Floodlights Trends in Disclosure of Environmental Licences and Compliance Data*, March 2013; Centre for Environmental Rights, *Barricading the Doors: The latest on our work on transparency in environmental governance in South Africa*, February 2013, Centre for Environmental Rights, *Money Talks: Commercial Interests and Transparency in Environmental Governance*, November 2014, http://cer.org.za/programmes/

289. The Promotion of Administrative Justice Act 4 of 2000 was promulgated to give effect to section 33 of the Constitution. The Act gives effect 'to the right to administrative action that is lawful, reasonable, fair and to the right to written reasons for administrative action'.[1081] An administrative action is defined as any decision taken, or failure to take a decision by an organ of state when exercising a power in terms of the Constitution or exercising a public power or function in terms of any other legislation.

A natural or juristic person other than an organ of state exercises an administrative function if it exercises a public power or performs a public function.[1082] The Act is important to the energy industry, as some sections of the industry can be regarded as government-regulated and others as semi-government regulated. They will have to comply with the provisions of this Act. However, industries that do not fall under government control can make use of the Act to control unreasonable decision-making by government when, for example, a licence or permit is refused.

---

transparency (accessed 10 Jan. 2015); Centre for Environmental Rights, *Full Disclosure: The Truth about Corporate Environmental Compliance in South Africa*, November 2016, http://fulldisclosure.cer.org.za/ (accessed 12 May 2019).

1081. Preamble.

1082. Section 1. The executive powers of the national executive, the provincial executive and municipalities are excluded from the definition, as are the legislative powers of these bodies, the judicial functions of a judicial officer or court, a decision to continue or discontinue a prosecution as well as any decision taken in terms of the Promotion of Access to Information Act 2 of 2000.

Part VI. Interaction Between Energy Law and Tax Law

290. The Department of Treasury's budget of 2019/20 shows that individuals contribute the largest portion of the tax revenue (ZAR 552.9 billion), while the taxes raised from corporates came to ZAR 229.6 billion. The contribution of indirect taxes, which includes value added tax, is ZAR 360.5 billion%.[1083]

291. Current fiscal policies link with the energy sector. There are five main categories of fiscal transfer – each energy sub-sector is treated differently. All sectors are subject to value added tax, with the exception of certain petroleum products. Private sector companies in the coal, liquid fuels, gas and renewable sectors pay income tax. Public utilities such as municipal electricity suppliers do not pay tax. In 1998, Eskom became a tax liable and dividend-paying entity.

292. In some sectors, especially the petroleum sector, special taxes and levies apply. The fuel levy contributes to more than 40% of the pump price of petrol and diesel. A levy is also placed on the price of aviation fuel.[1084] The levy on electricity sales by generators over a certain size is used to raise funds for the National Electricity Regulator.[1085] The synthetic fuels industry had substantive tariff protection in the past, which had a direct effect on the price of consumer fuel. In 2013, this represented a 224.5 c/l levy on petrol and 205.5 c/l diesel.

293. The public sector electricity suppliers (Eskom and municipalities) extract surpluses from some of their electricity consumers to cross-subsidize others (e.g., municipal services and former historically disadvantaged townships). These transfers represent a hidden tax, which is not subject to direct fiscal control by the government. The effect is that levies and taxes make up a high percentage of the retail

1083. National Treasury, *Budget Review 2019*, 20 Feb. 2019 http://www.treasury.gov.za/documents/national%20budget/2019/review/FullBR.pdf (accessed 12 May 2019).

1084. *See*, e.g., Government Notice R1052 in *Government Gazette* 38367 of 22 Dec. 2014.

1085. *See* the *Draft National Electrification Levies Bill* of 2000. The Bill is to impose levies to be paid into the National Electrification Fund. The fund will be used to assist the provision of electrification connections to households in South Africa. Eskom as well as municipalities will be able to apply for funding. By July 2019 the Bill has not been introduced into Parliament yet.

price of some fuels and a lower proportion in others. The price of coal includes only the 14% value added tax, and in the case of the informal domestic coal market, no tax is collected.[1086]

In 2003, the then DME published an *Electricity Basic Services Support Tariff (Free Basic Electricity) Policy*.[1087] In case of liquid fuels such as paraffin, no value added tax is added to make it affordable to poorer communities. Liquefied petroleum gas is still taxed as it is mainly used for commercial purposes. The use of liquefied petroleum is, however, monitored to determine whether policy changes will be necessary to assist the domestic sector; 50 kWh of grid electricity per month is provided free to poor households. According to the policy, approximately '56% of households connected to the national grid (in Eskom's licensed areas) consume less than 50 kWH of electricity per month'. This is more than the last quintiles of the population that can be classified as poor. It is suggested that this amount of energy per month is enough for lighting, media access and limited cooking. Some municipalities also introduced the provision of free electricity ranging between 20 kWh and 100 kWh per month. The funding for these allocations comes from the municipality itself, intergovernmental transfer allocation and cross-subsidization by the customers of distributing municipalities.

Approximately 88% of South African households are connected to the electricity grid. Where this is not possible, renewable energy resources are investigated and installed. Government also instals solar geysers on houses that are built for the poor. In rural areas where there is no electricity connection, renewable energy is provided to poorer communities.[1088] Municipalities have indigent policies that determine the price of subsidies and payment for services, if at all.[1089] Households using less than 150 kWh electricity per month may, for example, apply for a free basic electricity allocation. In 2002, it was estimated that the free allocation of electricity amounted to approximately ZAR 600 million. The monies were provided from national collected revenue and cross-subsidies by high electricity consumers.

In 2008, the then DME published the South African *Electricity Pricing Policy*.[1090] According to the policy, 'Government seeks to achieve an appropriate balance between meeting social equity, economic growth and environmental goals.'

1086. *White Paper on the Energy Policy of the Republic of South Africa* – Government Notice 3007 in *Government Gazette* 19606 of 17 Dec. 1998.

1087. General Notice 1693 in *Government Gazette* 25088 of 4 Jul. 2003.

1088. *See also* Department of Energy *Solar water heating*, http://www.energy.gov.za/files/swh_frame.html (accessed 13 Jan. 2015); Department of Energy, *Non-grid electrification guidelines*, 19 Mar. 2012, http://www.energy.gov.za/files/policies/electrification/NON%20GRID%20ELECTRIFICATION%20POLICY%202012.13.pdf (accessed 13 Jan. 2015); Department of Energy, *Policy Guidelines for the Electrification of Unproclaimed Areas*, 2 Jan. 2011, http://www.energy.gov.za/files/policies_frame.html (accessed 13 Jan. 2015), Department of Energy, *Schools and Clinics Electrification Policy Guidelines*, 2 Feb. 2010, http://www.energy.gov.za/files/policies/electrification/schools%20and%20clinis%20policy%202010-11.pdf (accessed 13 Jan. 2015), Department of Energy, *Policy Guidelines for the Electrification of Farm Dweller Houses*, 2 Feb. 2010, http://www.energy.gov.za/files/policies/electrification/updated%20farm%20dweller%20policy%202010.pdf (accessed 13 Jan. 2015).

1089. *See also* Department of Energy, *Free Basic Alternative Energy Policy*, Government Notice 391 in *Government Gazette* 29760 of 2 Apr. 2007.

1090. Government Notice 1398 in *Government Gazette* 31741 of 19 Dec. 2008.

A balance is to be found between affordable prices to households and low-cost electricity for industry. South Africa has more or less 1,100 domestic tariffs in existence, due indirectly to the culture of non-payment and electricity theft.

Cross-subsidization is based on inter-tariff cross-subsidization (one class of customers subsidize another class by being over-charged); intra-tariff cross-subsidization (high volume users subsidize low volume users) and geographic cross-subsidies (consumers nearer to point of generation pay the same tariff as consumers in distant geographical locations – from low-cost to high-cost areas). The true cost is not reflected. Revenue levied on electricity sales applied to other municipal services is regarded as a levy or tax. The determination of levies or taxes must be transparent.

294. Electricity pricing principles include the time-use principle, the development of cost-effective technology, incentives to promote the effective utilization of energy and the potential of the use of renewable energy sources.

In the policy, it is foreseen that in the medium to long-term the true cost of electricity generation and distribution should be reflected in the price of electricity excluding tax and levies. Consumers will pay separately for energy distribution and services (so-called energy wheeling charges). However, the fact that the electricity will not be affordable for some consumers will be taken into account. The externality of environmental costs was not taken into account by the policy as the National Treasury was at that stage undertaking research on the effectiveness of energy subsidies and taxation.

295. The Income Tax Act 58 of 1962[1091] contains a few measures that can be seen as tax incentives to protect the environment. Regional electricity distributors that are owned by a specific person and water service providers are exempted from the payment of normal tax.[1092]

The Act allows for general deductions.[1093] The expenditure to acquire an exploration or production licence may, for example, be deducted (section 11(1)(gD)). It is also possible to deduct tax for funding received for certified emissions reductions in terms of Cleaner Development Mechanism (CDM) Projects (section 12K). In terms of section 11B, expenditure for the purpose of scientific research for the development of a business may also be deducted. The South African Council for Scientific and Industrial Research (CSIR) must, however, certify that the research can be regarded as 'scientific'. Research on alternative energy uses or proper environmental protection can, therefore, possibly be deducted.

Certain new machinery, plants, implements, utensils and articles that are used for the first time by the taxpayer and used directly in the manufacturing process or for the production of renewable energy (including biodiesel and bioethanol), wind power, solar energy, hydropower and energy from biomass comprising organic waste, landfill gas or plant material) may be deducted in terms of section 12B. The

1091. *See also* D. Meyerowitz, *Meyerowitz on Income Tax 2003/2004*, paras 11.1, 11.19, 11.43–11.51 (The Taxpayer 2004).
1092. Section 10(1)(t)(viii) and (ix).
1093. Section 11.

court has decided that 'manufacturing process' also includes the processing of metal scrap waste, water purification works and soil conservation works.[1094] The Taxation Laws Amendment Act 15 of 2016 inserted section 12U. In terms of this section to allow a deduction for the construction of roads and the erection of fences (as well as improvements thereto) related to renewable energy (including wind, solar, hydro-power producing electricity of no more than 30 MW, as well as 'biomass comprising organic wastes, landfill gas or plant material').[1095]

Provision is also made for deductions in respect of pipelines used for the transportation of natural oil including liquid or solid hydrocarbon or combustible gas or its refined by-products as well as electricity transmission lines.[1096] Some deductions are allowed for the income derived from mining operations as well as for expenditure occurred during prospecting operations (section 15).

In 2013, the National Treasury introduced tax incentives for energy-efficiency measures.[1097] If a person can prove energy-efficiency savings, he or she may apply for a tax allowance in terms of section 12L(5) of the Income Tax Act 58 of 1962. The person (who may include an industry) have to register with the South African Energy Development Institute (SANEDI) as someone who wants to claim this allowance.[1098] The energy savings must be calculated by a measurement and verification professional as set out in SANS 50001.[1099] The baseline energy consumption must be determined in terms of ISO 50001.[1100]

296. In terms of section 8(1) of the Conservation of Agricultural Resources Act 43 of 1983, the Minister of Agriculture, Forestry and Fisheries may with concurrence of the Minister of Finance establish a scheme in terms of which assistance may be granted to land users by means of subsidies in respect of, *inter alia*, the construction of soil conservation works. Section 17A of the Income Tax Act 58 of 1962 provides for deductions of expenditure that was incurred for the construction of soil erosion works. Although a form of a direct tax incentive, it does not necessarily bring about soil conservation by landowners.[1101]

297. Several other environmental taxes have been introduced. International passengers have to pay ZAR 180 per passenger flying to Botswana, Lesotho, Namibia

---

1094. *Secretary for Inland Revenue v. Hersamer (Pty) Ltd* 1967 3 SA 177 (A); *Blue Circle Cement Ltd v. Commissioner for Inland Revenue* 1984 2 SA 764 (A); *Secretary for Inland Revenue v. Safranmark (Pty) Ltd* 1982 1 SA 113 (A).
1095. Also *see* Anon., *Environmental Support*, 56(2) Income Tax Reporter (31 Mar. 2017) 105–106.
1096. Section 12D. Expenditure for mining operations may also be deducted – s. 15.
1097. Government Notice R971 in *Government Gazette* 37136 of 19 Dec. 2013, as amended by Government Notice R186 in *Government Gazette* 38541 of 6 Mar. 2015 – Regulations in terms of s. 12L of the Income Tax Act, 1962, on the allowance for energy efficiency savings amended with effect from 1 Apr. 2015.
1098. SANEDI is established in terms of s. 7 of the National Energy Act 34 of 2008.
1099. SABS South African National Standard SANS 50001:2011 Energy Management Systems – this standard is based on the ISO50001 Energy Management System standard.
1100. *See also* W. Du Plessis, *Energy Efficiency and the Law: A Multidisciplinary Approach*, 111 South African Journal of Science (2015); ASSAf, *The State of Research, Development and Innovation of Electric Energy Efficiency Technologies in South Africa* (Academy of Science of South Africa, September 2017) DOI http://dx.doi.org/10.17159/assaf.2017/0017.
1101. *See* D. Meyerowitz, *Meyerowitz on Income Tax 2003/2004*, para. 12.198 (The Taxpayer 2004).

and Swaziland and all other international flight passengers ZAR 238. In 2004, a plastic bag levy was introduced[1102] and an electricity levy in 2009. The electricity levy is partially used to rehabilitate roads that are damaged by coal trucks and partially to subsidize solar heaters. There is also a levy on the use of incandescent light bulbs to encourage users to switch to more energy-saving bulbs.[1103] A CO_2 vehicle emissions tax is placed on passenger vehicles and double cabs to encourage users to buy more fuel-efficient vehicles.[1104] The income from environmental taxes was ZAR 11,220 million in the 2017–2018 tax year. However, this funding is not dedicated for environmental purposes.[1105]

298. In 2012, the National Treasury proposed the introduction of an electricity levy on non-renewable sources to fund energy-efficiency initiatives.[1106] The NEMWA allows the Minister to make regulations dealing with 'incentives and disincentives to encourage a change in behaviour towards the generation of waste and waste management by all sectors of society'.[1107]

299. Government introduced a carbon tax in 2019.[1108] The proposed carbon tax will be introduced at the rate of ZAR 120 per tonne CO_2-eq. Already in December 2010, government acknowledged in a Discussion Paper on Reducing Greenhouse Gas Emissions: The Carbon Tax Protocol that South Africa ranked as 'among the top 20 countries measured by absolute carbon dioxide (CO_2) emissions'. In May 2013, the National Treasury published a *Carbon Tax Policy Paper*[1109] for public

1102. In 2018, the levy on plastic bags was increased with 50% in order to serve as a disincentive for littering – *see* Anon, *Environmental and Health Taxes*. 2018 57(2) *Income Tax Reporter* 54.

1103. *Ibid.* The levy was increased in 2018 to try to incentivize energy-efficient behaviour.

1104. *Ibid.* In 2018 the vehicle emissions tax was increased to 'R 110 for every gram above 120 gCO_2/km for passenger vehicles' and 'R150 for every gram above 175 gCO_2/km for double cab vehicles'.

1105. Anon, *Expected Changes to Environmental Taxes*, *Engineering News*, 12 Apr. 2019, https://www.engineeringnews.co.za/article/expected-changes-to-environmental-taxes-2019-04-11/rep_id:4136 (accessed 3 Jul. 2019).

1106. South African Revenue Services, *Tax Proposals Budget 2012* (SARS 2012), http://www.treasury.gov.za/documents/national%20budget/2012/sars/SARS%20Tax%20Proposals%20at%20a%20glance.pdf (accessed 13 Jan. 2015). Government Notice R770 in *Government Gazette* 33514 of 31 Oct. 2010 – environmental levy on new motor vehicles manufactured in or imported into South Africa.

1107. Section 69(1)(bb). The Regulations may only be issued after consultation with the Minister of Finance. An MEC may issue similar regulations – s. 70.

1108. Carbon Tax Act 15 of 2019. Also *see* the preceding discussions: P. Gordhan, *Budget Speech 2014*, http://www.gov.za/2014-budget-speech-minister-finance-pravin-gordhan-0 (accessed 13 Jan. 2015); The Davis Tax Commission, *First Interim Report on Carbon Tax for the Minister of Finance*, 13 Nov. 2015 file:///C:/Users/10063994/Downloads/carbon_tax_brief_.pdf (accessed 12 May 2019); M. Barnard, *Koolstofbelasting as voorgestelde ekologiese fiskalehervormingsmaatreël in Suid-Afrika*, *Litnet Akademies* (2016) http://www.litnet.co.za/koolstofbelasting-voorgestelde-ekologiese-fiskalehervormingsmaatreel-suid-afrika/ (accessed 16 May 2019).

1109. National Treasury, *Carbon Tax Policy Paper. Reducing Greenhouse Gas Emissions and Facilitating the Transition to a Green Economy*, 2013, http://www.treasury.gov.za/public%20comments/Carbon%20Tax%20Policy%20Paper%202013.pdf (accessed 13 Jan. 2015).

comment. This policy document proposed tax measures (punitive) and tax incentives for energy-efficiency measures and the introduction of renewable energy. Provision will have to be made for tax-free thresholds and offsets. The tax would be introduced for 'emissions that result directly from fuel combustion and gasification, and from non-energy industrial processes ...[including] carbon dioxide, methane, nitrous oxide, perfluorocarbons, hydrofluorocarbons and sulphur hexafluoride'. The tax was to be increased at a rate of 10 cents per annum until 31 December 2019 when a new tax regime would have been introduced on 1 January 2020. The gradual increases in carbon taxes should allow large intensive energy users to reduce their energy emissions or to introduce more energy-efficiency measures.[1110]

The Carbon Tax Act 15 of 2019, that followed the Discussion Paper, came into operation on 1 June 2019. The Preamble to the Act states that the Act is based on the polluter pays principle and should act as an incentive to reduce greenhouse gas emissions.[1111] Taxpayers that conduct an activity resulting in greenhouse gas emissions and that is listed in Schedule 2 of the Act transgressing the threshold mentioned in the Schedule is liable to pay carbon tax.[1112] The carbon tax will be 'R120 per ton carbon dioxide equivalent of the greenhouse gas emissions of a taxpayer'.[1113] The Act also provides for a tax-free allowance for fossil-fuel combustion under certain circumstances.[1114]

300. Liquid fuel prices consist of costs and government subsidies. By pricing fuel, government is able to influence the fuel mix by adjusting taxation levels. A difference is, for example, made between the prices of petrol and diesel. Fiscal and energy policies must, however, be aligned, as these policies can either hinder or accomplish government's energy objectives.

The use of special-purpose levies earmarked in the budget to fund regulatory and other agencies is considered, provided that the additional costs be borne by those benefiting from the activities of the agency. These levies are to be managed in a responsible manner, promoting the principles of accountability, transparency and fiscal integrity.

1110. This discussion on carbon tax is based on W. Du Plessis, *Energy Efficiency and the Law: A Multidisciplinary Approach*, 111 South African Journal of Science (2015). *See also* Promethium Carbon, Carbon Trading in South Africa Trading Offsets against the Proposed Carbon Tax, March 2014.

1111. 'Greenhous gas emissions' is defined for purpose of the Act as 'gaseous constituents of the atmosphere, both natural and anthropogenic, that absorb and re-emit infrared radiation, and includes carbon dioxide (CO2), methane (CH4), nitrous oxide (N2O), hydrofluorocarbons (HFCs), perfluorocarbons (PFCs) and sulphur hexafluoride (SF6)' – s. 1.

1112. Section 4(1) states: 'The carbon tax must be levied in respect of the sum of the greenhouse gas emissions of a taxpayer in respect of a tax period expressed as the carbon dioxide equivalent of those greenhouse gas emissions resulting from fuel combustion and industrial processes, and fugitive emissions in accordance with the emissions factors determined in accordance with a reporting methodology approved by the Department of Environmental Affairs.' Also *see* General Notice 275 in Government Gazette 40762 of 3 Apr. 2017 – National Greenhouse Gas Emissions Reporting Regulations, 2016. The tax amount is to be calculated according to the formula set out in s. 6 and may be increased from time to time.

1113. Section 5.

1114. Sections 7–13 read with Sch. 1. Section 13 allows for an offset allowance, for example. The percentage of allowance is however restricted – s. 8.

301. Local governments will be able to tax electricity via an excise tax. The regional electricity distributors will collect this tax on behalf of the municipalities. The tax will be shown separately from the electricity consumption portion of the consumer's bill. The government may exclude certain consumer segments from this tax and may consider the phasing out of this tax.

302. In 2002, the Gas Regulator Levies Act 75 of 2002 was published in order to provide for the imposition of levies by the National Energy Regulator. The purpose of the levies is to obtain funds to meet the general administrative and other costs of the Regulator.[1115] The levies are 'to be based on the amount of gas, measured in gigajoules, delivered by importers and producers to inlet flanges of transmission or distribution pipelines and paid by the person holding the title to the gas at the inlet flange'.[1116] The levies must first be published for public comment. The Regulator must also provide reasons for the imposition of the levy. The Minister may approve or disapprove (with reasons) the proposed levies. The Regulator may only impose the levies after approval by the Minister of Energy in concurrence with the Minister of Finance.[1117] If a levy is not paid on the day it becomes due, interest will accrue. The interest is based on the uniform interest rate determined in terms of section 80(1)(b) of the Public Finance Management Act 1 of 1999.[1118] A levy lapses five years after imposition. Reimposition must be approved according to the procedure set out above.[1119]

303. In terms of the Petroleum Pipelines Act 60 of 2003, the National Energy Regulator must set as a condition of a licence the tariffs to be charged by a licensee. The tariff must be based on a systematic methodology applicable on a consistent and comparable basis, it must be fair, non-discriminatory, simple, transparent, predictable, stable and should promote access to affordable petroleum products.[1120]

The Petroleum Pipelines Levies Act 28 of 2004 allows the National Energy Regulator to impose levies to meet the authority's general and administrative costs. The levies must be based on 'the amount of petroleum, measured in litres, delivered by importers, refiners and producers to the inlet flanges of petroleum pipelines and must be paid by the person holding the title to the petroleum immediately after it has entered the inlet flange'.[1121] As is the case with the Gas Regulator Levies Act,

1115. Section 2. As of May 2005 the Act had not been put into operation but it will come into force on 1 Nov. 2005.
1116. Section 2(2).
1117. Section 2(3)–(5).
1118. Section 4.
1119. Section 5.
1120. Section 28. *See*, for example, Government Notice 40 in *Government Gazette* 37256 of 24 Jan. 2014 – Levy and Interest Payable on Petroleum Pipelines Industry.
1121. Section 2(1).

the Regulator must first publish the proposed levies for comment. Similar procedures as set out above in the case of the Gas Regulator Levies Act are to be followed.[1122]

1122. Section 2(2)–(8). The imposition of levies lapses five years after the day it was introduced – s. 5. The work of the Regulator may also be assessed to determine whether its performance is adequate – s. 6.

Part VII. Interaction Between Energy Law and Competition Law

304. Electricity generation and distribution are mainly done by Eskom, a government-controlled organization. There is no competition at this stage. The distribution of electricity is, however, fragmented and more than 2000 tariffs apply country-wide. A national tariff system and a move to implement cost-reflective tariffs have been proposed to ensure a more rational and equitable industry.[1123] There is some debate within the electricity sector to gradually introduce competition in the electricity market.[1124] The introduction of renewable energy and the connection of renewable energy plants to the national grid will in future also ensure a form of competition that has to be regulated by the NERSA. The government supports the idea of competition and the development of a Southern African Power Pool.[1125]

305. The Southern African Power Pool was created in 1996 by twelve Member States of SADC. The aim of the Pool is to 'facilitate the development of a competitive electricity market in Southern African region, give the end user a choice of electricity supply, to ensure that the Southern African region is the region of choice for investments by energy-intensive users, and to ensure sustainable energy developments through sound economic, environmental and social practices'.[1126] The Power Pool experiences a number of challenges, for example limited funding, lack of infrastructure, cannot meet the demand for energy and losses that are experienced.[1127]

South Africa ratified two SADC protocols, one on mining and one on energy. The purpose of these protocols is to ensure better cooperation in policy development and information as well as research in the energy and mining industry.[1128]

306. Gas distribution is still in an early phase. The production of gas is state-controlled, while the distribution is mainly done by Sasol. Future competition will

1123. D. Burger, ed., *South Africa Yearbook 2000/01*, 121–122 (Government Printer 2000).
1124. *Ibid.* at 475. Also *see* E. Steyn, *Electricity market restructuring: perspectives from abroad*, SA Mercantile Law 606–650 (2014).
1125. *White Paper on Energy.*
1126. Southern African Power Pool, http://www.sapp.co.zw/ (accessed 13 Jan. 2013). *See also* A. Klees, *Electricity Law in South Africa*, 57–58 (Juta 2014); N.J. Grobler, *Recent Developments in the Energy Sector of the Southern African Development Community (SADC)*, 8 Journal of Energy in Southern Africa (February) 15–17 (1997).
1127. Department of Energy, *Southern African Power Pool*, http://www.energy.gov.za/files/esources/electricity/electricity_powerpool.html (accessed 13 Jan. 2015).
1128. http://www.sapp.co.zw/ (accessed 13 Jan. 2013).

most probably be dealt with in terms of the Competition Act 89 of 1998, as is the case with petroleum, liquid fuels and renewable resources. All matters dealing with nuclear energy are at this stage still state-controlled but will most probably in future also be dealt with by the Competition Act. The National Energy Regulator has as one of its mandates to promote competition in the gas industry as well as the optimal use of available gas resources.[1129] A state-controlled entity in possession of a licence that sells any of its shares or assets to a privately controlled entity must do so by way of an open and transparent bidding procedure.[1130] The exploration and production of shale gas may bring a new dimension to the fore with regard to competition issues. One of the controversial clauses of the Mineral and Petroleum Resources Development Bill (B15B of 2013) deals with competition. In terms of the proposed section 86A, the state will have 'through the designated organ of state, a right to a 20% free carried interest in all new exploration and production rights from the effective date of such rights'. The state will also be able to participate in the acquisition at an agreed price and in production sharing agreements. The state will enter into a long-term joint operating agreement with the petroleum company and will have voting rights according to its interest. The state will have to appoint two representatives acting in the interest of the state. The Bill also proposes severe penalties in the case of contravention, for example refusal to provide information to the state mining activities and financial statements. A person not providing information will be held liable for 10% of its annual turnover and exports during the preceding financial year or to imprisonment of two years. Other transgressions (e.g., obstruction or hindering or opposing an authorized person, occupational detriment against an employer who disclosed information to the Minister of Mineral Resources and Energy or non-provision of information on request) will result in a fine of 5% of the annual turnover and exports during the preceding financial year or imprisonment of ten years.[1131] Although some competition will be allowed, it seems that the state will still ensure that it has control of the exploration and production activities of petroleum companies. In the consideration of applications for exploration and productions rights, the Department of Mineral Resources and Energy will take the manner in which the applicant complies with the Amended Broad Based Socio-Economic Empowerment Charter for the South African Mining and Minerals Industry. Competition within the mining and exploration and production industry will be allowed only if the provision is made for Black Empowerment.[1132]

307. The Petroleum Products Amendment Act 58 of 2003 prescribes the objectives that the Controller of Petroleum Products should take into account when issuing a licence. The objectives include among others the promotion of an efficient manufacturing, wholesale and retail petroleum industry, the facilitation of an environment conducive to efficient and commercially justifiable investment, the ensuring of the availability of petroleum products at competitive prices and the promotion of access to affordable petroleum products by low-income consumers for household

1129. Section 4(j)–(k) of the Gas Act 48 of 2001.
1130. Section 20 of the Gas Act 40 of 2001.
1131. Proposed amendments to s. 99 of the MPRDA.
1132. Proposed amendments to s. 80 of the MPRDA.

use.[1133] Before the promulgation of this Act, petroleum producers were not allowed to establish their own retail outlets. In terms of the new legislation, a company such as Sasol, for example, is now allowed to open retail facilities in its own name. The Act also provides for Black Economic Empowerment and in considering licences the Controller of Petroleum Products should promote the advancement of historically disadvantaged South Africans and should give effect to the Charter signed by the different petroleum stakeholders.[1134] The Minister of Mineral Resources and Energy must prescribe a system for the allocation of site and their corresponding retail licences and the supply of prescribed petroleum products to such licensees. The Controller will be bound for a period of ten years (or date set in the regulation) from the date of commencement of the regulation. The purpose of the Minister's regulation will be to transform the retail sector into one that has the optimum number of efficient sites, to ensure equilibrium between all participants in the industry, to promote efficient investment in the retail sector and the productive use of facilities. This he or she could do by limiting the number of sites and corresponding retail licences or by linking the total number of sites and licences to the mass or volume of prescribed petroleum products sold by licensed retailers.[1135] The Minister's regulation must, however, allow licensed wholesalers to trade with one another and to conclude agreements. He or she may also specify that petroleum products manufactured from coal, natural gas or vegetable matter which meets prescribed standards should be supplied to licensed retailers in preference to the supply of prescribed petroleum products produced from other raw materials.[1136]

308. The Competition Act 89 of 1998 provides for the establishment of a Competition Commission[1137] responsible for the investigation, control and evaluation of restrictive practices[1138] and merger control.[1139] A competition tribunal[1140] and a competition appeal court[1141] are established to adjudicate these matters.[1142]

The purpose of the Act is to promote and maintain competition in the country in order to promote 'the efficiency, adaptability and development of the economy, to provide consumers with competitive prices and product choices, to promote employment and advance social and economic welfare ..., to expand opportunities for South African participation in world markets and to recognize the role of foreign competition, to ensure that small and medium-sized enterprises have an equitable opportunity to participate in the community and to promote a greater spread

1133. Section 2A(3).
1134. Schedule to the Act.
1135. Section 2E(1)–(2). Before the amendment to the Act, General Notice 271 in *Government Gazette* 23163 of 25 Feb. 2002 specified the terms of reference for an independent third party to assist the Department of Energy in the profit monitoring of the marketing of petroleum of the oil industry.
1136. Section 2E(3).
1137. Established in terms of s. 19. *See* functions – s. 21. The commission has entry and search authority under warrant or without a warrant – ss 46–49.
1138. Sections 4 and 5.
1139. Chapter 3.
1140. Established in terms of s. 26 – *see* functions – s. 27. For orders of the tribunal *see* s. 60.
1141. Section 36 – *see* functions – s. 37.
1142. Sections 26–43.

of ownership of historically disadvantaged communities'.[1143] 'Public regulation' is defined as any 'national, provincial or local government legislation or subordinate legislation or any licence, tariff, directive or similar authorization issued by a regulatory authority or pursuant to any statutory authority'.[1144] 'Industry' is not defined.

The Act applies to all economic activity in the country or that might have an effect on the country. If an industry or sector of an industry is subject to the jurisdiction of another regulatory authority, the two authorities will have concurrent jurisdiction over the matter.[1145] Both restricted horizontal and vertical business practices are prohibited. Restrictive horizontal practices include the direct or indirect fixing of purchase or selling prices or any other trading conditions, the division of markets by allocating customers, suppliers, territories or specific types of goods or services and collusive tendering.[1146]

Vertical practices entail an agreement between parties in a vertical relationship, which has the effect of substantially preventing or lessening competition in the market. If a party to the agreement can prove that a technological efficiency or other pro-competitive gain resulted from the agreement, it will not be restricted. The practice of minimum resale price is also prohibited. A supplier or producer may, however, recommend a minimum sale price if it is clear that the recommendation is not binding, or if the price appears on the goods, the words 'recommended price' must be added.[1147]

A firm is regarded as a dominant firm if it has at least 45% of the market or at least 35% but less than 45% of the market (unless it can show that it does not have market power) or less than 35% of that market but has market power. A dominant firm may not charge an excessive price to the detriment of the consumers, refuse to give a competitor access to an essential facility when it is economically feasible to do so or engage in an exclusionary act.[1148]

A firm may apply to the competition commission to exempt an agreement or practice from the Act.[1149] Mergers are controlled in terms of Chapter 3 of the Act. A merger is defined as the direct or indirect acquisition or direct or indirect establishment of control over the whole or part of the business of a competitor or supplier.[1150] The competition commission must be notified of any proposed mergers. After consideration,[1151] the Competition Commission may approve the merger with

1143. Section 2.
1144. Section 1.
1145. Section 3(1) read with s. 3(1A).
1146. Section 4.
1147. Section 5.
1148. Sections 7 and 8(a)–(c). Exclusionary acts include *inter alia* the requiring or inducing a supplier or customer not to deal with a competitor; refusing to supply scarce goods to a competitor; selling goods or services on condition that the buyer purchases separate goods or services unrelated to the object of the contract, selling goods below their marginal or average variable cost or buying-up a scarce supply of intermediate goods or resources acquired by a competitor – s. 8(d). Price discrimination is also prohibited – *see* s. 9.
1149. Section 10. The Competition Commission is established in terms of ss 19–25 of the Act. In future the Act may also regulate complex monopoly conduct – the to be inserted s. 10A – Competition Amendment Act 1 of 2009 to be put into operation.
1150. Section 12.
1151. Section 12A.

or without conditions or prohibit the implementation of the merger. In the case of a large merger, the Competition Tribunal and the Minister of Trade and Industry must be informed.[1152] The tribunal can approve with or without conditions or prohibit the merger.[1153] Appeal is allowed to the competition appeal court.[1154] Decisions, judgments and orders of the Competition Commission, Competition Tribunal and Competition Appeal Court may be enforced as if they are orders of the High Court.[1155]

In most instances, the energy sector is subject to the decisions of their own regulatory authorities. Regarding matters of competition, however, the Competition Commission will have concurrent jurisdiction over the matter. The Competition Commission may also lodge its own investigations into competition issues in an industry that does not deal with a specific merger.[1156]

309. In 2012, the Independent System and Market Operator Bill (B9B-2012) was published. The Bill lapsed as it did not pass through Parliament before the 2014 elections and has to be reintroduced. The passage of the Bill was halted, as there were requests for a due diligence study as well as a cost-benefit analysis of the asset transfer and the establishment of this operator (ISMO). The Minister of Energy announced that the Bill will be reintroduced during the 2015 parliamentary session.[1157] The Bill surfaces again in 2019, but by December 2019, it has not been approved.

The Bill aims to, among others, establish ISMO as a state-owned company to trade electricity to ISMO customers and to manage tariff aggregation of generators in the sale of electricity.[1158] ISMO must buy electricity from generators and external traders in line with the *Integrated Resource Plan 2010–2030*. ISMO will be able to conclude agreements and decide on tariffs. It will take over the work of Eskom with regard to ensuring the uninterrupted supply of energy, make decisions on shutdowns for emergency and load-shedding, among other things.[1159] Eskom Holdings

---

1152. Section 14A. The Competition Tribunal is established in terms of ss 26–35, 51–60 of the Act. The Competition Tribunal may only impose administrative penalties and make certain orders – ss 58–59. With regard to the enforcement of the Act, *see* ss 64–68.

1153. Section 14.

1154. Section 17. The Competition Appeal Court is established in terms of ss 36–39, 61–63 of the Act.

1155. Section 64.

1156. *See*, for example, Government Notice 486 in *Government Gazette* 37740 of 20 Jun. 2014 – Market Inquiry into Liquefied Petroleum Gas Industry in terms of Ch. 4A of the Act; Government Notice 621 in *Government Gazette* 37903 of 15 Aug. 2014 – Terms of Reference for Market Inquiry into Liquefied Petroleum Gas; Competition Commission, *Liquefied Petroleum Gas (LPG) Market Inquiry Request for further Submissions* 27 Aug. 2015 http://www.compcom.co.za/wp-content/uploads/2014/09/LPG-Request-for-further-submissions_Final.pdf (accessed 12 May 2019).

1157. *See also* P. Saxby, *Constraints to 'Accelerating' IPP Programme will be 'Addressed' – Minister*, Issue 3668, Legalbrief Policy Watch, 14 Jan. 2015. On the IPP Programme, *see* A. Klees, *Electricity law in South Africa*, 273–278 (Juta 2014).

1158. Clauses 2–4.

1159. Clause 4. ISMO may also apply to be exempted from some of the provisions of the Companies Act 71 of 2008. The eventual Act will also provide for inspectors to oversee the implementation and enforcement of the Act – s. 34. On Eskom, *see* A. Klees, *Electricity Law in South Africa*, 278–291 (Juta 2014).

will be dissolved.[1160] Eskom is not able to buy electricity from Independent Power Producers (IPPs);[1161] this function was transferred to the Minister responsible for energy and the Department responsible for energy.[1162] The Minister will be able to issue directives if ISMO transgresses the law and may dissolve the board, bringing the independence of ISMO into disrepute.[1163] Although the Bill seems to deal with the establishment of an independent operator who has to purchase and distribute electricity, it will do more than that and it is questionable whether competition issues will be regulated properly. The relationship between the proposed ISMO, the National Energy Regulator, the Competition Commission, Electricity Regulation Act 4 of 2006 and public procurement legislation[1164] is also not clear.

310. A Draft Electricity Regulation Second Amendment Bill[1165] was published for comment in 2012. According to the Bill, NERSA will have to issue a licence if a competitive IPP procurement process has been conducted and finalized (despite any other provision in the Act).[1166] NERSA will not be able to grant a licence for new generation capacity if the Minister of Energy has not approved the application.[1167] The Minister may also prescribe the licence conditions and tariff requirements.[1168]

Klees[1169] is of the opinion that 'a "silent" power sector reform is already under way in South Africa ... While the REIPPPP promotes competition between IPPs "for the market", no competition "in the market" takes place'. According to him, several obstacles still remain including public-private partnerships that were concluded to generate alternative energy and the fact that Eskom still has a monopoly as a single buyer. He concludes that 'a first step towards a competitive environment

1160. Clauses 39–40.
1161. *See* Government Notices 1074–1076 in *Government Gazette* 36005 of 19 Dec. 2012 – IPP Procurement Programme, Baseload and Medium Risk Mitigation in terms of s. 34(1) of the Electricity Regulation Act 4 of 2006, as amended by Government Notice 731 in *Government Gazette* 39111 of 18 Apr. 2015. *See also* A. Klees, *Electricity Law in South Africa*, 278–291 (Juta 2014); General Notice 382 in *Government Gazette* 32122 of 17 Apr. 2009 – South Africa renewable energy feed-in tariff (REFIT): Regulatory guidelines 26 Mar. 2009 and Department of Energy, *Renewable Energy Independent Power Producer Procurement Programme*, http://www.ipprenewables.co.za/ (accessed 13 Jan. 2015).
1162. Government Notice R399 in *Government Gazette* 34262 of 4 May 2011, as amended by Government Notice 733 in *Government Gazette* 39111 of 18 Aug. 2015. *See also* A. Klees, *Electricity law in South Africa*, 267–272 (Juta 2014) – at this stage Eskom is the sole buyer of the generated electricity. According to Klees (at 270–271), the role players are the Minister of Energy (and the Department of Energy), Eskom, the IPPs and NERSA.
1163. Clause 36.
1164. *See* A. Klees, *Electricity Law in South Africa*, 242–265 (Juta 2014). The Renewable Energy Independent Power Producer Procurement Programme is partially exempted from the procurement legislation. *See also* General Notice R399 in *Government Gazette* 34262 of 4 May 2011.
1165. General Notice 905 in *Government Gazette* 34870 of 19 Dec. 2012.
1166. The to be inserted s. 13(5).
1167. New s. 13A. s. 33A will regulate the Minister in publishing an Integrated Resource Plan. Section 34 is also to be amended – more or less corresponding with the wording of the 2011 regulations. *See also* A. Klees, *Electricity Law in South Africa*, 272–273 (Juta 2014).
1168. New s. 14A.
1169. A. Klees, *Electricity Law in South Africa*, 293–294 (Juta 2014).

might have to allow IPPs to sell their power directly to private off-takers on a 'willing buyer, willing seller' basis, with no direct involvement of the state and thus without the 'government support' as provided for under the REIPPPP'.[1170]

1170. REIPPPP refers to the Renewable Energy Procurement Programme.

Conclusion

311. South Africa's legislation dealing with energy is fragmented. Specific topics are regulated by different acts, which may confuse developers. One of the major criticisms against South African energy legislation is that it also does not address the cycle of production, exploitation, transport, distribution and consumption. The topics are either not dealt with or to be found in different pieces of legislation. The pre-1994 dispensation was more focused on exploitation rather than taking into account people and the environment.

In the *White Paper on the Energy Policy of the Republic of South Africa*,[1171] the government commits itself to:

> promote access to basic energy services for poor households, in order to ameliorate the negative health impacts arising from the use of certain fuels(;) ... to work towards the establishment and acceptance of broad national targets for the reduction of energy-related emissions that are harmful to the environment and human health (and) ... to ensure a balance between exploiting fossil fuels and maintenance of acceptable environmental requirements.
>
> The government also foresees that the environmental costs are to be included in the price, even though cheap energy in the past benefited South Africa's foreign exchange. International standards may have an adverse effect on the country's future exports – the government, therefore, wants to find a balance between energy prices and sustainable environmental standards.

312. Since 1998 and even more so after 2005, there was an exponential growth in the number of acts, policies, strategies and subordinate legislation regulating not only energy matters but also the nexus between energy, the environment, health and safety. This growth can be accounted to the fact that South Africa is responding to its international and regional obligations as well as to section 24 of the Constitution.[1172]

1171. Government Notice 3007 in *Government Gazette* 19606 of 17 Dec. 1998.

1172. *See also* DEA, *Environmental Sustainability Indicators: Technical Report* 164–178 (Government Printer 2009), https://www.environment.gov.za/sites/default/files/docs/2009envirosustainability_indicators_global_stewardship.pdf (accessed 13 Jan. 2015).

Selected Bibliography

Alberts, R. & J. Moolman. *Protecting Ecosystems by Way of Biological Control: Cursory Reflections on the Main Regulatory Instruments for Biological Control Agents, Present and Future*. 9 Potchefstroom Electronic Law Journal 184 (2013).

Ashukem, J-C.N. *Setting the Scene for Climate Change Litigation in South Africa: Earthlife Africa Johannesburg v Minister of Environmental Affairs and Others [2017] ZAGPPHC 58 (2017) 65662/16*, 13/1 Law, Environment and Development Journal 35 (2017), http://www.lead-journal.org/content/17035.pdf.

ASSAf, *The State of Research, Development and Innovation of Electrical Energy Efficiency Technologies in South Africa* (Academy of Science of South Africa, September 2017) DOI http://dx.doi.org/10.17159/assaf.2017/0017.

Badenhorst, P.J. & M. Carnelley. *Application for a Mining License and the Audi Alteram Partem Rule*. 63 Tydskrif vir Hedendaags Romeins-Hollandse Reg 689 (2000).

Badenhorst, P.J., Pienaar, J.M. & H. Mostert. *Silberberg and Schoeman's The Law of Property* (4th edn, LexisNexis 2003).

Barnard, M. *The Role of International Sustainable Development Law Principles Enabling Effective Renewable Energy Policy in South Africa*. 15 Potchefstroom Electronic Law Journal 207 (2012).

M. Barnard, *Koolstofbelasting as voorgestelde ekologiese fiskalehervormingsmaatreël in Suid-Afrika, Litnet Akademies* (2016) http://www.litnet.co.za/koolstofbelasting-voorgestelde-ekologiese-fiskalehervormingsmaatreel-suid-afrika/ (accessed 16 May 2019).

Bhagavan, M.R. & S. Karekezi. *Energy for Rural Development* (Zed Books 1992).

Barrie, G.N. *South Africa and Nuclear Energy – National and International Legal Aspects*. Tydskrif vir Suid-Afrikaanse Reg 153 (1988).

Barrie, G.N. *The Nuclear Non-Proliferation Treaty on the Eve of the Fourth Review Conference*. Tydskrif vir Suid-Afrikaanse Reg 100 (1991).

Barrie, G.N. *Radioactive Waste Disposal: An International Law Perspective*. Tydskrif vir Suid-Afrikaanse Reg 177 (1989).

Blignaut, J. *Climate Change: The Opportunity Cost of Medupo and Kusile Power Stations*. 23 South African Journal of Energy 67 (2012).

Bosman, C., Kotzé, L. & W. Du Plessis. *The Failure of the Constitution to Ensure Integrated Environmental Management from a Cooperative Governance Perspective*. 19 SA Public Law 411 (2004).

Selected Bibliography

Bosman, C., Alberts, R. & C. Roos. *Integrated Waste Management,* 1055–1097. In N.D. King, H.A. Strydom & F.P. Retief, eds, Fuggle and Rabie's Environmental Management in South Africa (3rd edn, Juta 2018).

Bosman, C., Kidd, M. & R. Alberts. *Water Quality Management,* 995–1054. In N.D. King, H.A. Strydom & F.P. Retief, eds, Fuggle and Rabie's Environmental Management in South Africa (3rd edn, Juta 2018).

Bray, E. *Fragmentation of the Environment.* 10 SA Public Law 173 (1995).

Bray, E. *Clearing the Air – Industrial Polluters Beware.* 3 South African Journal of Environmental Law and Policy 211 (1996).

Bray, E. *Towards Sustainable Development: Are We on the Right Track?.* 5 South African Journal of Environmental Law and Policy 1 (1998).

Bray, E. *Administrative Justice,* 152–196. In A. Paterson & L.J. Kotzé, eds, Environmental Compliance and Enforcement (Juta 2009).

Bray, W. *Cooperative Governance in the Context of the National Environmental Management Act 107 of 1998.* 5 South African Journal of Environmental Law and Policy 13 (1999).

Bronstein, V. *Mapping legislative and executive powers over 'municipal planning': exploring the boundaries of local, provincial and national control,* South African Law Journal (2015): 639–663.

Centre for Environmental Rights. *Barricading the doors.* February 2013, http://cer.org.za/wp-content/uploads/2013/03/Barricading-The-Doors-Feb-20131.pdf (accessed 9 January 2014).

Centre for Environmental Rights. *Turn on the Floodlights Trends in Disclosure of Environmental Licences and Compliance Data.* March 2013, http://cer.org.za/programmes/transparency (accessed 10 January 2015).

Centre for Environmental Rights. *Money Talks: Commercial Interests and Transparency in Environmental Governance.* November 2014, http://cer.org.za/programmes/transparency (accessed 10 January 2015).

Chamberlain, L. *Beyond Litigation: The Need for Creativity in Working to Realise Environmental Rights* 13(1) LEAD Journal (2017) http://lead-journal.org/2017.htm (accessed 16 May 2019).

Couzens, E. *NEMA – A Step Closer to Coherence?.* 6 South African Journal of Environmental Law and Policy 13 (1999).

Couzens, E. & M. Lewis, *South Africa.* In K. Deketelaere et al., eds, Encyclopaedia of Laws: Environmental Law (Kluwer Law International 2013).

Crothers, C. *Levels of Winter Smoke Pollution in South Africa: Establishing a Need for Policy to be Developed.* 5 South African Journal of Environmental Law and Policy 141 (1998).

Department of Environmental Affairs, *Guidelines Series of the National Climate Change Response Monitoring and Evaluation System Volume 1* (June 2019).

De Wet, E. & A.A. Du Plessis. *The Meaning of Certain Substantive Obligations Distilled from International Human Rights Instruments for Constitutional Environmental Rights in South Africa.* 10 African Human Rights Law Journal 345 (2010).

Dixon, C. *The Puzzle of Media and Sector Legislation: Putting the Pieces Together to Create the Legal Picture for the Mining Industry.* 99 The Journal of the South African Institute of Mining and Metallurgy 149 (1999).

D'Oliveira, J.A. *Theft of Electricity: A Short Circuit? – S v. Ndebele*. 75 Tydskrif vir Hedendaags Romeins-Hollandse Reg 312 (2012).

Dube, L.T.N. *Wind Energy Potential in Maputaland*. 12 Development Southern Africa, No. 5 (October 1995) 625.

Dugard, J., et al., eds *Climate Talk – Rights, Poverty and Justice* (Juta 2013).

S.E. Uhunamure, N.S. & A. Musyoki, *Driving forces for fuelwood use in households in the Thulamela municipality, South Africa*, 28 Journal of Energy in Southern Africa (2017) http://dx.doi.org/10.17159/2413-3051/2017/v28i1a1635.

Du Plessis, A. *Understanding the Legal Context*, 11–40. In A. Paterson & L.J. Kotzé, eds, Environmental Compliance and Enforcement in South Africa (Juta 2009).

Du Plessis, A. ed. *Environmental Law and Local Government* (Juta 2015).

Du Plessis, A. *Climate Change, Public Trusteeship and the Tomorrows of the Unborn*, 31(2) South African Journal of Human Rights (2015): 269–293.

Du Plessis, A. *A Role for Local Government in Global Environmental Governance and Transnational Environmental Law from a Subsidiarity Perspective*, 48(2) Comparative and International Law Journal of Southern Africa (2015): 281–316.

Du Plessis A. & R. Alberts. *Cooperative Environmental Governance: At the Coalface of Sustainable Infrastructure Development in South Africa*, 29(2) Southern African Public Law (2014): 441–468.

Du Plessis, A. & O. Fuo. *Governing Authorities in the Same Boat and a Tale of Two Schedules: Marius Nel v Hessequa Local Municipality* (2015) 20 Commonwealth Journal of Local Governance 6076 (2017).

Du Plessis, A.A. *Land Restitution through the Lens of Environmental Law: Some Comments on the South African Vista*. 9 Potchefstroom Electronic Law Journal 1 (2006).

Du Plessis, A.A. *Public Participation, Good Environmental Governance and Fulfilment of Environmental Rights*. 11 Potchefstroom Electronic Law Journal 1 (2008).

Du Plessis, A.A. *Perceptive Approaches to the Interpretation and Realisation of South Africa's Constitutional Environmental Right*. 6 South African Journal of Environmental Law and Policy 129 (2009).

Du Plessis. A.A. *Adding Flames to the Fuel: Why Further Constitutional Adjudication is Required for South Africa's Constitutional Environmental Right to Catch Light*. 16 South African Journal for Environmental Law and Policy 75 (2009).

Du Plessis, A.A. *A Government in Deep Water? Some Thoughts on the State's Duties in Relation to Water Arising from South Africa's Bill of Rights*. 19 Review of European Community and International Environmental Law (RECIEL) 316 (2010).

Du Plessis, A.A. *Local Environmental Governance and the Role of Local Government in Fulfilling 24 of the South African Constitution*. 21 Stellenbosch Law Review 265 (2010).

Du Plessis, A.A. *South Africa's Constitutional Environmental Right Generously Interpreted: What is in it for Poverty?* 27 South African Journal on Human Rights 299 (2011).

Selected Bibliography

Du Plessis, A.A. and A. van der Berg, *RA Le Sueur v Ethekwini Municipality 2013 JDR 0178 (KZP): An Environmental Law Reading*, 25(3) Stellenbosch Law Review (2014): 580–594.

Du Plessis, A.A. *The 'Brown' Environmental Agenda and the Constitutional Duties of Local Government in South Africa: A Conceptual Introduction, Potchefstroom Electronic Law Journal* (2015): 1845–1880.

Du Plessis, A.A. *The Promise of 'Wellbeing' in Section 24 of the Constitution of South Africa*, South African Journal on Human Rights (2018) https://doi.org/10.1080/02587203.2018.1475116.

Du Plessis, A.A. *Local Government and the Pursuit of Urban Sustainability in South Africa,* 263–281. In N.D. King, H.A. Strydom & F.P. Retief, eds, *Fuggle and Rabie's Environmental Management in South Africa* (3rd edn, Juta 2018).

Du Plessis, L.M. *An Introduction to Law* (3rd edn, Juta 1999).

Du Plessis, W. *Integration of Existing Environmental Legislation in the Provinces.* 2 South African Journal for Environmental Law and Policy 23 (1995).

Du Plessis, W. *Inligtingsreëlings in Duitsland.* 61 THRHR 85 (1998).

Du Plessis, W. *Reg op Omgewingsinligting in die Europese Gemeenskap.* Tydskrif vir Suid-Afrikaanse Reg 222 (1998).

Du Plessis, W. *Right to Environmental Information in the USA.* 5 South African Journal for Environmental Law and Policy 115 (1998).

Du Plessis, W. *Enforcement of Environmental Rights by Way of a Right to Information.* 20 *Obiter* 92 (1999).

Du Plessis, W. *'n Reg op Omgewingsinligting in Nederland.* 10 Stellenbosch Law Review 36 (1999).

Du Plessis, W. *Legal Mechanisms for Cooperative Governance in South Africa: Successes and Failure.* 23 SA Public Law 87 (2008).

Du Plessis, W. *Hichange – A New Direction in Environmental Matters? – Hichange Investments (Pty) Ltd v. Cape Produce Co (Pty) Ltd T/A Pelts Products & Others.* 11 South African Journal of Environmental Law and Policy 135 (2004).

Du Plessis, W. *Recent Developments in the Use of Environmental and Energy Taxes in South Africa*, 217–337. In K. Deketelaere et al., eds, Critical Issues in Environmental Taxation (Oxford University Press 2007).

Du Plessis, W. *Access to Information*, 197–221. In A. Paterson & L.J. Kotzé, eds, *Environmental Compliance and Enforcement in South Africa: Legal Perspectives* (Juta 2009).

Du Plessis, W. *Cross-Border Gas Pipelines and Sustainability in Southern Africa*, 279–296. In J. Benidickson et al., eds, *Environmental Law and Sustainability after Rio* (Edward Elgar 2011).

Du Plessis, W. *Energy Efficiency and the Law: A Multidisciplinary Approach.* 111 South African Journal of Science (2015), http://dx.doi.org/10.17159/ sajs.2015/20130302#2013-0302.

Du Plessis, W. *Regulation of Hydraulic Fracturing in South Africa: A Project Life-Cycle Approach?* 18(5) Potchefstroom Electronic Law Journal (2015): 1440–1478.

Du Plessis, W. *Energy Efficiency: The Progress of Policy, Legislation, and the Role of the Courts in South Africa*, 24 South African Journal of Environmental Law and Policy (2019):175–204.

Du Plessis, W. & S. De la Harpe. *The Duty to Disclose and the Right to Refuse: Undefined Dilemma of Environmental Practitioners: South Africa and Other Jurisdictions.* 14 South African Journal of Environmental Law and Policy 83 (2007).

Du Plessis, W. & T. Murombo. *Energy*, 877–907, In A.A. Du Plessis, ed., *Local Government and Environmental Law in South Africa* (Juta 2015).

Du Plessis, W. & J. Nel. *Environmental Framework Law: A Strategy Towards Integrating Pluralist Legislation.* 90 Archiv für Sozialphilosophie 197 (2004).

Du Plessis, W. & J. Nel. *Driving Compliance to and Enforcement of South African Legislation by Means of a Hybrid of 'New' Environmental Governance Instruments*, 259–285. In P. LeRoy, eds, Compliance and Enforcement in Environmental Law (Edward Elgar 2011).

Du Plessis W. and J.M. Pienaar, *Illegal Mining: The Continued Struggle for Mineral Resources, Communities and the Environment,* in C. Rautenbach (ed), In the shadow of an African Boabab (Juta 2018.

Du Toit, L. *Promoting Clean Development Mechanism Implementation in South Africa: Law and Policy.* 24 SA Public Law 33 (2009).

Faure, M. & W. Du Plessis, eds. *The Balancing of Interests in Environmental Law in Africa* (Pretoria University Press 2011).

Feris, L. *Constitutional Environmental Rights: An Under-utilised Resource.* 24(1) South African Journal on Human Rights 29 (2008).

Feris, L. *The Socio-economic Nature of Section 24(b) of the Constitution: Some Thoughts on HTF Developers (Pty) Ltd v. Minister of Environmental Affairs and Tourism 2006 5 SA 512 (T).* 23 SA Public Law 194 (2008).

Feris, L. *Compliance Notices, a New Tool in Enforcement.* 9 Potchefstroom Electronic Law Journal 53 (2006).

Feris, L. *The Human Right to Sanitation: A Critique on the Absence of Environmental Considerations,* Review of European, Comparative & International Environmental Law (RECIEL) 24(1) (2015).

Ferreira-Snyman A. & W. Du Plessis. *Grondwetlike waardes, die openbare administrasie en die reg op toegang tot omgewingsinligting.* 67 Koers 1 (2002).

Ferreira, G., Du Plessis, W. & K. Van der Walt. *A License to Mine, Audi Alteram Partem and NEMA.* 6 South African Journal of Environmental Law and Policy 245 (1999).

Ferreira, G.M. *Constitutional Values and the Application of the Fundamental Right to a Clean and Healthy Environment to the Private Law Relationship.* 6 South African Journal of Environmental Law and Policy 171 (1999).

Ferreira, G.M. *Grondwetlike waardes en sosio-ekonomiese regte met verwysing na die reg op 'n skoon en gesonde omgewing*. Tydskrif vir Suid-Afrikaanse Reg 285 (1999).

Ferreira, G.M. *Volhoubare ontwikkeling, regverdigbare ontwikkeling en die fundamentele reg op 'n skoon en gesonde omgewing*. Tydskrif vir Suid-Afrikaanse Reg 434 (1999).

Field, T-L. *Realizing the National Environmental Act's Potential to Bring Polluters to Book.* 121 South African Law Journal 772 (2004).

Fourie, W., ed., *Implementing Sustainable Development Goals in South Africa: Challenges and Opportunities*, Report, University of Pretoria, August 2018.

Selected Bibliography

Freedman, W. *Environmental Conservation and the Concept of Ownership as an Absolute and Unrestricted right.* 8 South African Journal of Environmental Law and Policy 128 (2001).

Freedman, W. *Environmental Conservation and the Concept of Ownership as an Absolute and Unrestricted Right: Minister of Public Works and Others v. Kyalami Ridge Environmental Association and Another.* 8 South African Journal of Environmental Law and Policy 128 (2001).

Freedman, W. *The Constitutional Protection of Property, the Conservation of the Environment, and the Doctrine of Constructive Expropriation.* 9 South African Journal of Environmental Law and Policy 61 (2002).

D. French and L.J. Kotzé, eds, *Sustainable Development Goals: Law, Theory and Implementation* (Edward Elgar 2018).

Fuggle, R.F. & A. Rabie. *Environmental Management in South Africa* (Juta 1992).

Fuo, O. *The Right of Access to Sufficient Water in South Africa: Comments on Federation for Sustainable Environment and Others v. Minister of Water Affairs and Others.* 20(2) Murdoch University Law Review 21 (2013).

Gilder, A. & E. Swanepoel, *Climate Change,* 745–803. In N.D. King, H.A. Strydom & F.P. Retief, eds, *Fuggle and Rabie's Environmental Management in South Africa* (3rd edn, Juta 2018).

Glazewski, J. *Environmental Law* (2nd edn, Butterworths 2005).

Glazewski J. & L. Du Toit, eds, *Environmental Law* (2nd edn, LexisNexis 2013).

Glazewski J. & L. Du Toit, eds, *Environmental Law* (2nd edn, Service Issue 2, LexisNexis 2014).

Glazewski J. & L. Plit, *Towards the Application of the Precautionary Principle in South African Law*, Stellenbosch Law Review (2015): 190–219.

Grobler, N.J. *Recent Developments in the Energy Sector of the Southern African Development Community (SADC).* 8 Journal of Energy in Southern Africa 15 (February 1997).

Hamann, R. *South African Challenges to the Theory and Practice of Public Participation in Environmental Assessment.* 10 South African Journal of Environmental Law and Policy 21 (2003).

Hanks, J. *Achieving Industrial Sustainable Development in South Africa: What Role for 'Self-Regulatory' and 'Co-regulatory' Instruments.* 5 South African Journal of Environmental Law and Policy 298 (1998).

Hartzer S. & W. Du Plessis, *The Liability of Historical Mine Authorisation Holders for Rehabilitation of Old Order Mine Dumps*, Southern African Public Law (2014): 469–493.

Henderson, P.G.W. *Some Thoughts on Distinctive Principles of South African Environmental Law.* 8 South African Journal of Environmental Law and Policy 139 (2001).

Hoexter, C. *Administrative Law in South Africa* (2nd edn, Juta 2012).

Donna Hornby et al., *A Harvest of Dysfunction: Rethinking the Approach to Drought, Its Causes and Impacts in South Africa,* Oxfam South Africa (October 2016)

Humby, T. *The Black Sheep Comes Home – Incorporating Mining into the Environmental Impact Assessment Regime under the National Environmental Management Act, 1998.* 24 SA Public Law 1 (2009).

Humby, T., et al. *Introduction to Law and Legal Skills in South Africa* (Oxford University Press 2012).

Humby, T. *Maccsand in the Constitutional Court: Dodging the NEMA Issue [Discussion of Maccsand (Pty) Ltd v. City of Cape Town 2012 4 SA 181 (CC)]*. 24 Stellenbosch Law Review 55 (2013).

Humby, T. *Bengwenyama Trilogy: Constitutional Rights and the Fight for Prospecting on Community Land.* 15 Potchefstroom Electronic Law Journal 165 (2012).

Humby, T. *Hands on or Hands Off? The Constitutional Court's Denial of a Provincial Municipal Planning Role*, Journal of South African Law (2015): 178–188.

Jeffrey, L. *Challenges Associated with Further Development of the Waterberg Coalfield.* 106 The Journal of the South African Institute of Mining and Metallurgy 453 (2005).

Kidd, M. *Integrated Pollution Control in South Africa – How Easy a Task?* 2 South African Journal of Environmental Law and Policy 37 (1995).

Kidd, M. *Environmental Law* (Juta 1997).

Kidd, M. *Environmental Law* (2nd edn, Juta 2011).

Kidd, M. *The National Environmental Management Act and Public Participation.* 6 South African Journal of Environmental Law and Policy 21 (1999).

Kidd, M. *Vaal Environment Saved? The Director: Mineral Development, Gauteng and Sasol Mining (Pty) Ltd v. Save and Others.* 6 South African Journal of Environmental Law and Policy 149 (1999).

Kidd, M. *The Constitutional Court's Dilution of NEMA: Minister of Public Works and Others v. Kyalami Ridge Environmental Association and Another.* 8 South African Journal of Environmental Law and Policy 117 (2001).

Kidd, M. *Of Gas Pipelines and Sour Judicial Air: Merebank Environmental Action Committee v. Executive Member of KwaZulu-Natal Council for Agricultural and Environmental Affairs.* 8 South African Journal of Environmental Law and Policy 135 (2001).

Kidd, M. *Alternatives to Criminal Sanction in the Enforcement of Environmental Law.* 9 South African Journal of Environmental Law and Policy 21 (2002).

Kidd, M. *Some thoughts on Statutory Directives Addressing Environmental Damage in South Africa.* 10 South African Journal of Environmental Law and Policy 201 (2003).

Kidd, M. *Liability of Corporate Officers for Environmental Offences.* 18 SA Public Law 277 (2003).

Kidd, M, Retief, F and R. Alberts. *Integrated Environmental Assessment and Management*, 1213–1277. In N.D. King, H.A. Strydom & F.P. Retief, eds, *Fuggle and Rabie's Environmental Management in South Africa* (3rd edn, Juta 2018).

Kidd, M. *Administrative Law*, 209–261. In N.D. King, H.A. Strydom & F.P. Retief, eds, *Fuggle and Rabie's Environmental Management in South Africa* (3rd edn, Juta 2018).

King N., Strydom H, and F.P. Retief, eds, *Fuggle & Rabie's Environmental Management in South* Africa (3rd edn, Juta 2018).

Klees, A. *Electricity Law in South Africa* (Juta 2014).

Kleyn, D. & F. Viljoen. *Beginner's Guide for Law Students* (4th edn, Juta 2010).

Kloppers, H. & W. Du Plessis. *To be Destitute or to Benefit – Corporate Social Responsibility and Mining in South Africa*, 269–283. In M. Langton & J. Longbottom, eds, *Community Futures, Legal Architecture: Foundations for Indigenous Peoples in the Global Mining Boom* (Routledge 2012).

Kotzé, L.J. *Revisiting the South African Integrated Pollution Prevention and Control (IPPC) Regime: A Critical Survey of Recent Developments*. 22 SA Public Law 34 (2007).

Kotzé, L.J. *The Judiciary, the Environmental Right and the Quest for Sustainability in South Africa: A Critical Reflection*. 16 Review of European Community and International Environmental Law (RECIEL) 298 (2007).

Kotzé, L.J. *Phiri, the Plight of the Poor and the Perils of Climate Change: Time to Rethink Environmental and Socio-economic Rights in South Africa?*. 2 Journal on Human Rights and the Environment 135 (2010).

Kotzé, L.J. *A Critical Survey of Domestic Constitutional Provisions Relating to Environmental Protection in South Africa*. 14 Tilburg Foreign Law Review 298 (2008).

Kotzé, L.J. *Enforcing Liabilities and Responsibilities for Pollution Prevention and Remediation: A Legal Reflection on the Legacy and Future of the Mining Industry in South Africa*, 475–499. In L. Paddock et al., eds, Compliance and Enforcement in Environmental Laws: Towards More Effective Implementation (Edward Elgar 2011).

Kotzé, L.J. *Global Environmental Constitutionalism in the Anthropocene*, Hart Publishing Co (2016)

Kotzé, L.J. *Environmental Law and Governance for the Anthropocene*, Hart Publishing Co. (2017).

Kotzé, L. & R. Bates. *Similar but Different: Comparative Perspectives on Access to Water in South Africa and Australia*. 15 Denver Water Law Review 221 (2012).

Kotzé, L.J. & C. Bosman. *A Legal Analysis of the Proposed Waste Discharge System in Terms of South African Environmental and Water Law Framework*. 27 Obiter 128 (2006).

Kotzé, L.J. & A.A. Du Plessis. *Some Brief Observations on Fifteen Years of Environmental Rights Jurisprudence in South Africa*. 3 Journal of Court Innovation 157 (2010).

Kotzé, L.J. & A. Du Plessis. *A Gold Rush to Nowhere? The Rights-based Approach to Environmental Governance in South Africa's Mining Sector in Question*, 47 Verfässung und Recht in Übersee 447 (2014).

Kotzé, L.J. & W. Du Plessis. *Absolving Historical Polluters from Liability through Restrictive Judicial Interpretation: A Matter of (misguided) Principle*. 18 Stellenbosch Law Review 161 (2007).

Kotzé, L.J. & L. Feris. *Trustees for the Time Being of the Biowatch Trust v. Registrar, Genetic Resources and Others: Access to Information, Costs Awards and the Future of Public Interest Environmental Litigation in South Africa*. 18 Review of European Community and International Environmental Law 338 (2009).

Kotzé, L.J. & N. Lubbe. *How (Not) to Silence a Spring: The Stilfontein Saga in Three Parts*. 16 South African Journal of Environmental Law and Policy 49 (2009).

Kotzé L.J. and O. Fuo, *Domestic Manifestations of International Law's Right to Water: A Comparative Analysis of Emerging Rights Obligations in Finland and South Africa,*' 25 African Journal of International and Comparative Law (2017): 261–292.

Kotzé, L.J. & A.J. Van der Walt. *Just Administrative Action and the Issue of Unreasonable Delay in the Environmental Impact Assessment Process: A South African Perspective.* 13 South African Journal of Environmental Law and Policy 39 (2003).

Lawrence, R. *How Manageable is South Africa's New Framework of Environmental Management?.* 6 South African Journal of Environmental Law and Policy 61 (1999).

Lerm, H. *Fracking: an energy dream come true or an environmental nightmare?,* 36 Obiter (2015): 41–56.

Mabiletsa, M. & W. Du Plessis. *Impact of Environmental Legislation on Mining in South Africa.* 8 South African Journal of Environmental Law and Policy 185 (2001).

Madubansi, M. & C.M. Schakleton. *Changes in Fuelwood Use and Selection Following Electrification in the Bushbuckridge Lowveld, South Africa.* 105 Journal of Environmental Management 416 (2007).

Mathenjwa M. *The constitutional obligations imposed on a provincial government in instances where a municipality cannot provide basic services as a result of a crisis in its financial affairs*, Journal of South African Law 59 (2015).

Mauger R. and Barnard, M. *Addressing Fragmentation in the South African Renewable Energy Governance Effort – French lessons to be learned* 29(1) Journal of Energy in Southern Africa (2018).

Mettler, J, & K. Smith. *Bulk Electricity Prices, Exemptions & the Demise of Local Democracy.* 10 Local Government Bulletin 4 (2008).

Meyer, T.C., et al, *Soil, Land and Agriculture,* 283–350. In N.D. King, H.A. Strydom & F.P. Retief, eds, *Fuggle and Rabie's Environmental Management in South Africa* (3rd edn, Juta 2018).

Meyerowitz, D. *Meyerowitz on Income Tax 2003/2004* (The Taxpayer 2003).

Milton, J. *Sharpening the Dog's Teeth: of NEMA and Criminal Proceedings.* 6 South African Journal of Environmental Law and Policy 53 (1999).

Molete, T. *Environmental Risk Exposures – A Thorny Issue for Mine Closures.* January/February The Journal of the South African Institute of Mining and Metallurgy 55 (1999).

Muir, A. *The Le Sueur case and a local government's constitutional right to govern: case notes, SA Public Law* (2015): 556–579.

Murcott, M. *The Role of Administrative Law in Enforcing Socio-Economic Rights: Revisiting Joseph.* 29 South African Journal of Human Rights 481 (2012).

Murombo, T. *Beyond Public Participation: The Disjuncture between South Africa's new EIA Law and Sustainable Development.* 11 Potchefstroom Electronic Law Journal 106 (2008).

Murombo, T. *From Crude Environmentalism to Sustainable Development: Fuel Retailers Association of Southern Africa v. Director-General Environmental Management, Department of Agriculture, Conservation and Environment, Mpumalanga Province and Others.* 125 South African Law Journal 488 (2008).

Selected Bibliography

Murombo, T. *Legislative Mandates for Sustainable and Renewable Energy Use*, 103–115. In E. Kiderlen et al., eds, The Sustainable Energy Resource Handbook Vol. 2 The essential guide (Alive2green 2011).

Murombo, T. *Legal and policy barriers to renewable and sustainable energy sources in South Africa*, The Journal of World Energy Law & Business doi: 10.1093/jwelb/jww001 (2016).

Nel, J. *Unsustainable EIA Partnerships: Poorly-defined Rights, Roles, Responsibilities and Duties of EIA Stakeholders*. 8 South African Journal of Environmental Law and Policy 103 (2001).

Nel, J. *EIA Partnerships in the SADC Region: Learning Points for South Africa from Mozambique's EIA Regulations*. 8 South African Journal of Environmental Law and Policy 95 (2001).

Nel, J. & W. Du Plessis. *ISO14001 and Environmental Law*. 8 South African Journal of Environmental Law and Policy 51 (2001).

Nel, J. & W. Du Plessis. *Unpacking Integrated Environmental Management – a Step Closer to Effective Cooperative Governance?*. 19 SA Public Law 181 (2004).

Nel, J. & W. Du Plessis. *An Evaluation of NEMA Based on a Generic Framework for Environmental Framework Legislation*. 8 South African Journal of Environmental Law and Policy 1 (2001).

Nel, J. & L.J. Kotzé. *Environmental Management: An Introduction*, 1–32. In H. Strydom & N.D. King, eds, *Fuggle and Rabie's Environmental Management in South Africa* (2nd edn, Juta 2009).

Nel, J & R. Alberts. *Environmental Management and Environmental Law in South Africa: An Introduction*, 1–55. In N.D. King, H.A. Strydom & F.P. Retief, eds, *Fuggle and Rabie's Environmental Management in South Africa* (3rd edn, Juta 2018).

Ngobese, P. & J. Cock, *Development and the Environment*, 256–272. In P. Fitzgerald, A. McLennan & B. Munslow, eds, *Managing Sustainable Development in South Africa* (2nd edn, Oxford University Press 1997).

Norman, R., et al. *A Comparative Risk Assessment for South Africa in 2000: Towards Promoting Health and Preventing Disease*. 97 South African Medical Journal 637 (2007).

Oosthuizen, M., Van der Linde, M. & E. Basson, *National Environmental Management Act 107 of 1994 (NEMA)*, 125–207. In N.D. King, H.A. Strydom & F.P. Retief, eds, *Fuggle and Rabie's Environmental Management in South Africa* (3rd edn, Juta 2018).

Paterson, A. *Co-managing South Africa's Conservation and Land Reform Agendas: Evaluating Recent Initiatives to Resolve the Unruly Interface Thrust upon South Africa's Protected Areas*. 17 South African Journal of Environmental Law and Policy 97 (2010).

Paterson, A. *Clearing a Path towards Effective Invasive Control: the Legal Conundrum*. 9 Potchefstroom Electronic Law Journal 1 (2006).

Paterson, A, *Biological Diversity*, 519–572. In N.D. King, H.A. Strydom & F.P. Retief, eds, *Fuggle and Rabie's Environmental Management in South Africa* (3rd edn, Juta 2018).

Paterson A. & J. Glazewski. *Protected Areas and Community-Based Conservation Africa*, 3-21–3-62. In J. Glazewski & L. Du Toit, eds, Environmental Law in South (LexisNexis 2013).

Peart, R. & K. Govender. *Natural Resources Policies for the New Millennium: is South Africa Moving towards a more Sustainable Path?*. 8 South African Journal of Environmental Law and Policy 39 (2001).

Peckham, B. *Some Thoughts on the Regulation of Hazardous Waste Disposal in South Africa*. 1 South African Journal of Environmental Law and Policy 85 (1994).

Pienaar, G.J. & A.J. Van der Walt. *Law of Property* (4th edn, Juta 2002).

Retief, F. & L.J. Kotzé. *The Lion the Ape and the Donkey: Cursory Observations on the Misinterpretation and Misrepresentation of Environmental Impact Assessment in the Chronicles of Fuel Retailers*. 15 South African Journal of Environmental Law and Policy 139 (2008).

Ridl, R. & E. Couzens. *Misplacing NEMA? A Consideration of some Problematic Aspects of South Africa's New EIA Regulations*. 13 Potchefstroom Electronic Law Journal 80 (2010).

Rudman, J., Gauché P. and K.J. Esler, *Direct Environmental Impacts of Solar Power in Two Arid Biomes: An Initial Investigation*. 113(11/12) S. Afr. J. Sci. (2017) http://dx.doi.org/10.17159/ sajs.2017/20170113.

Rumble, O., et al, *Air Quality*, 401–457. In N.D. King, H.A. Strydom & F.P. Retief, eds, *Fuggle and Rabie's Environmental Management in South Africa* (3rd edn, Juta 2018).

Scheepers, T. *A Practical Guide to Law and Development* (Juta 2000).

Scheepers, T.E. & W. Du Plessis, *House of Traditional Leaders: Role, Problems and Future*. 3 Potchefstroom Electronic Law Journal (2000) 73.

Scholes R., et al, eds, *Shale Gas Development in the Central Karoo: A Scientific Assessment of the Opportunities and Risks*, CSIR/IU/021MH/EXP/2016/003/A (CSIR 2016).

Scholtz, W. *Milieuconvenanten, oftewel omgewingbestuursamewerking-sooreenkomste, as self-regulerende instrument in die omgewingsreg: 'n regsvergelykende ondersoek* (LLD Thesis, Leiden University 2001).

Smithen, A.A. *Environmental Considerations in the Preparation of Bankable Feasibility Documents*. 99 The Journal of the South African Institute of Mining and Metallurgy 317 (1999).

Snyman, E., et al. *An Integrated Environmental Management System for the North West Province – Final Report Phase II* (North-West University 2004).

Soltau, F. *The National Environmental Management Act and Liability for Environmental Damage*. 6 South African Journal of Environmental Law and Policy 21 (1999).

Stein, R. *Regulation of Waste Management in South Africa – A Case for Integration*. 4 South African Journal of Environmental Law and Policy 253 (1997).

Steyn, E. *Electricity market restructuring: perspectives from abroad*, SA Mercantile Law (2014): 606–650.

Strydom, H. *Is the End of Environmental Law's laissez-faire Make-Up in Sight?*. Tydskrif vir die Suid-Afrikaanse Reg 599 (2003).

Selected Bibliography

Strydom, H.A. & N.D. King, eds, *Fuggle and Rabie's Environmental Management in South Africa* (2nd edn, Juta 2009).

Strydom, H.A. & E. Cairncross, *Energy*, 459–517. In N.D. King, H.A. Strydom & F.P. Retief, eds, Fuggle and Rabie's Environmental Management in South Africa (3rd edn, Juta 2018).

Summers, R. *Common-Law Remedies for Environmental Protection*, 339–369. In A. Paterson & L.J. Kotzé, eds, *Environmental Compliance and Enforcement in South Africa* (Juta 2009).

Tladi, D. *Corporates and the Flexible Mechanisms in the Climate Change Regime: The Privatisation of Sustainable Development?*. 32 South African Yearbook of International Law 396 (2007).

Tladi, D. *Of Course for Humans: A Contextual Defence of Inter-generational Equity*. 9 South African Journal of Environmental Law and Policy 177 (2002).

Tladi, D. *Strong Sustainable Development, Weak Sustainable Development and the Earth Charter: Towards a More Nuanced Framework of Analysis*. 11 South African Journal of Environmental Law and Policy 17 (2004).

Toxopeüs M. & L.J. Kotzé. *Promoting Environmental Justice Through Civil-Based Instruments in South Africa*, 13/1 Law, Environment and Development Journal 47 (2017), http://www.lead-journal.org/content/17047.pdf.

Van der Schyff, E. *Unpacking the Public Trust Doctrine: A Journey into Foreign Territory*. 13 Potchefstroom Electronic Law Journal 122 (2010).

Van der Schyff, E. *Who Owns the Country's Mineral Resources? The Possible Incorporation of the Public Trust Doctrine through Section 3(1) of the Mineral and Petroleum Resources Development Act 28 of 2002*. Journal of South African Law 757 (2008).

Van der Schyff, E. *Water and the Public Trust Doctrine – the South African Perspective*. 4 The Journal for Transdisciplinary Research in Southern Africa 339 (2008).

E. van der Schyff, *Property in Minerals and Petroleum* (Juta 2016).

Van der Walt, A.J. *The Law of Neighbours* (Juta 2010).

Van der Walt, A.J. *Constitutional Property Law* (3rd edn, Juta 2011).

Van Horen, C. & A. Eberhard. *Energy, Environment and the Rural Poor in South Africa*. 12 Development Southern Africa 197 (1995).

Van Reenen, T.P. *Environmental Policy-Making and Effective Environmental Administration*. South African Journal of Environmental Law and Policy 35 (1994).

Van Reenen, T.P. *Constitutional Protection of the Environment: Fundamental (Human) Right or Principle of State Policy?*. 4 South African Journal of Environmental Law and Policy 253 (1997).

Van Wyk, J. *Development in Protected Areas*. 17 SA Public Law 163 (2002).

Van Wyk, J. *Fracking in the Karoo: Approvals Required?*. 25 Stellenbosch Law Review 34 (2014).

Van Wyk, J. *Planning Law* (2nd edn, Juta 2012).

Van Wyk, J. *The Law on Planning and the Environment*, 1131–1176. In N.D. King, H.A. Strydom & F.P. Retief, eds, *Fuggle and Rabie's Environmental Management in South Africa* (3rd edn, Juta 2018).

Van Wyk J. and P. Steyn, *Planning Law Casebook* (Juta 2015).

Van Zyl, D.H. *Geskiedenis van die Romeins-Hollandse Reg* (Butterworths 1983).
Viljoen, G. *South Africa's Water Crisis: The Idea of Water as Property as Both a Cause and a Solution*, 21 Law, Democracy and Development (2017): 176–200.
Wepener, V, Malherbe W. and N.J. Smit, *Water Resources in South Africa,* 351–400. In N.D. King, H.A. Strydom & F.P. Retief, eds, *Fuggle and Rabie's Environmental Management in South Africa* (3rd edn, Juta 2018).
Willis, C.B. et al., *Review of Policies and Legislation Influencing the Sustainable Use of South Africa's Sustainable Indigenous Woodlands*. 7 South African Journal of Environmental Law and Policy 171 (2000).
Winstanley, T. *The Final Constitution and the Environment*. 4 South African Journal of Environmental Law and Policy 135 (1997).
Winstanley, T. *Environmental Impact Assessments: One Year Later*. 5 South African Journal of Environmental Law and Policy 387 (1998).
Witbooi, E. *Restrictive Environmental Measures: (when) Do They Justify Compensation for the Property Owner?*. 8 South African Journal of Environmental Law and Policy 215 (2001).
Witbooi, E. *Plastic Bag Regulation in South Africa: Just a Load of Rubbish?*. 10 South African Journal of Environmental Law and Policy 67 (2003).
Young, M. *Are We Greening Our Court Rooms? An Analysis of the Recent Decisions in Magaliesberg Protection Association v. MEC: Department of Agriculture, Conservation, Environment and Rural Development*. 19 South African Journal of Environmental Law and Policy 63–73 (2012).

Selected Bibliography

Index

The numbers here refer to paragraph numbers.

Index

Index

Made in United States
North Haven, CT
04 November 2026

21743906R00124